Praise for *Read the Bi*

In the church's dry desert of biblical illiteracy, this book is a drink of cold, refreshing water. With pastoral sensitivity and practical skill, George Guthrie is equipping us to know, understand, and apply the treasures of God's Word in a way that will transform our lives and our communities for the glory of our God. I wholeheartedly recommend *Read the Bible for Life* for every Christian and every leader in the church.

—David Platt, pastor of The Church at Brook Hills, Birmingham, Alabama and *New York Times* best-selling author of *Radical*

In a culture where biblical illiteracy continues to spread like the proverbial plague, George Guthrie has introduced a healing medicine in the form of *Read the Bible for Life*. This overview of the Bible's nature and content will be welcomed in churches intent on developing biblically grounded followers of Christ. The book's conversational approach provides an easy entry for a generation that tends to read only headlines. With fresh insights for the longtime student of God's Word and accessible material for the new student, it is a resource I recommend for all believers.

—Ed Stetzer, coauthor of *Transformational Church*

The genuine give and take of conversation is key to the Christian community's deeper grasp of the Scriptures. *Read the Bible for Life* is a celebration of biblical conversation between friends who really love the Word. Hopefully, lots of people will join in.

—Michael Card, award-winning musician and author

READ THE BIBLE FOR
LIFE

READ THE BIBLE FOR
LIFE

Your Guide to Understanding &
Living God's Word

GEORGE H. GUTHRIE

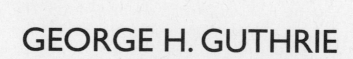

PUBLISHING GROUP
Nashville, Tennessee

978-0-8054-6454-2

Published by B&H Publishing Group
Nashville, Tennessee

Dewey Decimal Classification: 220.07
Subject Heading: BIBLE—STUDY AND TEACHING \
CHRISTIAN LIFE \ SPIRITUAL LIFE

1 2 3 4 5 6 7 8 9 • 16 15 14 13 12 11

DEDICATION

To my children, Joshua and Anna
May you ever be people of the Word

ACKNOWLEDGMENTS

As I look back over the past eighteen months in which this project has moved from conception to delivery, it strikes me that it has been born in and through vibrant community.

From the beginning of our conversations on a biblical literacy initiative, the gifted leaders at LifeWay, President Thom Rainer and the heads of various divisions, have embraced me as a partner in ministry. My longtime friend, Brad Waggoner, now the executive vice president of LifeWay and the publisher of B&H Publishing Group, believed in the importance of the book from the beginning and kept me laughing along the way. Shepherding the manuscript, editor Thomas Walters nudged with a "rod" now and then, but mostly guided gently with a steady "staff" of encouragement. With good grace, designers Diana Lawrence and Jon Rodda put up with an extraordinary amount of back-and-forth discussion on the book cover, listening to my concerns and hopes and guiding the process to a good conclusion.

My dear friend, Jack Kuhatschek, now the executive vice president and publisher at Baker Books, has long encouraged me to address the problem of biblical illiteracy in the church. It was Jack's idea to do the book in a narrative interview style, and the initial feedback I have gotten from family, friends, and students seems to indicate that his finely tuned "publishing" sense was spot on.

I cannot say enough about Union University, where I have been privileged to teach for the past two decades. Out of their love for the church and their keen vision for a Christian university, President David Dockery, Provost Carla Sanderson, and my dean, Gregory Thornbury, have given me life-space in which to write and have cheered me on each step of the way. My extraordinarily gifted colleagues in the School of Theology and Missions, often took time away from their own writing projects to talk to me about mine. The two women who really run the School of Theology and Missions (and my unofficial "design consultants"), Christy Young and Marianna Dusenberry, have given generous feedback on the cover and the initiative logo. A colleague in Union's Art Department, Melinda Eckley, freely gave of her time and nailed the cover design, as well as the initiative logo (and got a wedding dress in the bargain!). My students walked with me in community through the whole process, reading early drafts of various chapters, discussing ideas vetted in class lectures, offering feedback on design issues, and praying for me to endure.

Louise Bentley, still my teacher, offered encouragement and editing expertise at the eleventh hour, and David Wickiser and Lauren Bogdan, former students, did a great deal of work in helping me craft the Bible reading plans in the appendix.

Those interviewed in the book, have given much time because they believe in the project and the broader initiative. Needless to say, the book would not have been possible without their expertise and their time. For what I have learned from them in the process I am deeply grateful. My personal reading of the Bible will never be the same.

Of course, special mention must be made of my wonderful wife, Pat, and our children, Joshua and Anna, who read parts of the manuscript and gave loads of feedback on all aspects of the project. They are my nearest and dearest discussants on the Bible as we attempt to read it and live it together.

To all these I give thanks.

To God alone be glory.

George Guthrie
Jackson, Tennessee
Summer 2010

CONTENTS

Part Three: Reading the New Testament

Part Four: Reading the Bible in Modern Contexts

Invitation to a Conversation

 Could we sit down for a conversation? As I write this introduction, I am tapping away on my laptop in a popular coffee shop, and I would love it if we could have a cup of coffee and talk about the Bible. How to read it well. How to understand it. How to live it. Or perhaps we could sit in front of our fireplace at home, eating my wife's chocolate-chip scones and sipping hot tea. There is nothing better than a rich conversation with a friend about important matters, and it is made all the better over a hot drink; a little music in the background doesn't hurt either. But since you are where you are at the moment and I am where I am, we will just have to make do, meeting in the pages of this book. So grab a coffee or tea, find a comfortable chair, and let's have our conversation.

Why I Wrote This Book

Let me tell you why I went to the trouble of writing this book. To be honest, I really didn't have time to write it, but I felt strongly that it *needed* to be written—almost *demanded* to be written—and written as soon as possible. There are two main reasons.

It Is Important That We Read the Bible

First, I believe with all my heart, on a number of levels, that *it is important that we read the Bible and read it well.* When I say "we," I am not just thinking about those of us who are committed followers of Jesus Christ, although I want to speak to my fellow believers in just a moment. I mean "we" as in everyone touched by the English language or Western culture (and that includes the vast majority of people in the world these days). In *The New Dictionary of Cultural Literacy*, E. D. Hirsch writes:

> No one in the English-speaking world can be considered literate without a basic knowledge of the Bible. Literate people in India, whose religious traditions are not based on the Bible but whose common language is English, must know about the Bible in order to understand English within their own country. All educated speakers of American English need to understand what is meant when someone describes a contest as being between David and Goliath, or whether a person who has the "wisdom of Solomon" is wise or foolish, or whether saying "My cup runneth over" means the person feels fortunate or unfortunate.[1]

Whether you are describing someone as "the salt of the earth," or saying that you have "fought the good fight," or suggesting that a friend "go the extra mile," or speaking of a small amount as "a drop in the bucket," or saying, "I escaped by the skin of my teeth," you are speaking the language of the Bible. You and I have picked up such phrases along the way from newspapers, movies, and the chatter swirling around us as we have listened our way through life, but these phrases are cultural hand-me-downs, woven into the English language by long exposure to the King James Version of the Bible or through important works of literature, which in turn borrowed the language of the Bible. For instance, did you know that there are more than thirteen hundred documented quotations and allusions to the

Bible in the writings of Shakespeare? Shakespeare at times wrote with a quill in his right hand while the Bible was in his left.

It is not surprising, therefore, that in one 2005 survey 98 percent of high school English teachers suggested that students who are biblically literate have an edge academically over those who are not, and in 2006 English professors from the top universities in the United States agreed that "regardless of a person's faith, an educated person needs to know the Bible," saying that the Bible is "indispensable" and "absolutely crucial" for a person who wishes to be considered well educated.

However, not only has the Bible marked literature and the English language, it also has shaped political and social realities that we take for granted. Until English translations of the Bible began to be produced in the fourteenth century, the Bible was locked away in the gilded cage of the Latin tongue and locked up so well that many priests in England did not have the skills necessary to read and understand it, much less teach it to others. In *Wide as the Waters: The Story of the English Bible and the Revolution It Inspired,* Benson Bobrick notes that access to the Bible, brought about by the sacrificial work of Bible translators like John Wycliffe and William Tyndale, taught people to think, and the wide reading of the Bible led to an explosion in the printing of books. This rise in literacy eventually brought down the unjust powers of the day. Bobrick writes, "Once the people were free to interpret the Word of God according to the light of their own understanding, they began to question the authority of their inherited institutions, both religious and secular, which led to reformation within the Church, and to the rise of constitutional government in England and the end of the divine right of kings."[2]

As Western culture continued to develop, the Bible gave impetus for movements that have made the world a better place. Thomas Cahill, in *The Gifts of the Jews,* comments:

> Without the Bible we would never have known
> the abolitionist movement, the prison-
> reform movement, the anti-war movement, the
> labor movement, the civil rights movement,

the movement of indigenous and dispossessed
peoples for their human rights, the anti-apart-
heid movement in South Africa, the Solidarity
movement in Poland, the free-speech and pro-
democracy movements in such Far Eastern countries as South Korea, the Philippines, and even
China. These movements of modern times have
all employed the language of the Bible.[3]

However, not only has the Bible been a culture-shaping influence in the past. It continues to be the best-selling book in the
world year after year and thus constitutes a powerful world-shaping
force to this day. Each and every year about 25 million copies of
the Bible are sold in the United States, and some 100 million copies are sold around the world. Globally, another 400 million copies
of all or part of the Scriptures are distributed by the United Bible
Societies. Such figures dwarf and put in perspective even cultural
phenomena of the moment, like the Harry Potter series. As Boston
pastor of the early twentieth century, A. Z. Conrad, suggests, the
Bible "outlives, out lifts, outloves, outreaches, outranks, outruns all
other books."[4] Consequently, if we look at the role of the Bible in
the world from the standpoint of language and culture, it is important that we understand the literature of the Bible.

Now let me speak directly to those of us who consider ourselves to be followers of Jesus (and the rest of you are welcome
to listen in; this stuff might be pertinent for you someday).
My brothers and sisters, you know that for us the Bible is not
just another influential body of literature. It is a "living" book
because it comes from and leads to a living Lord. Hebrews 4:12
reads, "For the word of God is living and effective and sharper
than any double-edged sword, penetrating as far as the separation of soul and spirit, joints and marrow. It is able to judge the
ideas and thoughts of the heart." In other words, God's Word,
wielded by the Holy Spirit, has the power to sort us out spiritually, to surprise and confront us, growing us in relationship with
our Lord Christ.

Thus, reading the Bible ought to at once be as encouraging

as a mother's gentle touch and, at moments, as unsettling and disturbing as a violent storm. In his work entitled *Eat This Book,* Eugene Peterson rightly notes concerning the Bible, "We open this Book and find that page after page it takes us off guard, surprises us, and draws us into its reality, pulls us into participation with God on his terms."[5] This should be our experience of reading the Bible as we move from dry duty, beyond a checklist Christianity, slogging through the "reading of the day," to an experience of the Bible that might be called a "disrupting delight." If we are not being moved in heart and moved to new places in life—new levels of obedience to God—we are not *really* reading the Bible the way God wants us to.

Whereas the Bible has affected our culture and language, it defines and develops us as Christ followers. Take away the Bible and we cease to exist. It is both foundation and fuel of spiritual vitality for a Christian. Accordingly, there are many reasons we as believers need to read the Bible on a consistent basis. We need to read the Bible *to know the truth. We want to think clearly about what God says is true and valuable* (2 Pet. 1:20–21). We read the Bible *to know God in a personal relationship* (1 Cor. 1:21; Gal. 4:8–9; 1 Tim. 4:16). We read the Bible *to live well for God in this world, and living out His will expresses our love for Him* (John 14:23–24; Rom. 12:2; 1 Thess. 4:1–8; 2 Tim. 3:16–17). We read the Bible *to experience God's freedom, grace, peace, and hope* (John 8:32; Rom. 15:4; 2 Pet. 1:2). We read the Bible *because it gives us joy* (Ps. 119:111). We read the Bible *to grow spiritually, as we reject conformity to the world and are changed by the renewing of our minds* (Rom. 12:1–2; 1 Pet. 2:1–2). We read the Bible *to minister to other Christ followers and to those who have yet to respond to the gospel, experiencing God's approval for work well done* (Josh. 1:8; 2 Tim. 2:15; 3:16–17). We read the Bible *to guard ourselves from sin and error* (Eph. 6:11–17; 2 Pet. 2:1–2). We read the Bible *to be built up as a Christian community with others in the body of Christ* (Acts 20:32; Eph. 4:14–16).

The Holy Spirit produces these outcomes in the life of the believer, using the Word to grow us in spiritual maturity. Not surprisingly, in a recent survey of churchgoers by LifeWay Research, the number one predictor of spiritual maturity among those who regularly attend church was *reading the Bible daily.* As the great minister and philanthropist George Müller put it, "The vigor of our spiritual life will be in exact proportion to the place held by the Bible in our life and thoughts."[6]

I say it again, my first reason for writing this book is that *it is important that we read the Bible and read it well.*

We Are Not Reading the Bible

Second, *we are not reading the Bible.* I wish you could hear my tone through these letters I am dropping down on the page. I don't want to sound alarmist, critical, or preachy. I *am* excited that you have joined me in this conversation, and I don't want to lose you here. But let me speak frankly. I am concerned about where we are currently in terms of our reading of the Bible, and I want you to be concerned with me. Let me say it again: *we are not reading the Bible,* much less reading it well.

I have been struck by this fact as I have worked with bright young college students at my university where the average score on the ACT for incoming freshmen is over twenty-five. We just had 120 prospective students on our campus last weekend, all of whom had scored over thirty-one on the ACT. (For those of you not connected to the academic world, that's *very* good.) My students are exceptionally bright, and the vast majority, though not all, come out of the church.

For several years I have been conducting brief biblical literacy exams at the beginning of my New Testament Survey course. The questions on the exam are straightforward, multiple-choice queries such as: Which of these books is from the New Testament? Whom did Pontius Pilate release during Jesus' trial? How many temptations did Jesus experience in the wilderness? Where would you look in the Bible to find the Sermon on the Mount?

Last fall the average score on the exam was 57 percent. The averages from classes over the past few years have ranged between 50 percent and 70 percent, but most of the time the average is closer to 50 percent. This is not unique to my students but is consistent with what other professors are finding at top Christian universities all over the United States. Our students, even those coming out of the church, simply are no longer grounded in the basics of the Bible's story. In just a moment I will suggest why I think this is, but let me paint the picture of our current situation a bit more broadly for you.

My students mirror a striking cultural phenomenon that pervades the English-speaking world. At least for the past half century biblical literacy has been in a whirlpool-like spiral downward, sucking a basic understanding of the Bible's stories and once-familiar phrases into a blank space in the culture's collective mind. It used to be that a public speaker could make allusions to key stories of the Bible and assume that most of his or her audience would catch them. No more. For instance, in 2001 Dick Meyer, a CBS News commentator, had a puzzled response to such an allusion in President Bush's inaugural address. Meyer confessed, "There were a few phrases in the speech I just didn't get. One was, 'When we see that wounded traveler on the road to Jericho, we will not pass to the other side.'" Meyer concluded, "I hope there's not a quiz."[7]

Speaking of growing biblical illiteracy in the broader culture, George Lindbeck comments: "The decline of biblical literacy has been abrupt and pervasive. . . . The decline affects intellectuals and non-intellectuals, the religious and the non-religious, those inside the churches and those outside, clergy and laity."[8] In his recent book *Religious Literacy: What Every American Needs to Know—and Doesn't*, Stephen Prothero writes, "The Gospel of John instructs Christians to 'search the scriptures' . . . , but little searching, and even less finding is being done."[9] Prothero reports that more than 10 percent of Americans believe that Joan of Arc was Noah's wife. Only 50 percent can name one of the four Gospels and less than half can name the first book of the Bible.

Literary critic George Steiner adds: "As any high-school or college teacher will testify, allusions to even the most celebrated biblical texts now draw a blank. . . . The King James Bible and the

Luther Bible provided much of our civilization with its alphabet
or referential immediacy, not only in the spheres of personal and
public piety but in those of politics, social institutions, and the
life of the literary and aesthetic imagination."[10]

In other words, the Bible is in a slow fade from our collective
conversation, not only in the realm of spiritual and church life
but also in the realms of politics, social institutions, literature,
and the arts.

If you are a practicing Christian, you may be thinking, *Surely
those of us who attend church regularly do much better than the average
person on the street!* I'm afraid not. As indicated by my students'
performance on biblical literacy quizzes, we aren't getting it
either. Ask one hundred church members if they have read the
Bible today, and eighty-four of them will say no. Ask them if they
have read the Bible at least once in the past week, and sixty-eight
of them will say no. Even more disconcerting, ask those one hundred church members if reading or studying the Bible has made
any significant difference in the way they live their lives. Only
thirty-seven out of one hundred will say yes.

Since we as Christians should be "people of the Book," something is wrong with this picture. We should know the Bible well,
but we really don't. All of the polls show that those who claim to
be evangelical Christians only do marginally better than their
nonbelieving neighbors when asked questions about the content
of the Bible, and a biblical view of the world is not making inroads
into how we think about and live our lives. Hymn writer William
Cowper's words come to mind: "While thousands, careless of
the damning sin, Kiss the Book's outside who ne'er look within."
Brothers and sisters, we simply must do better. Our biblical illiteracy hurts us personally, hurts our churches, hurts our witness,
and, thus, hurts the advancement of the gospel in the world.

Why Is This Happening?

You might be asking, "So, why is this happening?" My guess is
that many factors are causing the current slide into ever deeper
levels of biblical illiteracy. Let me mention four.

First, *reading generally is on the decline,* in spite of the fact that Amazon.com and myriads of other book outlets are pouring millions of volumes into the streets every year. A significant portion of the population simply does not read anything beyond clips in the newspaper, or brief magazine articles, or bits and blogs on the Internet. In fact, according to a 2003 study by the U.S. Department of Education one out of seven American adults functions at or below basic literacy levels.[11] Also, a 2004 study by the National Endowment for the Arts, entitled "Reading at Risk," found that only 56.6 percent of American adults had read a book in 2002, a four percentage point drop from a decade earlier; and the reading of literary works is in an even steeper rate of decline. This, of course, is going to affect the way we read (or don't read) the Bible. It also says something to those of us who are parents about the importance of teaching our children to love and read books if we want them to be readers of the Bible.

Second (and this probably contributes to the first reason), *technology may be hurting our ability to read.* Many of us have plugged a literacy-numbing network of technology into our brains, and in various ways this seems to be affecting our reading of the Bible. In an *Atlantic Monthly* article entitled "Is Google Making Us Stupid?", Nicholas Carr laments what the Internet is doing to our brains. He suggests that our click-and-skim interface with technology makes for shallow reading and thinking, eroding our ability to do sustained reading of more substantive material. He writes:

> Immersing myself in a book or a lengthy article used to be easy. My mind would get caught up in the narrative or the turns of the argument, and I'd spend hours strolling through long stretches of prose. That's rarely the case anymore. Now my concentration often starts to drift after two or three pages. I get fidgety, lose the thread, begin looking for something else to do. I feel as if I'm always dragging my wayward brain back to the text. The deep reading that used to come naturally has become a struggle.[12]

Now please understand me. I am no iPhone-smashing
Luddite, who thinks all technology should be sworn off by the
faithful. My iPhone is right here with me as I write, thank you
very much, and I constantly use the Internet for all kinds of
helpful research, including the writing of this introduction.
(Carr's article was just a click away!) But there is a thin line
between using technology as a constructive tool and bowing to it
as a hot-wired god to whom I sacrifice way too much of my time,
my mind, and my spiritual energy. Consider that a 2009 Nielsen
Report showed that the average American watches 153 hours of
television per month (about 5 hours per day; up 20 percent over
a decade ago), and television sets are on in the average household
for a whopping 8 hours 21 minutes per day. Hours more are spent
online. It is little wonder that we struggle to find time and emo-
tional/mental/spiritual space for reading the Bible. We are going
to have to start turning off and tuning out in order to make room
in our lives and hearts for God's Word. If we will give just one-
tenth the time the average American spends watching TV each
day, we can read through the Bible in a year's time.

This brings us to a third reason we don't read the Bible: *we are
distracted and overextended in our schedules.* Jesus once told a story
about seeds and soils (Mark 4:3–20), using graphic word pictures
to describe the different levels of *receptivity* people have toward
God's Word, and the parable is very pertinent for us today. Jesus
used the picture of a farmer broadcasting seed along the edge
of a field. Some seed falls on the hard-packed path alongside
the field, so the seed can't penetrate the soil; some falls on rocky
ground that has little topsoil, so the plants starve; some falls in
the weeds that choke the life out of the plants; and some falls
in fertile soil that offers a good environment for seed and plant
growth. As Jesus tells the story, you can almost feel the breeze on
your face as that breeze scatters some of the seeds to the edges of
the field. Where the seeds fall provides graphic word pictures of
the human heart as it interfaces with God's Word.

Notice that in three of the four word pictures, the problem
is *space.* There is not enough space for the seed or the plant that

grows from it to thrive. I am a gardener, and I can tell you the number one factor for growing a beautiful, productive garden has to do with preparation of the soil, and among other things you want your soil to be what gardeners call a rich, friable *loam*— not too clayish and not too sandy. This kind of dirt provides just the right amount of space for all the elements of good soil, moisture, minerals, air, and heat, to do their magic in interacting with the seed.

I want to suggest that as we interact with God's Word we too need space in our lives—life space and heart space. In other words we need enough space in our schedules every day to sit, read, and think about the Bible; and we need space in our hearts to take it in and respond to it appropriately. Believe it or not, in about twenty to thirty minutes per day, you can read through the entire Bible in a year. That is life space. But we also need what I call "heart space," especially for those who want to read the Bible to grow spiritually. In Jesus' story of the seeds and the soils, the hard-packed soil represents a hard-packed heart that does not listen to God. The shallow soil portrays shallowness of heart. The weed-choked soil parallels a congested heart clogged by worries or wants. All of these spiritual conditions affect our reading of the Bible. So we need to make more space in our lives to learn how to read the Bible better, space to listen to the Bible daily, and space to respond to it well. In fact, biblical literacy is as much about learning how to respond to the Bible as it is about knowing the details of the Bible's stories. With Robert Hutchins, I would suggest that true literacy—the kind that matters—brings about clearer thinking and informed action.[13] Thus, true biblical literacy involves an interaction with the Bible that changes the way one thinks and acts, and that kind of interaction takes time.

Fourth, *we don't know the Bible's grand story or how its parts work.* Let me explain. The vast majority of people in our churches have no frame of reference, no overarching narrative, which holds all the bits and pieces together. Not surprisingly, the most common comment from my students who have just finished a

Bible survey course is, "I never understood how everything fit together before!" Of course, understanding the overarching story of the Bible is part of what it means to *be* biblically literate. Yet our failure to teach people the story of the Bible makes their ongoing growth in biblical literacy hard sledding. The Bible ends up being a jumble of stories, psalms, proverbs, prophecies, and strange passages that don't make sense because they do not fit into a grand narrative. When a person doesn't get *the story*, all the little stories, and psalms, and parables have no point of reference by which we can understand them. Thus, we are going to have to teach people *the story* if we are going to reverse current trends in biblical illiteracy.

On the other hand, neither have most people been trained to read the parts of Scripture well. Since about 1995 I have asked every "Introduction to Bible Study" class I have taught at Union University, "How many of you have ever attended a church that has offered a class or seminar on how to read, study, or interpret the Bible well?" Normally, I have about twenty-five students in that course, and I have never had more than seven hands go up. The normal count is three or four. Most people have never received training in how to read the various literatures found in the Bible and, having understood what they have read, how to bring the truths of Scripture to bear on modern life.

A psalm is different from Paul's letters. Revelation is different from Leviticus. A prophecy cannot be read the same way you read a parable. Reading the Bible is much more meaningful and enjoyable as we learn how these different parts of the Bible work and the impact they were to make on their original audiences. In other words, we are going to have to learn how to *understand* the Bible, reading the various parts according to how the authors were intending to communicate their messages.

Imagine an alien plopped down on Earth with the ability to read English but with no understanding of how a comic strip works differently from a coupon. Or how a novel works differently from a historical textbook, or how a poem is different from a prescription. Many of us are that alien, plopped down in the Bible's literature with little sense of how to navigate the various kinds of literature we find there. Understandably we are befuddled and befogged, and no one likes being confused. It is little wonder we don't read the Bible more. Learning how to read the Scriptures well can help us move from confusion to joy in our Bible reading.

These are a few reasons we are struggling currently with biblical illiteracy, but the question is, of course, what can we do about it? Although I am concerned about where we are in terms of reading the Bible, I am excited about one way we might address the problem.

What This Book Tries to Do

Read the Bible for Life is part of a biblical literacy initiative (also called Read the Bible for Life) being carried out by LifeWay Christian Resources and B&H Publishing Group. We have developed several tools to help individuals and churches grow in reading, understanding, and living the Bible more effectively. Two of these tools, *Reading God's Story: A Chronological Daily Bible* and *A Reader's Guide to the Bible*, help a person read through the story of the Bible over the course of a year. There are also audio resources for those who want to listen to the Bible being read. Two other tools are the book you have in your hands and a video curriculum that presents some of the content of this book in a form conducive to group study. To learn more about these tools and the Read the Bible for Life initiative, see the last few pages of this book and visit www.readthebibleforlife.com.

This book particularly focuses on reading the *parts of Scripture well* and the *practice of reading the Scripture well in various contexts of life. Read the Bible for Life* is filled with conversations carried on over a period of about eighteen months with my wife, a couple of pastors, a close friend who is a musician and minister of the Word, and a bunch of bright scholars who have spent their lives studying the parts of Scripture about which I interviewed them.[14] Almost all of these scholars are friends of mine and know a lot more than I do about their areas of specialty. I can sincerely say

I learned a lot through these conversations, and I am excited about sharing them with you. In each conversation we try to get to the heart of how to read the Bible more effectively, both in terms of the kinds of literature we are reading and the various contexts of our lives. At the end of each chapter, you will find a summation of the main points made in the chapter, several conversation questions for you to discuss with others, and a transformation exercise by which you can put the principles of that chapter into practice in the coming week.

The book is laid out in four parts, and each part has four chapters. Part 1 deals with foundational issues, including the topics: "Reading the Bible as a Guide for Life," "Reading the Bible in Context," "Reading the Bible in Translation," and "Reading the Bible for Transformation." Part 2 concerns "Reading the Old Testament," with chapters on the Old Testament stories, the Law, the Psalms and Proverbs, and the Prophets. Chapters on "Reading the New Testament" are found in part 3 and include "Reading the New Testament Stories," "Reading the Teachings of Jesus," "Reading the New Testament Letters," and "Reading Revelation." Finally, in part 4 we focus on various contexts in which we might read the Bible. We will talk about reading the Bible with the church, with the family, for personal devotions, and in times of sorrow and suffering.

At the back of the book, you will also find two Bible reading plans I hope you find helpful. As you read *Read the Bible for Life*, do so with the Bible in hand, tracking with the Scripture itself as we incorporate specific passages into our discussions. Take time to process the principles you find in each chapter by discussing these principles with others, using the conversation questions at the end of each chapter; and apply what you are learning, using the transformation exercises. Above all, begin to make space each day for reading the Bible! J. C. Ryle has written:

> Begin reading your Bible this very day. The way
> to do a thing is to do it, and the way to read the
> Bible is actually to read it. It is not meaning, or
> wishing, or resolving, or intending, or thinking

about it; that will not advance you one step. You
must positively read. . . . If you cannot read yourself, you must persuade somebody else to read
to you. But one way or another, through eyes or
ears, the words of Scripture must actually pass
before your mind.[15]

As we read on a daily basis, growing in our skill in Bible reading, the rhythm of a life lived deeply in God's Word will become
as nurturing as our daily meals, as spiritually strengthening as
daily exercise, and as emotionally satisfying as a good-morning
kiss from a spouse. It takes discipline, but Bible reading can come
to be a discipline of delight if we open our hearts and lives to it.
So pour yourself another cup, and join me as I walk across the
room or across campus or fly across the country to discuss how
we might begin to *Read the Bible for Life*.

PART ONE

Reading the Bible:
Foundational Issues

CHAPTER 1

Reading the Bible as a Guide for Life

A Conversation with David S. Dockery

I will instruct you and show you the way to go;
with My eye on you, I will give counsel.

—Psalm 32:8

 We all need guidance at points in our lives. Sometimes we are confronted with big decisions, like whom to marry or whether to accept a job offer. At other times small decisions clamor for attention, like which camera to buy or at which hotel we should stay while on vacation. I am a firm believer in research and, for example, take full advantage of *Consumer Reports* or the ratings on Amazon.com. Yet how to live life well finds inadequate coverage by even the best books on Amazon's virtual shelves. For a whole-life guide, nothing beats the Bible, still the best-selling book of all time. However, there are good ways and bad ways of accessing the Bible's wisdom, so I invited Dr. David S. Dockery to sit down for a chat about how we should read the Bible as a guide for life.

David serves as the fifteenth president of Union University where I teach. Not only is he the best university president I know of, but he is the best university president I can imagine. David is a scholar who has written or edited dozens of books. Having won awards in the classroom, he has the heart of a teacher, and his vision for university education has won him accolades from

Christian leaders across the country. God has graced David with many gifts including an extraordinary measure of wisdom for dealing with people, for building community, and for navigating difficult situations.

Yet the word *difficult* is too mild for what our university experienced on February 5, 2008. That night an F4 tornado tore through our campus, causing close to $45 million in damage. Having seen David Dockery lead us through that crisis moment, I could think of no better place to begin our discussion on "Reading the Bible as a Guide for Life." So on a bench in the middle of the fourteen dormitories built in the wake of the storm, we sat down to talk. The day was windy but beautiful, a mild spring day that made the night of the tornado seem like a crazy dream.

A Moment of Crisis

I started our conversation with, "Well, David, the weather today is quite different from what we experienced back on February 5, 2008. What do you remember about that night?"

David leaned forward, placed his elbows on his knees, and said, "That was a night we'll never forget on this campus, George. It was a time when we saw walls crumbling down—the campus literally within an eyelash of total ruin. I was in my office when the tornado struck the campus, and shortly thereafter, about 7:04 p.m., my phone began to ring. I was told that the tornado had hit the residence life area. Two deans who were with me and I came out to the residence life area as quickly as we could. We saw devastation like we've never seen before. It was just unbelievable. Six academic and administration buildings were damaged. We lost sixteen residence life facilities.

"We saw students coming out of their rooms cut, bruised, disoriented, frightened, and not knowing what had happened. Twelve hundred students were in the dorms at the time. When the first emergency workers arrived on the scene, they phoned the hospital and told them to expect fifty to one hundred fatalities.

We took fifty-one students to the hospital that night, nine who were seriously injured; but by God's grace no lives were lost. God sustained us."

Thinking back to that night, I remembered sitting in a closet in my home about twenty minutes away from the campus. I tracked the tornado by radar on my laptop; it clearly was a tornado, a big one with a spinning, purple center. My family and I watched it carve its way through West Tennessee and head directly for the university. I said to my wife, Pat, and the kids, "That has got to be going right over Union." So we prayed that God would keep our students safe. The night was a night of chaos.

Yet one of the things that people have said was most striking about the night of the tornado was the poise of our students. Over the next few days a number of students were interviewed on television. The big media stations like CNN, FOX News, and ABC were looking for interviewees who were falling apart and panicking, but that's not what they found. Our students were amazingly poised. I asked Dr. Dockery about that response.

A young female student came walking down the sidewalk, certainly wondering what the professor and president were doing having a conversation in the middle of the afternoon, in the middle of the dorm area. As she walked on by, David noted, "At 6:00 on the morning following the storm, media from every national network were here. We did interviews that morning with FOX, NBC's *Today* show, ABC's *Good Morning America*, and with CBS's *The Early Show*. We did a national press conference with MSNBC, and then they started talking with our students, just pulling students aside at random.

"An hour or so later, one of the major network producers came to talk with me. He said, 'Have you prepared or scripted these students?' I said, 'Sir, we are just—we're barely trying to hold our life together here, and we're in emergency mode, and I don't have any idea who you've talked to.' He said, 'Well, they're echoing everything you said during the first interviews.' I said, 'That's not because they listened to me or we scripted them; that's just the nature of the Union University community. Our students live their lives grounded in Christ and the Bible, and even in this kind of situation, they respond in light of who God is and in light of the bigger picture rather than just out of their own concerns.' The news outlets came here thinking they were going to find stories of despair—they told us so. All they found were stories of hope. Hope sustained us and carried us through, hope that only comes from the promises of God and His wonderful faithfulness which is revealed to us in His Holy Word."

By God's grace we rebuilt our campus. The dorms were built in about *six months*—no small feat—and $17 million was raised to make up the difference between what insurance would cover and what the new, state-of-the-art dormitories would cost to build. David commented, "God has provided for us, and the people of God became His agents of grace and mercy to us. We've been able to do it without sustaining long-term debt for the institution, and we have been able to provide these beautiful facilities for our students for years and decades to come. It is a 'thanks be to God' moment at Union University."

The Bible as a Foundation

I wanted us to begin to get at the role of the Bible in helping the school navigate such a crisis. We walked over to the Penick Building and continued our conversation in a podcast studio set up by our tech staff at the school. On our way there we passed another building under construction, its foundation reaching deep into the earth to provide stability. As we picked up the conversation, I asked, "What were ways the Bible laid the foundation for our community, preparing us for the aftermath of the tornado? How was that foundation manifested during that spring?"

Dr. Dockery responded, "We had a common commitment as a community to the Bible as the Word of God. We believe it is an inspired Word, that it is true and trustworthy, and that it has authority for our lives. Out of that commitment the Bible began to speak to us in fresh ways. It gave us comfort in the midst of our discouragement. It gave us guidance in the midst of our confusion. It gave us direction as we anticipated what would come next for this university. It has been an amazing thing to see students recommit themselves not only to God but to God's Word, not just for the moment but as an ongoing commitment of life."

Embracing a Biblical View of the World

To read the Bible as a guide for life, we must first embrace the Bible's view of reality. What does it say is true about God, about us as human beings, and about the world around us? As I think about the response of our community during the spring after the tornado, the Bible was at the center of the attitudes and actions of those involved in the recovery process. At Union we talk a lot about growing in a biblical worldview. These are not empty, ivory-tower words for us. Reading the Bible as a guide for life is not primarily about methodology but rather an approach to living all of life from the standpoint of a biblical view of the world. We don't just go to the Bible during times of crisis. We live it daily, and when the crises come, the Bible continues to fill our thoughts and guide us, just as it has been doing all along. I asked Dr. Dockery to comment on what it means to grasp and live this biblical view of the world.

David rested his hands on the table in front of him, the buttons on his ever-present sport coat clicking lightly against the table's edge. Leaning forward, he commented, "First, we must be committed to the Great Commandment, loving God with all our heart, soul, mind, and strength, as well as loving one another as ourselves. We see God as Creator; we understand the devastation that has happened to the world because of sin; and we grasp what Jesus Christ did by coming to the earth as God in the flesh, redeeming us from our sin and giving us hope, forgiveness of sin, promise for the future, and the hope of eternal life. These are not just theological platitudes. They are reference points by which we understand life and the things that go on around us.

"It is because of sin that our relationship with God has been distorted. It is because of sin that our relationship with others has been frayed. We recognize that because of sin even our relationship with ourselves and with nature has been disoriented. What Jesus Christ did to redeem us and reconcile us with God, with one another, with ourselves, and with all of creation begins to make sense as we focus on the Word of God. The Bible becomes more than an ancient book, an account of a meaningless series of events in history. It becomes the wonderfully relevant Word of God for us today. We learn to interpret the Bible, but we also learn to let the Bible interpret us in light of what it says is true about the world."

At the center of our university stands a clock tower. You can see it from almost any place on campus. After the storm the tower, though battered, still stood, its hands frozen in place at 7:02, the precise moment the tornado struck on that fateful night. As I thought about David's words, I responded, "I guess when people are in crisis, facing real pressure in life, what is central to their lives really stands out. Part of what I hear you saying is that when we think about the Bible as a guide for life, it's not a matter of just having a few handy principles that we apply. The Bible really is at the center, providing an orientation to life, which directs us in all we do and helps us face the challenges of life."

David nodded as he took a deep breath and continued, "I think that is what happened on February 5 on this campus. It was not that suddenly we ran to the Scriptures to see what we should do. This was a community that was grounded in the Scriptures, and the Scriptures guided us in responding appropriately."

Life Habits

As we talked, I thought about our students, who are from over thirty countries of the world, from a wide variety of ethnic and socioeconomic backgrounds, and will be going into a broad range of professions—medicine, education, ministry, politics, business, and law among them. Yet many of them have a common bond in their commitment to Christ and this vision of orienting their lives around God's Word. They want the Bible to guide them. So I asked Dr. Dockery to discuss habits that are necessary if Christ followers are to embrace this Bible-centered view of life. "How can we cultivate a life oriented to the Bible, which enables us to handle the various decisions and crises we face?"

David thought through the question and replied, "Well, first and foremost we must develop a habit of reading the Bible on a regular basis, reading it with an openness to what God would say to us. We need to begin by finding a readable translation. I would encourage a person to go to a Christian bookstore, find a readable translation of the Bible, and begin to read it. Read the overarching story of what God has done for us in Christ. Then develop the habit of reading a portion of Scripture every day, perhaps using a Bible reading plan (like one provided in the appendix of this book). As you read, ask questions. What do I see? What should I learn? What is God telling me? What does God want me to do?

"Once the habit of Bible reading is established, move on to the next level, reading the Bible with a view of studying it more seriously. Use a good Bible dictionary or commentaries, or read a good study Bible, which will help you understand the grand themes of the Bible. It will help us greatly if we will get involved in a Sunday school class or a Bible study group. Individual time in God's Word is important, but we were not made to be 'Lone Ranger' Christians. We need to study and discuss God's Word in community with others as well. Also, we need to be part of a church where the Bible is being preached faithfully, hearing the full counsel of God as Paul describes it in Acts 20:27. In short, we need to put ourselves in situations in which we're taking in the Word of God, in which we read it, hear it, study it, meditate upon it, and memorize it so that it is a meaningful part of our lives. I don't think we can overestimate the importance of those kinds of habits."

Problems to Avoid

As I thought about Acts 20, which David had just mentioned, I thought about the difficulties that can arise as we read the Bible. In that chapter of Acts, Paul addresses leaders of the Ephesian church and notes that false teachers would come from among those very leaders—and they had been trained by Paul himself! So I probed the issue with David. "As we deal with the Scriptures individually and in community, it is possible for us to get off track at times. What errors do we need to avoid?"

He responded, "I think at times we make mistakes in interpretation, and at other times we make mistakes in our application of Scripture. One mistake people make is jumping quickly from just reading the Bible to a personal application without deeper reflection on the original meaning of a passage. Sometimes we see this tendency in our students regarding their dating relationships, or as they're going through a difficult decision in determining their direction in life. We see it in families struggling with financial issues, with matters on the job, or with raising their children. It's easy just to read the Bible out of your own situation, and while I'm confident that God does speak to us in our particular situations, it's also possible to read into the Bible what we want to find there rather than letting the Bible speak to us."

I have known people who apply the Bible in this way. I have tried to apply the Bible in this way in the past! I commented, "So the method that simply opens the Scriptures and says, 'Wherever my Bible falls open, I'm going to shut my eyes and point my finger, and I'm going to take that as God's word for me today'— you're saying that's probably not the best way to go about getting direction from God?"

David shook his head, a slight smile creasing his face. "Not on a consistent basis. I don't believe that is the way God desires us to read His Word. He wants us to read it systematically, and I think, therefore, He wants us to read it over time so that we begin to understand it and know what the Bible says about various experiences in life.

"Another mistake we can make is reading parts of the Bible without understanding God's intention for each part. In other words, we need to read the Bible in context. Accordingly, we also need to learn to read appropriately the different kinds of literature found in the pages of the Bible. We read the Law books differently from the way we read Poetry; and we read the poetic books, like Psalms, differently from the Prophets; and we read Prophecy differently from historical narrative; we read narrative parts of Scripture differently from the Epistles in the New Testament; and we read Paul's letters differently from the book of Revelation. Understanding the different types of literature in the Bible is an acquired skill. As we read the Scriptures over and over again and get basic training (like this book!), the Bible begins to make sense."

Understand the Whole Story of Scripture

One vitally important aspect of reading the Bible in context is to grasp its overarching story. One reason we have a hard time understanding and living the parts of the Bible is because we really don't get the big picture, the overarching story. I asked David about the importance of grasping the Bible's big picture.

He answered, "I think we need to understand the big story from creation to the book of Revelation and understand that God has revealed Himself not only at particular times to particular people but has done so progressively. As time went on in biblical history, God revealed more and more aspects of His plan for humanity. We see progression, for instance, in the covenants He has made with people. He made a covenant with Abraham, which was amplified in the covenant with David, and then further amplified in the new covenant promised in Jeremiah. Covenant finds fulfillment when we begin to read Matthew 1 as Matthew traces the heritage and history of Jesus back through the covenants of the Old Testament. The covenants give us a framework for understanding God's agenda in forming a people who would follow Him, and we begin to see how the pieces of the Bible fit together. This big picture keeps us from lifting passages out of context or reading something into the Bible that is not there."

In thinking about the importance of reading the Bible in light of the overarching story, I commented, "It seems that some approaches to Scripture, whether we talk about legalism or liberalism, leave out different parts of the story. Is that another way we can go wrong in our reading of Scripture? Obviously, if we leave out parts of the story, we don't understand the story as a whole, and therefore we don't understand our place in the story appropriately."

Dr. Dockery responded, "That's well said, George. Legalists tend to emphasize the law and the importance of the law, whereas liberals want to, at times, dismiss the supernatural— prophesies and miracles—and focus only on the ethical teaching of Scripture. We need the whole of Scripture to find balance in our perspectives on who God is and how He wants us to live in the world."

I continued, "So as we understand the big picture of the story, then we begin to understand our place in the ongoing story of what God is doing in this world."

Be Encouraged by the Word

As we moved to the close of our interview, I wondered how David had seen the Scriptures provide encouragement to those around him, and I said, "Romans 15:4 says that those things written in former times, Paul specifically speaking about the Old Testament, give us encouragement so that we might have hope. As you look at our faculty, staff, and students here at Union, how do you see the Scriptures giving encouragement and hope to people in our community? How has the Bible provided encouragement as it has provided guidance?"

David answered, "We see God's faithfulness and consistency as He has worked in the lives of our spiritual ancestors in the Bible. We see how people of the Bible responded in different situations, so when we're going through times of discouragement, we can respond accordingly. A person might read about the life of David or might read the Psalms, like Psalm 27, and all of a sudden he finds a word from God that brings him encouragement. Isaiah 6 speaks of the year that King Uzziah died, which obviously grabbed the headlines of the news during that time. But in the midst of that crisis, Isaiah was led to worship, not to despair. Through that passage of Scripture, we are challenged to face our crises with worship rather than despair. That is what happened here at Union following the tornado. People were encouraged by the Word even as they were led by the Word.

"So I think that is what Romans 15:4 is all about. It's seeing how God has worked in the past and allowing God's Word to guide us, trusting in God's faithfulness. We realize that our faithful God is going to connect with us and speak to us in our situation and community today as He did with people in the Bible. Romans 15:4 is something we can hang onto. We gain encouragement from hope, and hope comes from the promises of God that are found in His Word."

As we talked, it was clear to me that finding guidance through God's Word really is a "whole life" process. An eighteenth-century New Testament scholar named J. A. Bengel has said, "Apply yourself wholly to the Scriptures, and apply the Scriptures wholly to yourself."[16] Thus, reading the Bible as a guide for life is not so much a method, like the pagans would use when they would cut up chickens and read their intestines; it's really a lifestyle, lived in relationship with the Lord by His Spirit, lived out with other people in the community. It involves the whole of life as we try to grasp and interact with the whole story of Scripture and find our place in that story.

Conclusion

As David and I talked, I had been reminded that the rebuilding of our campus had an important back story: the Bible-oriented building of lives over time, lives oriented to the Bible's way of seeing and responding to life. We read the

Bible as Christians. We do not read the Bible as some magical book full of superstitious spells or as a talk-show-style, quick-fix manual for life. Rather, we read the Bible as God's Holy Word, a Word that speaks relevantly and authoritatively to all aspects of our lives as we take all of the Bible seriously. David helped us see a more holistic approach to reading the Bible as a guide. His wisdom, demonstrated so clearly in the weeks and months following the tornado at Union, clearly was grounded in his own reading, understanding, and seeking to live in light of God's Word.

Summary & Application

Summation

- Be committed to the Bible as the Word of God.
- Embrace a biblical view of the world, allowing the Bible to provide you with an orientation in life.
- Learn to interpret the Bible, and let it interpret you!
- Develop life habits like reading the Bible regularly, studying it with others, and attending a church where it is preached faithfully.
- Learn to read the Bible in context and according to its various kinds of literature.
- Understand the "big story" of the Bible.
- Finding guidance in the Bible is more about a whole-life commitment than about a methodology.

Conversation

1. What is the area in which you need God's guidance the most right now in life?
2. In what difficult situation or important life decision has the Bible been helpful to you or someone you know?
3. In this chapter George Guthrie notes that reading the Bible as a guide for life has more to do with a whole-life commitment than a methodology. Do you agree or disagree? Explain.

4. What do you think are the three most important truths in a biblical view of the world, and why would you point to those three?
5. What life habits related to the Bible are most important to you at this point in your life? What one habit might you develop that you think would be most life changing?

Transformation

This week read Psalm 25 in three different translations. Make a list of the things the psalmist says he will do, and then make a list of the things he asks God for or trusts God will do. Circle the items in these two lists that correspond to the greatest needs in your life right now. Pray, using the parts of this psalm as prayer to God, bringing your needs to Him.

CHAPTER 2

Reading the Bible in Context

A Conversation with Andreas Köstenberger

In the fifteenth year of the reign of Tiberius Caesar, while
Pontius Pilate was governor of Judea, Herod was tetrarch
of Galilee, . . . during the high priesthood of Annas and Caiaphas,
God's word came to John the son of Zechariah in the wilderness.

—Luke 3:1–2

One May my family and I traveled east from our home in Tennessee, through the Smoky Mountains, and came to the lovely campus of Southeastern Seminary in Wake Forest, North Carolina. I had been invited to teach there for a week by my friend, Dr. Andreas Köstenberger, who serves as professor of biblical theology and head of the Ph.D. program at Southeastern. He grew up in Vienna, Austria, and while a student at a university, had a fairly radical conversion experience when someone simply read the Bible to him. He remembers, "I was struck by the power of God's Word."

With a Ph.D. in economics already in hand, Andreas eventually decided to commit his life to studying and teaching that powerful Word. One of the foremost authorities in the world on the Gospel of John, Andreas has thought much about how we read and study the Scriptures. So, since we were going to be together for a few days while I taught his students the book of Hebrews, I asked if I could interview him about how our understanding of the various contexts of the Bible affect our reading of it. He graciously agreed. Sitting across from each other at a conference table in his spacious office, surrounded by scholarly tomes, we had our talk.

What Do We Mean by Context?

"Andreas, what do we mean when we talk about the 'context' of a passage?"

Pausing only a second to consider the question, Andreas answered. "Context refers to the circumstances that form the *setting* for an event, a statement, or a written text, by which that event, statement, or text can be rightly understood. Someone has said that 'context is king' when interpreting the Bible, because understanding various contexts is so important to our understanding of biblical passages or ideas."

I thought about how vital context is for even the most basic communication we experience every day. The word *hand* for instance can be used in many different ways in English, depending on the context. When the host of a variety show, calling for a response to a wonderful piano performance, encourages the crowd with, "Give her a hand!" we don't suddenly see people throwing the "hands" of a clock or mannequin hands onto the stage! Neither do we see people rushing onto the stage to help the pianist (as in "give her some help!"—another possible meaning for the sentence, "give her a hand"). Why? The audience knows from the context that the host is calling for applause.

The need to discern context is also true even in our closest relationships. Leaning into the microphone a bit, Andreas gave an example. "I have a close, wonderful relationship with my wife. Yet even in our communication I have to pay careful attention to context. When she talks to me, I need to make sure I interpret what she says in its proper context. I must grasp what she means to say based on the topic about which she has been speaking, her body language, where we are at the moment, and other clues; or I'm likely to read my self-interests into what she's saying, which would be misinterpreting her words."

I shot back with a smile, "And that means trouble!"

He laughed and nodded his head in agreement.

The same is true when we read the Bible. Our understanding of the contexts in which God spoke His Word has a profound impact on the way we hear what God wishes to say to us through that Word.

I asked Andreas, "So what, then, are the various contexts that affect our reading of the Bible?"

He answered, "There are at least four: literary context, cultural context, historical context, and theological context."

I suggested that we talk about each, perhaps looking at examples of how understanding these contexts can help us read the Bible better.

Literary Context: Where Does the Passage Fit? How Does It Function?

Andreas noted, "When we speak about 'literary context,' we mean the broader section of a literary work, which surrounds a particular passage we are reading or studying. In short, literary context refers to what comes before and after a passage, and we want to try to understand the role our particular passage plays in the development of the book we are reading. We want to ask, 'How does this passage fit and function in this book?' or 'Why did the author say this, in this way, at this point?'"

I asked Andreas if he could give us an example.

"Sure. At the beginning of John 2, we have the story of Jesus turning water to wine at a wedding. How this story is positioned in the book is important. As we begin John 2, Jesus has just come back to Galilee from Judea and has just called His first disciples (1:43–51). In fact, John's reference to 'the third day' in 2:1 is the third day since Jesus interacted with Nathanael, and Jesus' disciples were invited to go with Him to the wedding in Cana (2:2). So the water-to-wine story flows from what has been happening in the previous chapter.

"As for the relationship of this story to what follows in the Gospel, in 2:4 Jesus tells His mother, 'My hour has not yet come,' a statement made two more times over the next eleven chapters (7:30; 8:20). Not until 12:23–13:1 are we told that Jesus knew that His hour had come. Furthermore, John tells us that Jesus' miracle of turning the water to wine was the first 'sign,' or miracle that Jesus did and that as a result Jesus' disciples believed in Him (2:11). So the fact that this miracle was the first one makes it significant, and it elicits a response from His disciples who had started following Him in the previous chapter. In terms of literary context, it stands at the 'front door' leading into Jesus' ministry. We should ask why John records this story here in this way. He is crafting his story in a particular way for particular reasons. Also, the water-to-wine miracle is the first of seven signs in the book, the seventh of which is the raising of Lazarus from the dead (11:1–44). So, again in terms of literary context, we should look at this bigger picture of the way the Gospel story is unfolding and ask questions about the role the water-to-wine story plays. This is what it means to read in light of the literary context."

I commented, "So literary context means that we read the story carefully in light of the material that comes before it and after it, and we ask questions about what the author was trying to accomplish. It has to do with the way this story fits and functions in the bigger story."

Andreas responded, "That's right."

Understanding Cultural Aspects of the Bible

That made a great deal of sense, so I wanted to push on to discuss the next context Andreas had mentioned and asked, "What do we mean by 'culture' and 'cultural context'?"

Andreas leaned back in his chair and answered, "Culture has to do with attitudes, patterns of behavior, or expressions of a particular society; and these are aspects of the ancient world that have an impact on our understanding of the Bible."

I asked, "Do you mean issues like, What was worship like in the eighth century BC?, or What is a Pharisee?, or Why does Paul speak about head coverings?"

He nodded in agreement. "Or how people in first-century Palestine acted at funerals or weddings, or how they dressed, or what they ate, for example."

I thought about an aspect of clothing from our culture: wearing neckties. Depending on your age or the subculture to which you belong, you may or may not think of neckties as attractive, as "dressing up." Yet two hundred years from now people will likely look at pictures of us in neckties and respond, "What were they thinking? That looks pretty ridiculous, and neckties had no real function!" (Think about how you respond to the clothing of two hundred years ago.) Yet a necktie is a cultural artifact, a normal part of our culture that we mostly just take for granted. Or consider the way we eat. When my wife and I lived in England for a brief time a few years ago, we used a knife and fork like Brits, even scooping peas up on the back of the fork! When I was in China a year after my time in England, I ate with chopsticks. The way people eat is an aspect of culture.

I asked Andreas, "You're saying that in the first century AD, for instance, people had certain patterns of living and interacting that come through in the Bible, and we need to learn about those patterns to read the Bible well?"

"That's right. Let me point out a couple of examples from John's Gospel. We were just talking about the wedding at Cana in John 2. That's a wonderful example because here you have a small, intimate wedding. John tells us that Jesus' mother was there as well as His brothers and some of His disciples. The wedding was held in Cana, close to where Jesus grew up in Nazareth, and so the wedding probably involves a family that was close to Jesus' family and had invited them to the wedding. This may be why Mary steps in when a crisis ensues. She tells Jesus, 'They don't have any wine!'"

I asked, "Why was that such a crisis? I have been to many Baptist weddings that didn't have any wine!"

Andreas rested his arms on the table and leaned into the microphone. "We need to understand that it was not just a one-hour ceremony. A wedding often was a week-long ceremony, and the family was responsible for hosting their guests for the whole week. Running out of wine would have been embarrassing socially, reflecting negatively on the family's ability to celebrate the bride and groom properly. It would be like a family today failing to provide food and drinks at a wedding reception. Those attending would be embarrassed for the family. So essentially Mary was asking Jesus to preserve the honor of that family, in whom she seems to have had some vested interest. In that culture honor and shame were important concepts, much more important than in our culture."

I commented, "Yet what Jesus does is use this crisis as an opportunity both to bless the family (notice that the wine Jesus made was of the finest quality) and to reveal His true identity as the Messiah, to display His glory, as John puts it."

Andreas noted, "That story has many other nuances as well as theological implications, but you begin to see why knowing something of the cultural dynamics of that day is important. When we understand what was expected at a wedding or powerful social forces like honor and shame, the story begins to take on nuances of meaning we did not see before.

"Or take John 11 and the raising of Lazarus. Of course Lazarus had just died, and in this story we see Jewish customs that were characteristic of how people grieved over a deceased person. Sometimes the family of the deceased hired professional mourners who would wail as the funeral was underway. By contrast family members often sat *shivah*, or in mourning. They would sit in the house silently, and then relatives or friends would come and console them. We see this in John 11 when Mary sits in the house waiting for Jesus to call on her (11:20). She was just doing what was normal for the sister of a dead person at a funeral. She wasn't being disrespectful of Jesus or ignoring Him. When she gets up and goes to him, the mourners think she has gone to the tomb. But notice how the story focuses on Jesus rather than the dead person, because Jesus is the One with the answer the other characters in the story need. Mary going to Jesus and Jesus commanding that the stone be moved (over the objection that

Lazarus had already been in the grave for four days and would have stunk) show that the normal cultural patterns and thinking are being overturned. God's glory breaks into what would have been considered normal in that culture. Yet you have to know what is going on culturally to catch the nuances of how much God is bringing transformation to the situation."

Understanding Historical Context

As the southern sun outside heated up this lovely town, we began to warm to our topic, and I wanted to make sure we covered our bases. So I probed a bit further. "We've mentioned two aspects of context thus far: literary context and the cultural context of the Bible. What do we mean by 'historical context'?"

Andreas glanced at the shelves of books behind me, collecting his thoughts. On those shelves you would find many books on the history of the Jewish people in the ancient world, or volumes on the history of Rome, or the history of the Persians or Greeks. "First, historical context has to do with historical events in the biblical era, either events recorded in the pages of Scripture or events that form the backdrop for the biblical story. For instance, from a historical perspective, what historical events form the backdrop for the book of Amos, or Ezra, or the Gospel of John?"

I interjected, "So we need to understand Amos against the backdrop of the social and economic developments in Israel during the eighth century BC, or Ezra against the backdrop of the Babylonian exile in the sixth century BC"

He nodded his head in agreement and added, "We also need to grasp the broad sweep of biblical history. When we sit down to read a book of the Bible, we need to ask, 'Which stage of God's dealings with His people does this book address?' Just this morning, teaching on the book of Micah, I explained to my Sunday school class that Micah is not just a parable or allegory about human life. It is a book given by God through a prophet to His people Israel at a particular point in time and for specific reasons. So we first need to understand God's message to those original recipients before we can understand the relevance of God's message for us today. We need to ask: 'Who was this prophet? What events seem to form the backdrop of God's Word to His people at this place and time?'"

"Don't Know Much about His-to-ry"

As we talked, Sam Cooke's 1958 song "Wonderful World," where he sings about not knowing much about history, started playing in my head. I imagine that some of us may be intimidated by the idea that we need to bone up on our history a bit. It just seems so much easier simply to read the Bible and let it speak to us. You may be thinking, *Do I really need to go to the extra trouble?*

I asked Andreas, "What do you say to a student who comes to you and complains, 'Why can't I just read the Bible and let the Spirit speak to me?'"

He answered, "On the positive side, aspects of Scripture can be grasped intuitively by a believer who has the Spirit because the Spirit who inspired Scripture is the same Spirit who guides our reading. Many aspects of Scripture can be understood fairly well just by reading a passage carefully. But at the same time we need to remember that Scripture is an ancient text that has come down to us from millennia ago. With such an ancient text, we would expect to find certain words, events, concepts, and cultural features that are obscure to us. Even if we have a good translation, if we are not familiar with certain historical dynamics surrounding the text, we will miss dimensions of the Bible's meaning at points. God gave His Word in particular times, places, and ways; and learning about those times, places, and ways helps us read the Bible better.

"When I became a Christian, I wanted to learn how to study such things because I wanted to know what God was saying to me through His Word. I wanted to understand all of it, not just some of it. So passages like 2 Timothy 2:15 are dear to me: 'Be diligent to present yourself approved to God, a worker who doesn't need to be ashamed, correctly teaching the word of truth.'"

I asked Andreas about the payoff of such study. I wanted to know if he could give us an example of how understanding a historical event helps us read Scripture better. He pointed to the destruction of the temple in Jerusalem in AD 70.

The Destruction of the Temple as an Example

Beautiful buildings have always been important among people of faith since buildings express something about the value we place on our relationship with God. A beautiful building on a college or seminary campus, like the one we were sitting in at the moment, serves as a monument of sorts to the values of a people. Yet it is difficult for us to grasp how central, how important the temple in Jerusalem was to most Jews during the time of Jesus. It served as the center of the religion, the focal point of the Jewish festivals, and even a bank where wealthy Jews kept their material wealth. Understanding the place of the temple in Judaism of the day makes Jesus' words in the Gospels all the more potent. In Matthew 12:6 we read Jesus' proclamation, "But I tell you that something greater than the temple is here," words that would have seemed outlandish in the extreme given the central place of the temple in Judaism.

In addition, Herod the Great had expanded and beautified the temple and the temple complex beginning in about 19 BC, and many saw it as one of the most magnificent structures in the world at the time. This sentiment is reflected in a discussion between Jesus and His followers: "As He was going out of the temple complex, one of His disciples said to Him, 'Teacher, look! What massive stones! What impressive buildings!' Jesus said to him, 'Do you see these great buildings? Not one stone will be left here on another that will not be thrown down!'" (Mark 13:1–2).

That event prophesied by Jesus happened in AD 70 (some forty years after His death and resurrection) when the Romans, under the leadership of Titus—a general who would eventually become emperor—destroyed Jerusalem and her beloved temple. So ingrained is this event in the psyche of the Jewish people, the destruction of the temple is still mourned on an annual basis in the Jewish fast called *Tisha B'Av*. In one fell swoop the Romans destroyed the center of Jewish life and worship, indeed the geographical center of their existence as a people.

Andreas noted that the Gospel of John was written one to two decades after the destruction of the temple. This would have made Jesus' words in John 2:19–21 ring with power for the first readers. He said, "Destroy this sanctuary, and I will raise it up in three days." To this the Jewish leaders responded, "This sanctuary took 46 years to build, and will You raise it up in three days?" Their incredulity is understandable. All of them knew that the temple had been under construction as long as anyone could remember. John goes on to clarify that Jesus was speaking about His physical body. So Jesus commented on His own resurrection, drawing an analogy to the destruction of the temple, which He knew was coming some four decades later.

Andreas noted, "In Judaism of the first century, it was almost unthinkable to worship God without any reference to the temple since so much of Jewish worship centered around the sacrificial system. For instance, Passover had to be celebrated within the walls of Jerusalem since the Passover lambs were sacrificed at the temple. So once the temple was destroyed, the question was, how are God's people now going to worship God appropriately?"

I asked, "Did that question provide Christians in the late first century with an opportunity to bear witness to the gospel—that God had made Jesus' followers into a new kind of temple, one made up of people rather than of stone?" I was thinking of passages like Ephesians 2:21–22: "The whole building, being put together by Him, grows into a holy sanctuary in the Lord. You also are being built together for God's dwelling in the Spirit." And 1 Peter 2:5: "You yourselves, as living stones, are being built into a spiritual house for a holy priesthood to offer spiritual sacrifices acceptable to God through Jesus Christ."

Andreas agreed excitedly, "Talk about the perfect opening for the gospel. I look at John's Gospel as taking an opportunity to present Jesus as the new temple, if you will, as God's way to worship now that the temple had been destroyed. From the beginning of John's Gospel we get hints in this direction. If you remember, in the conversation Jesus had with the Samaritan woman in John 4, He said: 'Believe Me, woman, an hour is coming when you will worship the Father neither on this mountain nor in Jerusalem. You Samaritans worship what you do not know. We worship what we do know, because salvation is from the Jews. But an hour is coming, and is now here, when the true worshipers will worship the Father in spirit and truth. Yes, the Father wants such people to worship Him'" (John 4:21–23).

What Do We Mean by Theological Context?

From what Andreas shared, the importance of understanding certain historical events seems clear. It seemed to me, however, that we may have crossed over into yet another type of biblical context he had mentioned earlier—theological context. I asked him if that was the case.

Köstenberger smiled and said: "That is exactly right. When we speak about theological context, we are referring to the tapestry of theological themes in the story of the Bible. For instance, almost every important theological concept in the New Testament has a rich theological background in the Old Testament, and many are developed in various ways in the New Testament itself. So we are not just looking for the historical facts but also asking questions about what stories, or practices, or institutions tell us about God, or about ourselves as human beings, or the world in which we live. We also are asking about the development of those ideas over time, as God revealed truth progressively in the development of the biblical story."

I interjected, "So, for instance, we were talking about the temple. You are saying that the rich history of how God's people understood the temple in the Old Testament era is important for our understanding of Jesus' words about the temple in the Gospels and the temple theology we find in the rest of the New Testament."

Andreas agreed. "Right. The theological backdrop for our discussion of the temple in the Gospels goes all the way back to the beginnings of the Old Testament and the emphasis on God's desire to be present among His people. In Exodus, for example, the tabernacle clearly was constructed to facilitate this desire on God's part. When Solomon built the first temple, which was patterned after the tabernacle, God blessed it, but His blessing was conditional; if the people abandoned the Lord, God would cause the temple to be destroyed (1 Kings 9:8–9). Ultimately, we see from the New Testament that God's desire for the temple had to do with relationship with people, rather than a beautiful building. Christ's words about the destruction of the temple are given in a context in which the true purpose of the temple had been abandoned. This is why Jesus drove the money changers out of the temple complex.

"So the New Testament's teaching about Christians as the 'New Temple' (Eph. 2:21–22) forms an important development of the theology about the temple we see in the rest of the Bible. Ultimately God answers His own desire to be present among people by working out a way for Him to live in them, by the Holy Spirit. Yet passages like Ephesians 2:21–22 have a rich theological context that spans the whole Bible. This idea is developed even further at the end of Revelation when the dwelling place of God 'is with humanity, and He will live with them. They will be His people, and God Himself will be with them and be their God' (Rev. 21:3).

"Thus, at any given point in Scripture, we can ask, 'How does this passage or theme relate to the development of theological ideas in the rest of the Bible?' That is how we tune into the theological context."

What Tools Can Help Us with Learning about Context?

Each of these four aspects of context obviously can play an important part in helping us read the Bible better. So I asked

Andreas, "How can people grow in their sensitivity to these con-
textual dynamics? What tools can they use?"

He began by pointing out the need to read the Bible extensively. "People need to have a plan to read through the Bible
regularly, and as you listen to a sermon or study the Bible for
yourself, ask yourself questions such as: 'What does this story tell
me about God? How does this passage fit into the bigger picture
of this book or the Bible as a whole?' Specifically look for characteristics of God that are revealed in the part of Scripture you
are reading. Begin to get a feel for the grand sweep of the story.
A study Bible can be enormously helpful as you read through
the Bible, giving you outlines for the books, help with the immediate literary context, historical background information, and
theological concepts. So I would encourage people to get a good
study Bible if they do not have one. But foundationally you need
to establish a life habit of reading the Bible consistently."

I have often suggested that the most foundational habit
people need to develop is the habit of reading through Scripture
consistently. If people read through the Bible every year over the
next five years or so, that habit would begin to give them the big
picture of Scripture. Their grasp of both literary and theological
context would be greatly enhanced, and they would grow in their
understanding of the historical context of the Bible.

Andreas continued, "A Bible dictionary is another wonderful
tool that can help with all of the contexts we have mentioned
in our discussion. Good commentaries address issues of historical and cultural background for a book or particular passages.
Commentaries also normally present an outline of a book, and
some of them discuss theology extensively. Especially in recent
years we have seen the rise of specialized commentaries that
focus specifically on historical-cultural background. A specialized tool like a backgrounds commentary can offer great insights
for your reading of Scripture."

I asked about use of the Internet. I know a lot of people
search the Internet to find information about the Bible. Much of
the information is helpful, but caution is needed.

Andreas shifted in his seat a bit, framing his words carefully. "I would be careful. With reputable publishers, historical facts have to be verified by at least two independent sources. Sometimes finding the evidence for some of the intriguing suggestions as to the background of a particular passage can be difficult. Something might sound great but be based on little or no evidence. Corroborating background and cultural information by using the best commentaries available is best."

I commented, "We are blessed, in the last thirty to forty years in evangelicalism, with wonderful tools—great commentaries published by good publishers, as you mentioned. We can be confident in those kinds of commentaries that we're going to be led in the right direction."

The Impact of Our Own Context on Our Bible Reading

Before we closed our interview, I wanted to ask Andreas how our cultural context affects our reading of Scripture. "Everyone has a historical-cultural context that affects the way we read the Bible. Doesn't this skew the way we read the contexts of the Bible?"

Andreas agreed that our context affects us extensively. "The key is to have a posture toward God's Word by which His Word is changing us in our context rather than our molding the Word to our cultural tastes and values. That is hard to do. We have to read with humility. And I think the beginning of humility is the fear of God. We have to believe in the authority of God's Word and be ready to adjust our lives to it."

I commented, "So there should be a sense of urgency. Urgent listening, if you will."

Andreas agreed. "Yes, in the sense of submission to truth and the striving for understanding the truth, as when God tells Timothy to handle God's Word correctly. This is why learning to read the Bible in context is so important. It helps us understand the Word so we can live it."

As we wrapped up our conversation, I thought about the context of our conversation. Here we were, sitting in an air-conditioned office on a hot summer day, in the southern part of the United States, at the beginning of the twenty-first century. Yet the Bible has affected both of us profoundly. This book written millennia ago, in vastly different cultural and historical circumstances from our own, compels us to spend our whole lives reading it, seeking to understand it, and living it. The theological truths God built into this book are deeper than the deepest ocean and higher than the heavens; they are universal in their implications, relevant for all people throughout the world, in spite of vastly different cultural situations. The Bible, read in light of its various contexts, can transform our contexts whatever they might be. Andreas had helped us learn more about how to read the Bible better and in context.

Summary & Application

Summation

- Context refers to the circumstances that form the setting for an event, a statement, or a written text, by which that event, statement, or text can be rightly understood.
- Understanding context is vital for all kinds of communication.
- Literary context refers to how a passage fits and functions in a book.
- Cultural context has to do with attitudes, patterns of behavior, or expressions of a particular society, which affect our understanding of a passage.
- Historical context has to do with historical events in the biblical era, either events recorded in the pages of Scripture or events that form the backdrop for the biblical story.
- Theological context refers to how a topic fits in the tapestry of theological themes in the story of the Bible.

- Tools like study Bibles, Bible dictionaries, and
  backgrounds commentaries can help us understand the
  various contexts of the Bible.

Conversation

1. In interpersonal communication, why do we consider
    it unfair to take a person's words "out of context"? How
    does this situation parallel a person's taking the Bible's
    words out of context?
2. What examples shared by Drs. Köstenberger and
    Guthrie in the chapter were most striking to you?
3. Read Philippians 2:1–11. What role does this passage
    play in its literary context?
4. What aspects of Philippians 2:5–11 relate to the
    cultural context of Paul's time? (Hint: What elements
    were a part of the broader culture, elements that non-
    Christians would have been familiar with?) How do
    these aspects of the passage contribute to the message
    in this passage?
5. How does Philippians 2:5–11 fit into the theological
    context of the Bible? (Hint: What theological themes
    here play a significant role elsewhere in the Scriptures?)

Transformation

*Read Philippians 4:8–17 in light of its literary, cultural, historical,
and theological contexts. Begin by reading about the book of Philippians
in the introduction to the book found in a good study Bible or a Bible
dictionary. (Go to a bookstore and buy one of these tools if you don't
own one!) Then read the passage carefully several times. Once you have
thought through the various contexts surrounding this passage, write out
your understanding of Paul's main point in Philippians 4:13. How might
you apply the passage to your life this week?*

CHAPTER 3

Reading the Bible in Translation

A Conversation with Clint Arnold and Mark Strauss

They read out of the book of the law of God,
translating and giving the meaning so that the
people could understand what was read.

—Nehemiah 8:8

Most of us do not think much about the important role Bible translation has played in our lives. Those of us for whom English is our primary language too easily take for granted both the ready access we have to the Bible and the superstore type variety of options we have in terms of translations. Yet, unless you read ancient Hebrew and Greek, you could not read the Bible for yourself—not one word of it—if it were not for that translation sitting at home on your nightstand. The fact is that you and I are indebted to many people who have worked hard to bring God's Word in its original languages over into our language in a way that speaks to us; and since about 1960 our options (for English translations particularly) have grown exponentially. Yet our many options also can be daunting. Which translation should you use for reading the Bible? Which for deeper study? Why do the various translations seem to differ at points? Which is a fit for where you are in your spiritual life right now?

I thought it would be helpful to discuss such questions with my good friends Clint Arnold and Mark Strauss. For the past few years the three of us have served together as editors of a

New Testament commentary series and have overlapped on various other projects. Clint is professor of New Testament Language and Literature and chair of the New Testament Department at Talbot School of Theology in La Mirada, California. Mark serves as professor of New Testament at Bethel Seminary San Diego. These two men have worked on translation projects as consultants or translators or both. So, e-mailing back and forth, we set a time and got together while at a meeting of the Evangelical Theological Society in Providence, Rhode Island. With the hum of the conference in the background, we found a reasonably quiet conference room in the convention center and sat down for a talk. Our conversation was peppered with laughter, thoughtful insights, and helpful suggestions on Bible translations.

Why So Many Translations?

As we settled into our seats, I asked my friends, "Mark and Clint, why do we have so many different English translations of the Bible?"

With a big smile on his face, Clint quipped, "Well, people like different colored covers!"

Mark laughed, and I responded, "I hope it goes beyond that!"

Clint continued, ". . . in leather, or hardback, or with different paper. Ironically, some people choose their Bible on such bases—just what feels and looks good; but there are other, much more important criteria we should consider when choosing a Bible. A lot of different translations are available, and they vary greatly in terms of approach."

Knowing that we would return to the question of how to choose a particular version of the Bible, I pressed, "OK, so why do we have so many translations?"

Translation Is Difficult

Mark chimed in, "The simplest answer is that translation is an inexact science. No translation is perfect, and translators have a natural tendency to seek to improve on what came before. We believe the Bible is the most important book of all time. It is God's Word, His revelation to us as human beings. It provides the answers to our deepest questions in life. So we should not be surprised that so many people work so hard to get it right and to get it into the hands of as many people as possible. Ultimately the reason there are so many translations is a positive one: a passionate desire to make God's Word accessible to people everywhere."

That made sense to me. Translation is not an exact science in part because language is so wonderfully flexible and complex. As any married couple knows, communication can be challenging, even when two people are speaking the same language! How much more so when we are moving from an ancient language to a modern one?

Mark continued, "In answer to the question, 'Why so many English versions?' there are at least two main reasons. One has to do with the development of any language over time, and the other has to do with different approaches to translation work."

Language Is Always Changing

Picking up on the fact that any language morphs over time, Clint leaned forward and said, "It's amazing how quickly our English language changes. Vocabulary changes, new words enter the world, and even grammatical structures—the way we say things—change. For example, we used the King James Version in church when I was growing up. I remember as a brand-new believer, sitting in church, hearing a pastor preach out of the New Testament book of James, 'Count it all joy when ye fall into divers temptations.' Now in the early 1600s, the word 'divers' meant 'diverse' or 'various,' but I didn't know that. I used to watch this underwater show called *Sea Hunt*, and I'm thinking of a scuba diver!"

I laughed and commented, "So you're imagining the guys with air tanks on their backs?"

Clint continued, "Yes, the picture entered my mind of a guy in the ocean looking for sea anemones. I couldn't imagine what kinds of temptations those divers might be facing, but of course I was hearing the passage in a way completely out of line with what James intended to communicate!"

Think about how much language has changed even in the past half century. *Cable* used to be something that held up a bridge; *remote* used to refer to a secluded spot; and a person *surfed* in the ocean rather than on a computer or a phone!

Mark leaned back, smiled, and continued, "Related to the fact that language is changing is the need for translations to address different audiences. Children read on a different level from adults. There are churched people who understand traditional biblical language, and others who have never attended church much but are open to learning more about the Bible. Certain translations have a more technical vocabulary. For a young child, however, you want something that's easier for them to understand."

As we talked, I also thought about experiences I have had internationally. Years ago, while in Singapore, I often found that my friends who spoke English didn't always understand my brand of Southern, American English! So I added, "And I guess that would go for cross-cultural situations as well? We tend to think of English translations as being used in North America, but a lot of English speakers around the world live in various cultural situations; I guess English translations for them would need to be sensitive to their cultural contexts."

Mark agreed. "People who speak English as a second language need translations that are sensitive to their situation. If they read a more literal translation, they can't understand it at all. Some versions were specially translated and developed for that purpose. Also, in many parts of the world, the British form of English has had more influence than American English."

I shifted in my seat a bit and said, "So the first reason we have so many English translations has to do with historical and cultural contexts; language is always changing, and the use of English varies among different groups of people. Let's talk about the other reason you mentioned, Mark."

Different Approaches to Doing Translation

I haven't mentioned this before, but Mark is a bundle of energy, a warm Christian scholar who is animated when he speaks. As we got into the issue of translation philosophies, he became even more excited, waving his arms as he explained the different approaches to translation.

"The second reason we have so many translations of the Bible concerns approaches to translation. Some people believe that a more literal, or 'formal equivalence,' version is the most accurate kind. Others (including me) believe that a 'functional equivalence' translation, one that seeks to capture the meaning of the text in clear and natural language—the way the reader normally would speak—tends to be a better translation for most people. All of us should agree that different kinds of translation, formal equivalence and functional equivalence, are helpful in different situations."

For scholars, like Mark and Clint, these subjects are basic. Yet perhaps a bit of explanation is in order. The Old Testament was originally written in Hebrew (with a small part being written in Aramaic, a language in the same family of languages as Hebrew); and the New Testament was written in Greek. All translators of the Bible work with these languages in order to bring God's Word over into English (or any other language). So, when Mark speaks of a formal equivalence translation or a functional equivalence translation, both approaches work with Hebrew in the Old Testament and Greek in the New, and both want to be faithful to what the Hebrew or Greek text is communicating. The difference between the translation approaches concerns how best to communicate what the original authors of the Bible wrote, as Clint explains.

Clint smiled at Mark's enthusiasm and added, "A basic question here is this: Should the translator place priority on the exact form of the original text (formal equivalence) or on clarity of the English expression (functional equivalence)? If the emphasis is placed on exactly following the wording of the original languages, readability suffers. Yet, if the translator stresses readability, literalness is sacrificed, and much more of the trans-lator's interpretations come through in the translation. *Every* translation involves interpretation because the translator has to make decisions about word meanings, grammatical structures, and other matters; strictly speaking, no translation is truly literal, and can't be because the structure and use of words vary greatly when we move from an ancient language to English."

I asked, "Could you explain a bit more about the two differ-ent approaches to translation?"

Clint thought for a minute, then picked up the conversation, "A formal equivalence translation will try, as much as possible, to use an English word that closely corresponds to each Hebrew or Greek term. It will also try to approximate the grammatical forms of the sentence, matching nouns with nouns, verbs with verbs, etc."

Thinking about how differently the Greek language works when compared to English, I said, "Yet, if you try to follow a word-for-word correspondence when moving from the biblical languages to English, the translation wouldn't make much sense, would it? You have already said that the two languages are differ-ent in many ways."

Clint nodded his head in agreement. "It would be gibberish. It would not make much sense. It would be a collection of words that might mean something, but it would be wrong if we just went word by word in the same grammatical structure. For instance, if we translated John 1:18 very literally, it would read, 'God no one has seen ever: only begotten God the being into the bosom of the father that one explained.' That is literal but does not make a good translation. But that is not what a formal equivalence translation is doing."

"So," I interjected, "what we mean by a formal equivalence translation is one that, while seeking to communicate as clearly as possible in understandable English, attempts to stay as close as possible to a word-for-word correspondence with the Hebrew or Greek."

Moving on, I said, "So we have more formal translations that are trying to track with word meanings consistently and patterns of words. Tell us more about functional equivalence translations."

Mark explained that the point with functional equivalence translations is to determine the function or the meaning of words and translate accordingly; in other words, the key questions are, what was the author trying to say, and how do we express that best in English? He continued, "The example I always use, since I'm from San Diego, comes from the Spanish language. In Spanish you say '¿*Cómo se llama?*' Most people would say a good translation of that phrase is 'What's your name?' But a literal translation of that question would be 'How yourself call?' Notice that this translation changes the verb 'call' (*llama*) to a noun, 'name,' and the word order in the question is changed. Would we say that 'What's your name?' is not an accurate translation because I changed the words around in bringing this question over into English? No. A good translation communicates the meaning, and that is what a functional equivalence translation is trying to do. By the way, Bible translators throughout the world, who are translating the Bible into hundreds of different languages, normally use this approach."

Clint added, "With functional equivalence we want to hear the sense of the passage like the original hearers of the New Testament would have heard it and in line with what the author intended to communicate."

Are Translations "God's Word" to Us?

I thought for a moment about the love that each of the three of us has for God's Word. All three of us hold to the authority of Scripture; we believe that every word of Scripture was inspired by God. We are men under the authority of God, and we want to be true to Scripture. We want to obey what God is saying to us, and I think we, like most of the believers we know, want to hear what God is saying to us through the Scriptures. So I raised the question of "authority" when it comes to translations. After all, our life as Christians in the church should be grounded on

God's Word, so we need to know we can trust the Bible we have in hand.

"Now, it sounds like when we're talking about translations, we're saying there are variables, questions of interpretation, and decisions to make when we translate God's Word from Hebrew and Greek into English (or any other language for that matter). So how can we speak to people about reading their NIV, HCSB, ESV, or NLT translation as the Word of God? How do we talk about authority when we speak of bringing the Greek and the Hebrew over into English? What do you say to a student or a church member who comes up and says, 'Are you saying that what I have in my hand is not the Word of God?'"

Clint nodded his head soberly, grasping the gravity of the question, then answered, "You want to reassure the person that what they have in their hand is the very Word of God, and the Scripture was given to be understood, but interpretation is part of the process. This was true even in the first century. When Paul went to the synagogues in Ephesus or Rome, for example, he was using a translation of the original Old Testament text. The original Old Testament text was written in Hebrew, and Paul was using a translation of the Old Testament in Greek (remember, the New Testament was in the process of being written during Paul's time), and yet he called what he was using, 'the Word of God.' On many occasions he stood in synagogues, or among believers in a church, and quoted (the Greek translation) or interpreted the words of the Old Testament for them. He also challenged Christian leaders, like Timothy, to do sound interpretation (2 Tim. 2:15). So believers from the beginning of the Christian movement understood that translation and interpretation were built into the process of dealing with God's Word. God in His wisdom gave us His Word in human language, yet the early Christians still received it as God's authoritative Word!"

I commented, "So Paul actually gives us an example to follow because he worked with a translation—the Greek version of the Old Testament—and both practiced and encouraged sound interpretation, in order to communicate with other people who were using that translation." As I thought about it, as the Christian movement spread across the world, translation of the Bible was done as a part of spreading the gospel and Christian teaching. People needed the Scriptures in their own language. So, when we do translation work today, as committed Christians, we are carrying on a great tradition that started two thousand years ago.

Mark chimed in, "Right! And think about the question you just asked. You said, 'How can we speak to people about reading their NIV translation or their NLT translation as the very Word of God?' Now think about that phrase—the Word of God. Well of course we know that the word *word* here is a translation of the Greek word *logos*. But the Greek word *logos* doesn't always mean a 'word.' It can mean 'a word,' but it also means 'a message.' Throughout the New Testament it frequently refers to a message. So when I hand someone an English Bible and say, 'This is the Word of God,' I'm not saying, 'These are the exact words of God' because the specific words that God originally inspired were in Hebrew and Greek. But I can say, 'This is the message of God'; this is the meaning of those Hebrew and Greek words, those specific statements, sentences, paragraphs, and books. So when we say 'the Word of God,' we're talking about the message, the meaning of the text as it came to us. Every English translation translates all of the words of God because those words are in Hebrew and Greek, but it retains the Word of God, the message from God, if it in fact communicates the meaning of the text accurately."

How Do Translations Get Produced Today?

I wanted to move us on to other issues, so I said, "OK, interesting stuff. It sounds like Bible translation is not an easy process, but it is an important process. So how do translations get done today? Do a couple of guys go into a room and just work it out, or what is done?"

Clint stated, "It's not just one person sitting alone in a room in isolation; normally teams of people work on almost any translation. Other teams review the final translation for accuracy. There are checks upon checks upon checks so that what you end up with is a good translation."

Clint and Mark went on to point out that in this team approach to producing a translation, an individual or a small group translates a book like Mark's Gospel, and an editor reviews their work. Then the translation is handed over to other scholars who review the translation and editors who evaluate the translation in terms of English style and grammar. So most translations really are a community project. This type of process not only catches mistakes made along the way but also guards against theological or interpretive bias. The outcome is that we have a number of excellent translations today, translations that are accurate and communicate well. These should be received as a gift to the church.

Heroes of Translation Work

I thought about the fact that translation work was not always this organized and this well supported in the history of the church. In church history, as well as international contexts today, people have paid a tremendous price to translate the Bible into the languages of common people. So I asked, "Can you think of an example, from church history or from the contexts of international missions, of someone who has paid a great price to translate the Bible, a person who exemplifies the value and cost of getting the Bible into a form that communicates with people?"

Mark lit up in response to this question. "My favorite story is that of William Tyndale. Tyndale was the first to produce a printed version of the New Testament in English that was translated directly from the Greek. He was a brilliant Greek and Hebrew scholar, and his version became the model for all English versions that followed. Much of the specific, well-known wording of the King James Version originally came from

Tyndale's translation. Tyndale was passionate about getting God's Word into the hands of common people. He once said, 'If God spares my life, my goal is to make the farm boy who pushes a plough know more Scripture than the Pope himself.' And this is what he did! Yet when Tyndale did his work, it was illegal to publish the Bible in any language except Latin—the language used by the Catholic Church in worship. The common folk couldn't read Latin (and many of the priests couldn't read the language well either), and the church of Tyndale's day did not want commoners to read their Bible. They feared they would find things in the Bible that didn't match up with the church's teaching.

"Because of persecution, Tyndale was forced to flee England for Europe. His work was published in 1526, and copies were smuggled back into England. The people loved it! Not only was it accurate; it was also readable. It was written in their language, the language of the heart. The people of England bought up all the copies and wore them out through use. Few copies of the original Tyndale edition have survived today because people read them until they fell apart! Wouldn't it be great if we could say the same about our Bibles today?

"But Tyndale's enemies bought up as many copies as possible and destroyed them. So Tyndale simply took the royalties he made and published even more! Sadly, Tyndale's opponents pursued him to Europe. He was betrayed, kidnapped, imprisoned, tortured, and eventually executed; he was strangled to death, and his body was burned. Tyndale believed so passionately in the Bible that he was willing to give his life so that people could hear God speak to them in their own language. His translation had an amazing impact, laying a foundation for English Bible translations that would come along through the centuries. He is a true hero of the faith."

Translation Work Elsewhere in the World

We tend to think of English translations of the Bible. As we moved toward wrapping up our time together, I asked Mark and

Clint, "Do most people in the world have a translation of the Bible in their language? What can we do to help others have the Bible in their languages?"

Mark responded, "This is a great question. While dozens of English versions are widely available, many languages and people groups do not have a single word of Scripture in their own language. That is a tragedy! Groups like Wycliffe Bible Translators, the United Bible Societies, the International Bible Society, New Tribes Mission, and many others work tirelessly to get the Bible into every language of humanity. According to Wycliffe's statistics, there are 6,912 languages around the world. Of these, 2,251 do not yet have a single verse of the Bible in their own language! It is critical to finish the task of making the Bible available to every man, woman, and child around the globe. I encourage people to support these missions!"

Mark's point is well taken. How many copies of the Bible do you and I have lying around our homes? We can do three things in response. First, take time right now and thank God for your ready access to the Bible. Second, consider giving away the copies of the Bible around your house that you don't use. Your church or another ministry in your town or city probably could use copies of the Bible to share with the people who come through their doors. Finally, consider supporting one of the ministries Mark mentioned above. Courageous men and women around the globe need our help in making God's Word available to every person, no matter their language.

Summary & Application

Summation

- We should be thankful for the translations of the Bible we have at our disposal! We have many different translations because:
  - Translation is an inexact science.

- Translators continue to try to improve on what has been done in the past.
- Language continues to change over time so updated translations are needed for clear communication.
- Different translations are needed to address different audiences.
- There are different approaches to doing translation work.

- The Bible was originally written in Hebrew (the Old Testament) and Greek (the New Testament).
- Formal equivalence translations are more "word for word," trying to stay as close as possible to more literal meanings of the original words in a passage. Functional equivalence translations are more "thought for thought" and seek to communicate the original author's meaning as accurately and clearly as possible.
- Most translations today are done by teams of scholars.
- Various translations are helpful for various purposes, and everyone should have several translations on hand.

Conversation

1. What is your favorite translation and why? After reading this chapter, are there other translations you would like to investigate and why?
2. What surprised you in this chapter? What questions do you have now that you have read the chapter?
3. As a group, read Psalm 23 in three different translations. Discuss which translation of the passage you liked best and why. What details in the passage stick out to you as you hear the passage read in different translations?
4. What are the benefits of using one primary translation for broad reading of the Scriptures and for study? What are the disadvantages?

Transformation

Assignment 1: Take time this week to go to a bookstore and browse the various translations offered there, or search online for "Bible translations" and explore a Web site or two that make it possible to read the Bible in various translations.

Assignment 2: Read Romans 8 in four or five different translations and write out three verses from the chapter, in whichever translation you wish, that seem especially fresh to you at this time.

CHAPTER 4

Reading the Bible for Transformation

A Conversation with George H. Guthrie

But be doers of the word and not hearers only, deceiving yourselves.

—James 1:22

The Bible is unique among the books in the world, meant not only to inform us but also to transform us in ways that bring us closer to God and enable us to live more effectively for Him. Yet that change is contingent on our being "doers" of the Word of God rather than merely "hearers." In this chapter I carry out a conversation with myself and, believe me, this is not the first time this has happened! I have been teaching Introduction to Bible Study since the early 1990s and have thought a great deal about how we might apply the Bible to our lives and the challenges that surround that endeavor. In this conversation I discuss why thoughtful application might be difficult for us, steps to appropriate application of the Scriptures, various ways we can apply the Scriptures, and the key role application plays in God's agenda for our world.

My family and I live on five and a half acres north of Jackson, Tennessee. We love gardening flowers, fruits, and vegetables and watching the multitudes of birds that come to our feeders. Each year blue herons, wood ducks, and kingfishers visit our pond, and from March to July we host some twenty to thirty pairs of migratory purple martins, which raise their young on our property before making the long trip back to Brazil where they spend the winter. In the past few weeks we have had visits from raccoons, those masked critters that swipe our birdseed, a beautiful red fox that has helped himself to two of our ducks, and a deer, which, thankfully, came nowhere near our garden. Our conversation took place as we walked the quarter-mile trek around our property.

As we started our walk, I expressed my appreciation for finally having time to myself. "Dr. Guthrie, thanks very much for taking time to talk to me today."

"Well, George, I am beside myself that you would ask. Anytime. Really, *any* time. I am always available to you!"

What Do We Mean by "Application"?

As we walked past my tomato beds and toward the woods at the back of the yard, I raised the question, "What do we mean when we talk about application?"

Pausing just for a moment, Dr. Guthrie responded, "When we speak of application, we mean the thoughtful appropriation of biblical truth to our lives—how we take it in, embrace it, and adjust our lives to bring them in line with the truth of God's Word. Application really is a key to renewal and ongoing growth in the Christian life. Life gets exciting when we see God changing us on a consistent basis."

I was a bit puzzled as I thought about that definition, not because it was hard to understand but because application seems so obvious that everyone ought to do it almost automatically. So I said, "It would seem that application should be a no-brainer for us as Christians. Do we really need to spend time thinking about how to apply the Scriptures? Doesn't it just boil down to acting on what we hear?"

We now were walking past my tool shed. Dr. Guthrie looked at a shovel that had been propped up next to the door and shook his head a bit. "Look at that shovel. Whoever left it by the door could have just taken the few easy, extra steps and hung it in its place on the tool rack, but he didn't, and it probably was *you* who left it out!" he said with a smile. I laughed as I remembered propping the shovel up against the shed the day before.

Not as Easy as It Seems

Dr. Guthrie continued, "It might seem that application would be one of the easiest aspects of Bible reading and study, but it actually is one of the most difficult to do consistently and well. Just like your neglect of the shovel, I find that sound, specific application is easy for my university students to neglect."

Realizing he was right, I asked, "Why is that?"

We now had made our way around to the west side of the pond in front of our house. Dr. Guthrie reached down and took a rock, throwing it into the pond. Watching the ripples swirl outward from the splash, he commented, "First, we have our sin natures to contend with. Frankly I often find that I really don't want to adjust my life to bring it in line with God's Word; my heart tends to be rebellious or too lazy to act on what I know to be the truth. Paul writes, 'For the flesh has desires that are opposed to the Spirit' (Gal. 5:17 NET). In Jesus' parable of the sower (Mark 4:3–20), three of the four illustrations He offers have to do with 'heart problems' when it comes to receiving God's Word. Jesus describes hearts that are hard and unreceptive to God's Word, hearts that are shallow and turn from God's Word when things get difficult, and hearts that are congested, in which worry and desire for material things elbow out the Word. If I am having a hard time focusing on God's Word, I ask myself, 'What is the condition of my heart right now?' So one reason we struggle with applying the Bible to our lives is our spiritual condition: we aren't really spiritually receptive to what God has for us."

We walked right under our purple martin houses, which are about ten to fifteen feet in the air, supported by a metal rack designed to keep predators away from the martins' nests and young. In the past month a Cooper's hawk has been raiding the colony, at times carrying off an unfortunate bird that was a bit too slow to evade the hawk's acrobatic maneuvers. Wanting to probe more deeply the challenges we face in living well in the Scriptures, I asked, "What else keeps us from applying the Word to our lives?"

Dr. Guthrie responded, "A second factor—and I see this as a pervasive problem in the Western church—we have been trained to be vague, mushy, and general in our treatment of Scripture rather than clear and specific. C. S. Lewis once noted that Jesus never dealt in vague, idealistic gas in His teaching but rather demanded specific changes in life. Consider how specific many of Jesus' instructions are in the Sermon on the Mount: Don't be angry (Matt. 5:22); don't lust (5:28); give up your coat (5:40); go two miles (5:41). Jesus meant for people to put His words into action in specific, tangible ways. Our problem is that we think it is enough just to grasp general concepts as if taking in the Word of God is a mental exercise. Jesus, rather, meant our interaction with the Word to be a life exercise. Therefore I have started challenging my students to stay away from 'VIGs' (vague, idealistic gases!). Rather than saying, 'I need to love people more' in a noncommittal way, we should consider, 'What am I going to do today, or this week, to demonstrate love to a specific person?' Instead of saying, 'I need to have more faith,' we should think through how we might express our faith specifically today. Applications often should be tangible, measurable, and specific. At the end of the day or week, I should be able to look back and say, 'I worked that into my life in this way.' This is when we see life begin to change in exciting ways."

Needing a bit more clarity, I asked, "How do you think we have been trained to be vague rather than specific in our applications?"

"Well, George, many Christians hear the Bible taught several times per week and walk away saying, 'That was great,' or 'I didn't get much out of that,' without ever considering what they need to do to act on what they have heard. When a person has done that year after year, it becomes habit. We, as teachers, too often do not help our listeners think through the specific implications of the truth we have communicated. Therefore, some go to church and Bible studies week after week and never adjust any aspects of their lives to bring them in line with God's Word. They have a vague idea they should, but they are not used to thinking specifically how to do so. Therefore, we have trained them to be hearers of the Word and not doers, to allude to James 1:22. James says people in that situation 'deceive themselves,' by which he means that they think they are on the right track spiritually but aren't. In reality this dynamic constitutes one of the greatest crises for the contemporary church. Scripture simply is not changing us, making us different from those around us who do not profess faith, and they know it. By our lack of application of the Word in meaningful ways, we are sending a message to the world that reads, 'Christianity really is irrelevant to life.'"

As we continued our walk and rounded the southern end of the pond, we walked past hickory trees, pines, oaks, mulberries, ash, maples, a magnolia, and other species of trees. The variety brought to mind another question, so I asked, "When you speak of acting on biblical truth, what forms does that take?"

Dr. Guthrie nodded his head knowingly, took off his cap, and wiped his brow since the morning was beginning to warm. He then continued, "I have emphasized tangible *actions* in our application of Scripture because active application of biblical truth is so neglected in many people's experience of the Bible. When we speak of actions, we probably think of activities like washing the dishes for my wife or taking my child out for a meal and a talk, and these are appropriate and needed. However, other facets of application need to be considered. Some biblical passages, like Psalm 19:1–4, call us to worship, and the most appropriate application is to fall on our knees and spend time praising God. Other passages draw us into thanking God for specific gifts in life. Still other biblical texts might consist of a particular teaching about God, and our response should be to make a decision to change our thinking about that aspect of theology. Finally, when we meditate on the Scriptures, thinking deeply about their truths, turning specific concepts over and over in our minds, this is an aspect of appropriating the truth. As we read the Bible consistently year after year, so that its thoughts become our thoughts, that is an important form of application. So our application can, and should, take various forms."

We made our way around to the back porch and took a seat in a black wicker rocking chair. Pat, my wife, made us mint tea to quench the thirst built up during our walk, but I was ready to move on to the meat of the conversation. "What, then, are the steps to appropriate application in general?" I asked.

Dr. Guthrie rocked for a moment, reached down to scratch Beauty, our chocolate lab, who in terms of energy is just one step above a rug, and spoke carefully, "Let me begin by giving a point of clarification. We should not think about application as a series of steps we do at the end of our reading or study of the Bible. The seeds of right application are planted at the beginning of the time we sit down to read the biblical text, in the soil of our attitudes and our posture toward the Word. Are we receptive? Are we committed to hearing God's truth and acting on it? I teach my students to spend a brief time in prayer at the beginning of their Bible reading or study, submitting themselves to God and crying out to Him for discernment. In this way we begin to move toward application from the beginning. At the same time, too many of us rush right to application without thinking through what the text is actually teaching. Imagine the Sunday school class in which a passage is read, then the teacher says, 'What does this passage mean to you?' The responses often consist of people sharing what they see as the implications of the passage, but if the passage has not been understood, the applications are going to be baseless. In short, *sound application must begin with sound interpretation.*"

"So we must read well to live well?" I commented.

Dr. Guthrie smiled and said, "You took the words right out of my mouth!"

I continued, "So once we have learned to read the text well, how do we move to thoughtful application?"

Ticking the points off on his fingers, Dr. Guthrie ran down the list. "Begin with *clarifying the main point or points of the passage*

and how the original audience was to apply the truth communicated.
Write out the main point if that helps. Sometimes the main point
is obvious and clearly stated. I mentioned Psalm 19 earlier. When
verse 1 states, 'The heavens declare the glory of God, and the sky
proclaims the work of His hands,' the language is figurative, but
the truth proclaimed is straightforward. The creation of God
reflects the glory of God. The original audience was being called
to worship God. Yet at other times we need to think more carefully about the main point."

I interjected, "Hopefully the rest of this book will help with
understanding how to get at sound interpretation of more difficult passages."

"Once you are fairly clear on the main point of the passage
and what the original audience was being challenged to do in
response," Dr. Guthrie stated as he raised a second finger, "*think
through both the similarities and differences between you and the original
readers of the passage.* In a passage like Psalm 19:1, the similarities are: we both worship the God of Israel, we both can observe
nature, etc. Differences are there as well. For example, I live in
the twenty-first century, not hundreds of years before the time of
Christ. If I live in the city, I might note that it is difficult to see
the stars at night from where I live. If I am dealing with a passage
having to do with idol worship, I could point out that people in
my immediate circle do not struggle with worshipping stone or
wood statues; their idols tend to take different forms!"

A hummingbird suddenly swooped in for a drink of red nec-
tar from the hummingbird feeder. We paused just for a moment
to let the beautiful little bird drink. Then, taking another sip of
iced tea, I asked, "Why is it important to note the differences and
similarities we have with the original audience?"

Dr. Guthrie put his hands behind his head and watched the
hummer soar out above our bamboo grove on the east side of
the property. He answered, "Because the specific applications
of a biblical truth by the original audience might be carried out
in relation to a specific aspect of their culture, like the wearing
of tunics, for example. We need to be thoughtful about what

aspects of a biblical passage are meant to be transferable to us and which are simple, cultural differences. Take that bamboo; in one way it is analogous to the principles of Scripture since it has various applications in various cultures around the world today. In China it may be used for scaffolding in a building project, a use you never will see in the United States. Here in West Tennessee, most people, if they use bamboo at all, will use it to stake their tomato plants or perhaps to build a trellis of some kind. We have bamboo in common with our Chinese friends and yet different applications. When we deal with Scripture, we have certain things in common with the biblical audience like our need to hear the truth and to understand the principles being taught. The principles of Scripture are universally relevant. I may not wear a tunic, but I do wear and value clothing. If I am dealing with Jesus' command to give a person my tunic, the principle is important for me to understand and live even though I don't wear a tunic."

At this point we got up and walked out into the garden area, strolling around raised beds of potatoes, squash, tomatoes, corn, beans, and other vegetables, as well as fig and apple trees. "OK, Dr. Guthrie, what's next?"

Reaching down to pluck a shoot of nut grass out of the sunflower bed, he replied, "Third, *think through various contexts of your life to which the passage might apply.* You might think about home, work, school, public life, personal life, relationships, church, etc. These garden beds each have a slightly different environment to meet the growing needs of the different flowers, vegetables, or fruit growing in them. Some need soil that is slightly more acidic or sandy. Some do better in soil that actually is less fertile. Each environment is different. In our lives we have different needs in our various contexts. For instance, my application to love others is going to be different between home and work. In both places I need to express love, but how I put that into practice is applied in different ways."

"So the shape of my applications," I remarked, "will be determined somewhat by the various contexts of my life?"

Nodding his head in agreement, Dr. Guthrie continued, "Fourth and finally, *think about a specific application of the biblical truth to your life.* For instance, back on our example of Psalm 19:1, my application could be personal: 'Spend time this morning praising God for the various ways His creation reflects His glory.' Or my application could be relational: 'The next time Bob mentions what a beautiful day it is, take the opportunity to share a word of witness with him about how the beauty of creation points to God's talent in creating it.' The key is to be specific enough that you can actually act on that truth in the near future. Such action is a vital way of embracing God's truth, of expressing real faith" (see James 2:14–17).

Conclusion: Being Open to Hear

As we moved toward wrapping up our conversation, I could see the importance of being specific in working on application, but I asked, "Does this get a bit overwhelming if every biblical truth I hear or read compels me to specific action?"

He responded, "I think the key questions are: Am I open to hearing what the Spirit is saying to me through the Word in ways I need to adjust my life? And am I characterized by making adjustments to my life based on God's Word? If we just have one or two areas in our lives each week in which we are thoughtfully making specific application of biblical truth, it would make a profound difference in the way we live and in our witness to the watching world. It is not easy, but there is no substitute for being 'doers of the Word.'"

As we headed for the house, I commented to Dr. Guthrie that I saw eye to eye with him more than all the other friends with whom I had talked for this book. He laughed and said, "I'm not surprised."

Summary & Application

Summation

- Application is the thoughtful appropriation of biblical truth to our lives—how we take it in, embrace it, and adjust our lives to bring them in line with the truth of God's Word.
- Application can be difficult to do consistently because of our sinfulness and because many of us have been trained to think in terms of "vague, idealistic gases" (VIGs) rather than specific action.
- Application might take the form of a tangible action, worship, meditation, or adjusting our theology.
- Sound application must begin with sound interpretation.
- The steps to application are:

  - Begin with clarifying the main point or points of the passage and how the original audience was to apply the truth communicated.
  - Think through both the similarities and differences between you and the original readers of the passage.
  - Think through various contexts of your life to which the passage might apply.
  - Think about a specific application of the biblical truth to your life.

- Don't get overwhelmed. Work toward being characterized by making specific application at least one to two times per week.

Conversation

1. What is one specific application of biblical truth you have made to your life in the past month? How has that made a difference in your life?
2. According to Dr. Guthrie, specific application can be difficult to do well and to do consistently. What

reasons does he give for this difficulty? What are other challenges to applying the Scriptures?

3. What might be examples of how we treat the Scriptures too generally?

4. How might the non-Christians you know respond if all the Christians around them started living out biblical truth in profound ways? Do you know of examples of a non-Christian being impacted by believers living out biblical truth in an authentic way?

5. Of the four main steps Dr. Guthrie shares for moving toward sound application, which is the most difficult for you and why?

6. Read James 2:14–17. What might be a specific, tangible application of this passage for us as individuals or as a group?

Transformation

As you read your Bible this week, listen to a sermon or Bible study, or study the Word yourself, use the four steps to application given in this chapter to identify at least one specific way you can apply biblical truth to your life. Be prepared to share your application(s) with the group next week, or share your applications with a friend.

PART TWO

Reading the Old Testament

CHAPTER 5

Reading the Old Testament Stories

A Conversation with Bruce Waltke

When your son asks you in the future, "What is the meaning of the decrees, statutes, and ordinances, which the LORD our God has commanded you?" tell him, "We were slaves of Pharaoh in Egypt, but the LORD brought us out of Egypt with a strong hand."

—Deuteronomy 6:20–21

 I love great stories. My favorites include Dickens' *David Copperfield*, with its verbose Mr. Micawber and the unflappable (except for "the donkeys!") Aunt Betsy Trotwood, and the epic *Lord of the Rings* trilogy. I grieve the passing of my children's growing-up years when we would sit and enter the worlds of *If You Give a Mouse a Cookie*, *Winnie the Pooh*, *Good Night Moon*, and (one I can still quote verbatim through several pages) *Moo Moo Peekaboo*. As Joshua and Anna got older, we went through the wardrobe into Narnia, romped through the woods in Redwall, and walked the fields of England, learning about animals with James Herriot. I still love these books because they do what they do so well, drawing the reader into other worlds, other places and times and ways of thinking or imagining.

Large portions of the Old Testament come to us in the form of stories. They call us into a world both foreign and familiar, challenging us to find our place in a big story different from the small, boxed-in set of our personal, time-bound, culturally conditioned tales. They call us to enter God's grand story, which tells what He is up to in the world.

To gather us around the proverbial campfire and lead us into these stories, I could think of no one better than Professor Bruce Waltke, one of my favorite Old Testament teachers and one of the premier Old Testament scholars in the world. The author of numerous books and articles, he is loved among fellow believers for his commitment to Christ and the church and widely respected among even secular scholars for his erudition, skills in Hebrew language and literature, and careful work on the text of the Bible. Listening to him explain an Old Testament story is like sitting down with a wise Jewish grandfather who thoughtfully expounds the truths of the universe in a casual Jersey accent. One of the last scholars I interviewed for this book, I met Professor Waltke at a November meeting of the Evangelical Theological Society in New Orleans, Louisiana. We also videotaped the interview, capturing the words from this thoughtful man on camera. So, surrounded by bright lights and a camera crew, we sat down for our talk. In the city of beignets, battles, and Bourbon Street, we discussed the fascinating, rough-and-tumble world of Old Testament stories.

First Principles for Reading the Old Testament Stories Well

God Is the Main Hero of the Old Testament Stories

I began our conversation by asking Professor Waltke, "Why have the Old Testament stories stood the test of time?"

He thought for a moment and then began with a smile, "We're all interested in stories just as we all love a good joke. We love the tension of a good story, and the Old Testament stories have plenty of tension. But primarily the Old Testament stories have stood the test of time because the main hero of the story is God, and He is eternally relevant for our lives. In the story of Moses, we are told that God's name means 'I Am.' This tells us that He is the ultimate reality. He always was, He is, and He will be."

I interjected, "He's never out-of-date."

Professor Waltke agreed. "He's never out-of-date, and who He really is has been revealed to us in Scripture. He says, in essence, 'You have to know Me as I reveal Myself to you, a God of grace, a God of love, a God of truth and holiness, a God of justice, everything your heart needs.'"

I added, "So as we read the Old Testament stories, we need to keep in mind, first of all, that these stories have God as the main actor; and we need to ask, 'What is this story revealing about God?'"

The professor responded, "That's exactly right. God has revealed much to us in the form of these stories about Himself, and He is the main point. When we are reading about Adam and Eve, or Joshua and Jericho, or David and Goliath, we need to remember that *we are not* the main point of the stories. We too often begin by asking, 'What does this story tell me about me?' God is the main point. Keep that in mind."

I thought that a helpful point. Generally, I tend to be self-centered in life, and I live in a me-oriented culture and time in history. My most fundamental questions as I read the Bible tend to slip into a form of "What's in it for me?" So I need the Old Testament stories to reorient me toward a bigger view of God, who always is at the heart of these stories. At the same time these stories obviously are meant to connect with us as human beings. So I asked Professor Waltke about how they draw us as human beings and confront us with the issues of life while keeping the focus on God.

The Old Testament Stories Parallel Our Lives

He answered, "The stories often have at their core the struggles of people to believe God, to trust Him, and I think we all face those struggles; so the stories ring true for us. Also, almost every story has a protagonist, usually the good guy, and his opposition, the antagonist, usually the bad guy. Consequently a tension in the story moves it toward a climax in which this tension between good and evil comes to a critical moment. This is true for our lives as well. The Old Testament stories are not primarily about us, but they do parallel our lives. We struggle to live by faith. Sometimes, in a climactic moment of our own stories, we find the reality of God's presence with us in the midst of our difficulties, just as the characters in the Old Testament did. So the Old Testament stories can really speak to us in ways we understand."

As Professor Waltke spoke, it dawned on me that many of the dynamics we see in the Old Testament stories are familiar to most of us since we have been reading, or watching, or listening to stories all of our lives. Good guys and bad guys, crises and climaxes, the struggle of a main character to trust that the story will have a good ending—all of these are common to great stories such as those by Dickens or Dostoevsky, Tolkien, Tolstoy, or Twain. These great stories are great because they speak with unmistakable relevance to our lives. We identify with emotions such as hope, despair, longing, or fear in the characters of good stories because we experience those same emotions. Even fantasy works this way. G. K. Chesterton once said, "Stories about dragons are important, not because dragons are real but because they show us that dragons can be beaten." So, as we begin to ask, "What does this story tell me about God?" we can also ponder, "How do I fit into God's story?"

A Good Story Has Tension

I wanted to explore a bit more the idea of tension as central to a good story. I remember watching children's movies with my daughter when she was younger. A story would come to a scary part, a crisis. The music changed, and things seemed to be going wrong. I could tell Anna was getting a bit upset as she snuggled up close to me, sometimes shutting her eyes. Knowing what was coming, I often would turn to my sweet little five-year-old and say, "It's OK. This is the crisis, but things are going to get better!" Knowing the ending of the story really helped.

I commented to Professor Waltke, "As we read the Old Testament stories, we may be unsettled by tension in a story or puzzled by the tension we experience as we are reading it. We might not understand why something is happening. A character in the story might be doing something we know is foolish. A story might take a tragic turn. But tension isn't necessarily a bad thing when we are reading the Bible, is it?"

He responded, shaking his head slightly, "No, tension is absolutely essential to life. We grow and develop through tension. Our character is shaped by it. If God answered our prayers immediately, relieving all of our tension in life, it would destroy us because we would see God as a tool to be used, like a genie in Aladdin's lamp. We would become even more selfish than we already are. By not rewarding virtue immediately, or punishing vice immediately, God develops our character. So tensions—living in a story in which there is a struggle between good and evil—are really necessary to our own development. In the same way, the tension we find in the Old Testament stories tells us something about how to live with tension in our own relationships with God."

I asked, "How do the Old Testament stories accomplish that?"

Shutting his eyes briefly, the professor shaped his words carefully. "The stories depict all aspects of life—the good and the bad. They tell about the great joys of following God, but they don't back up from the fact that life also can be hard and confusing. When we face difficulties or confusion in life, the stories of the Bible offer us perspective. They tell us, 'You are not alone in this experience.' We know from the stories of the Bible that what we are experiencing is normal for God's people and that God is still there for His people when they are experiencing such things. Also we see that these stories have a beginning and an ending; God has shaped the story from the beginning, and He is carrying it through to the end. So we see how the story being written by God turns out, and this gives us hope. Of course the reality of life is that we really never see how our part of the story turns out until we're with our Lord; only then will we be able to see all the ways God was working, sometimes especially through the difficult parts of our lives. As Hebrews 11 tells us, the heroes of the

Old Testament stories show us that trusting God is the right way
to live no matter what we are experiencing."

Joseph as an Example

I thought about the story of Joseph, found in the latter part of
the book of Genesis, as an example, and I mentioned that story
to Professor Waltke. "We read through those chapters of Genesis
and see Joseph put in prison. If we have read the story before, we
know what's coming. But if we read the details, Joseph actually
spends a number of years in prison just waiting. He was in what
I call the 'in-between time.' In the story he sits between the point
of injustice that has landed him in prison and the point of God
delivering him. So he is living in that moment of tension where
we live a lot of our Christian lives."

The professor commented, "Yes we do. I remember one time
in class we were reading Genesis 37 in the Hebrew text, and
I'd made the point that every detail in the story is there for a
purpose. We came to the part where Joseph goes up to see his
brothers at Shechem. When Joseph gets to Shechem, the brothers are not there. We're told he was wandering around in a field,
and a man happened to see him and gave him information about
his brothers.

"So a student in the class asked me, 'What's with this wandering around in the field? If all the parts of a story are important,
what's the purpose of that?' And I realized the purpose of it was
that we might understand that in God's providence, in His guiding of events, sometimes it seems like you're wasting time. Your
activities seem meaningless. But the reality is, if Joseph hadn't
wasted time there in Shechem, he would have arrived too early
for the Midianite merchants coming through. Since he had been
wandering around, he arrived at just the right moment to be
picked up by that bunch heading to Egypt where he would eventually be exalted and used by God to save a lot of people's lives,
including the lives of everyone in his family.

"I've had students tell me how helpful that was to them.
When they're going through life, and they seem to be spinning

their wheels, wasting time, God is at work. That is the wonderful thing about a story; you can identify with the characters, and you can see how it turns out, and that gives you hope. The stories give you and me transcendent values that the human heart is yearning for. The stories challenge us to trust God."

What Did Old Testament Storytellers Want to Accomplish?

Thus far in my talk with Bruce Waltke, we had discussed two absolutely critical points for reading the Old Testament stories well: the need to focus on God as the main character of the Old Testament stories and the need to note how these stories parallel our lives. I could see how these perspectives are most foundational for us as we enter the story of the Bible, actively engaged in reading the stories appropriately. We also had seen that the tension in these stories not only makes for good storytelling, it challenges us to live well in the midst of the tensions we experience in life. These insights were helpful and were beginning to offer fresh perspectives on how we could read the stories more effectively.

Yet there seemed to be one big assumption hovering backstage of our discussion like an actor anxious to step into the spotlight. We seemed to be assuming that these stories have purposes, goals the writers had in mind as they painted their word pictures of people, places, events, and outcomes. So I wanted us to explore the objectives the human authors of the stories seem to have had in mind as they were crafting their narratives.

The Stories Are Historical

In answer, Professor Waltke pointed to the work of Mier Sternberg, who has written on the art of the Old Testament stories. "According to Sternberg, there are primarily three objectives. The first objective of the Old Testament storytellers was *historical*. They were recording historical events; these are not fairy tales. These events actually happened. The writers point to specific times and places in order to anchor us as readers in real history. Even the genealogies, which many people dread as they read through the Old Testament, have the purpose of moving us from one point in history to another, as well as telling us a lot about the identity of the Old Testament characters and people groups. Generally, though, through the Old Testament stories we see how God has shaped history in specific ways to craft a people for Himself."

The Stories Reinforce the Covenant

The professor then moved to a second point concerning the purpose for the Old Testament stories. "This brings us to a second objective these writers had in mind. The storytellers wanted to communicate a *message*, and at the heart of the message is the covenant that God established between Israel and Himself. In that covenant relationship God is always calling for His people to trust Him on the basis of who He has revealed Himself to be, and this trust expresses itself in obedience. God says in effect, 'You will be My people, and I will be your God. I will take care of you and guide you; you can count on Me. But I am holy, and you must live in obedience to My ways and not simply do your own thing.'

"Of course, the problem with us as people—and we see this throughout the stories of the Old Testament—is that we want God's care without being careful with His covenant commands. So the stories of the Old Testament reinforce the covenant relationship between God and His people, and this is the glue that ties the whole Bible together. If we understand that the Bible is all about relationship with God, we will be getting at one of the main purposes for these stories."

I interjected, "So these stories are meant to pull us deeper into a faithful relationship with God. Can you give us an example of how we can read the stories in light of the covenant?"

Professor Waltke replied, "Certainly. At the beginning of the book of Judges, we have the story of the Israelites conquering the town of Bezek (Judg. 1:4–7). The king of the town was Adoni-bezek, and they cut off his thumbs and his big toes.

Adoni-bezek says, 'Seventy kings with their thumbs and big toes cut off have picked up scraps under my table. Now God has paid me back for what I did to them' (Judg. 1:7 NIV). Then, we are told, they brought him back to Jerusalem, and he died there.

"A number of commentators think Adoni-bezek is a great guy who understands God's justice, and they interpret this passage as primarily communicating the idea of justice. But this passage must be read in light of Deuteronomy 7 and the terms of the covenant. In Deuteronomy 7:2 the covenant instructions give specific directions for how to deal with the people of the land of Canaan: 'And when the LORD your God delivers them over to you and you defeat them, you must completely destroy them. Make no treaty with them and show them no mercy.' The Israelites were supposed to exterminate completely the evil incarnated in Canaanite society. So this passage in Judges 1 is not about justice; it is about Israel's failure to deal carefully with God's instructions under the covenant, and it sets the tone for Judges, which is a book about the utter failure of God's people. In other words, the way they dealt with this Canaanite king marks the beginning of the decline of Israel. Unless you understand the covenant of Deuteronomy 7, you really will misinterpret the story about Adoni-bezek in Judges 1, as many commentators do."

I interjected, "So in dealing with this Canaanite king, the Israelites do something that seems generally appropriate and even fits the sensibilities of our culture, but they are not careful with the Word of God."

Waltke responded, "That's right. The Israelites at this point are following the pattern of a Canaanite king, not the ways of God. And I see a similar dynamic in the church today. We're making small compromises, and we're becoming more and more like the world all the time because we don't deal with God's Word carefully."

The Stories Were Written as Art

I summarized, "OK, in terms of what the Old Testament storytellers were wanting to accomplish through the telling of these stories, you have pointed to a historical purpose and to an ideological purpose—to reinforce the message of covenant faithfulness. What was the third reason the Old Testament stories were written?"

The camera crew looked on intently, caught up in the conversation. They were focused on their craft, but they also were tuned into the discussion. Waltke's third point would be relevant for these videographers, who work with light and sound and images to convey powerful messages. The professor commented, "Now the third purpose the writers had for these Old Testament stories was *aesthetic*; they wanted to communicate in a way that was beautiful and compelling. In other words, the history and the messages about the covenant have been crafted so as to be works of art. They *prescribe* what God's people should do, but they also *persuade* by telling these stories well. One scholar has said, 'You don't know what the Bible means until you know *how* it means—how it was put together to communicate a message.'"

The Stories Have Structure

I asked if he could give us an example. Professor Waltke gladly agreed to do so. "Take the story of Solomon as told in the first twelve chapters of 1 Kings. It is crafted in what is called a 'chiastic' pattern. The first part of the story corresponds to the last part, the second part corresponds to the next to the last part, and so on. The story begins in 1 Kings 1 with Solomon inheriting the kingdom from his father, David. It ends in 1 Kings 12 with a born leader named Jeroboam taking a good portion of the kingdom away from Solomon's heir, Rehoboam. In chapter 2, Solomon's kingdom is established. In chapter 11, Solomon's kingdom is disestablished. In that chapter God says, 'Since you have done this and did not keep My covenant and My statutes, which I commanded you, I will tear the kingdom away from you and give it to your servant' (1 Kings 11:11). In chapters 3–4 we see Solomon's wisdom and literary gifts, which God uses for good. In chapter 10 Solomon's wisdom is misused for selfishness and splendor and his own glory. In chapters 5–6 Solomon builds the shell of the temple, but the utensils have not yet been crafted and set up. In 1 Kings 7:15–9:9 Solomon finishes the utensils for the temple and dedicates it."

With a twinkle in his eye, Waltke asked, "What, then, is left right in the middle of the story? In the middle Solomon interrupts building God's house/temple to build *his own* palace complex because he lost sight of God as his first love. This passage on Solomon's building his palace complex seems out of place, but it is significant that it is right in the middle of the story about Solomon's reign, and it serves as a turning point in the structure of these first twelve chapters of 1 Kings. In a story that is set up with this type of chiastic structure, the part right in the middle is the most important part, the main point. For Solomon, his palace and the palace of his Egyptian wife were given priority over finishing the setup of the temple and preparing it for worship services. This tells us something about Solomon's heart. When we come to 1 Kings 11, we find that his heart has been turned away from the Lord by his wives."

I remarked, "So we can clue into the main message of the story about Solomon's reign by understanding how the story is put together artistically, identifying the passage on the building of his palace complex as at the heart of the story." That was helpful to me. I have often wondered about Solomon's fall away from the Lord. How could someone who was so wise, who had heard God speak to him twice, be so spiritually dull just a few chapters later? What Professor Waltke pointed out about the structure of the story suggests that the seed of Solomon's fall was his putting the things of the earth before his worship of the Lord. At the end of the day, his heart, which began as that of the kindly Dr. Jekyl, became that of a diabolical Mr. Hyde. This is why his wives were able to turn his heart completely away from God. The crafting of the story provides the clue to this critical insight.

Professor Waltke then shared how relevant such an insight can be for us in our relationship with the Lord. "In the 1990s I taught on these chapters from 1 Kings at church and pointed out this interpretation of 1 Kings 7:1–14. This was at a time when the stock market was going gangbusters. An elder of the church told me that other elders had resigned from the church because they wanted to seize the moment and focus on making money. He said, 'I was thinking of resigning too until I saw what happened to Solomon in this passage. I decided I was not going to put my portfolio before the church, before God.'"

Further Help for Reading the Stories Well

Sometimes a key insight, like the structure of a passage, can flip the switch to our understanding of a story of the Old Testament. As with the church elder Professor Waltke just mentioned, that understanding can give us practical help in our Christian lives. So, as you and I read these stories, we should take note of how the stories are put together, and a good commentary or study Bible can be a tremendous aid in sorting out a story's structure. Reading carefully, we can begin by watching for an introduction and conclusion, key transitions in a story, or what seems to be the climax. As we begin to tune into the flow or structure of the story, we begin to understand the purpose of the story.

Yet, some stories are so difficult (dare I say horrible) on the surface that we struggle to grasp any redeeming qualities from them at all. I asked Professor Waltke, "How should we read the really difficult stories of the Old Testament? I think of the story of Jephthah's daughter in Judges 11. How do we approach those kinds of stories that jar us when we stumble upon them?"

How Do We Read the Difficult Stories of the Old Testament?

He thought for a moment, closed his eyes, and then began, "Well, when you hit a story like that, you may not have an answer to it right away. You might have to put it in your pocket and wait a few years until you're able to get some clarification on it. But begin by understanding the context. The time of the Judges was a time of chaos when the people of God did not know the Word of God and played fast and loose with the covenant of God. Keep that in mind."

I asked Professor Waltke if he would remind us about the details of the story.

"If you remember, Jephthah really is a negotiator as well as brave warrior. Jephthah's brothers have rejected him, and they don't want to share the inheritance with him because he is the son of a concubine. His brothers are the elders and captains of Israel at the time, but the Ammonites are threatening them. The brothers know they are not competent. They just want a good life. They don't want to risk themselves, so they call Jephthah to be their leader. He negotiates with them and tells them they are going to have to make him head of the family.

"Now Jephthah doesn't really have much faith in God. He has a hesitant faith that God is going to help him, even though God has given the Israelites covenant promises. So he makes a risky vow and says, 'Whoever or whatever comes out of the house, I'm going to devote to you, God. I'm going to sacrifice it to you if you give me the victory.' Now you have to understand that in this culture they often kept their animals in the house with them. He may have expected a bull or some other animal to come out of the house, but it was an absolutely stupid vow. When a warrior was returning from battle, the women would come out of the houses and celebrate the victorious hero. Who did he expect to come out of the house? So his daughter comes out. And then he says, 'You've been a disaster to me.' Notice how self-centered his response is. He is not concerned that he is going to take her life. He is saying, 'Poor me.' It's ironic and shows the nature of the man.

"So it's a horrible story. It shows the consequences of unbelief. Jephthah is not to be commended for this. And the fact of the matter is he had other options. He could have sacrificed himself. That would have been a possibility. He could have looked to God's priests to help him understand the law. The law left open the possibility of redemption when you could not or should not keep your vow. But he doesn't seek the priest for insight into the law. So, Jephthah illustrates how bad things were in Israel at the time. He shows us how not to live for God. He doesn't know

God's Word, and he doesn't have the proper faith. God works through him because God sometimes uses messed-up vessels. Yet Jephthah serves as an example of a fool during a time when people were not oriented to God's Word."

I responded, "So sometimes the biblical characters don't teach us what we should do. They may serve as stellar examples of what we shouldn't do."

"Right. And again, I'm evaluating his actions by the covenant. According to the covenant, you were not to take innocent life. Which is worse? Taking an innocent life or not keeping a vow? They are both bad. Because of his foolishness he is stuck with a pair of bad choices, but he doesn't know God's Word well enough to see a way out. So the tragedy of the story is ignorance of the ways of God. Jephthah's story serves as a challenge for us today as well. How many Christians today end up making devastating, foolish decisions that wreck their lives because they do not know the Word of God?"

Reading the Old Testament Stories in Light of God's Grand Story

A recurring theme in our conversation had been the problem of God's people not knowing God's Word well. So I asked Professor Waltke, "Could you comment on the importance of knowing the stories of the Old Testament as an important part of having a grasp on God's Word generally?"

Professor Waltke responded, "To appreciate the importance of these Old Testament stories, you have to *see the whole Bible holistically.* The framework of the Bible is a historical framework. The stories of the Old Testament lay a foundation for the grand, developing story of the whole Bible. So we will never understand the Old Testament stories apart from their place in the developing story of the Bible, and we never will really understand the Law, the prophets, the poetic literature, or the writings of the New Testament apart from the foundation laid by these Old Testament stories. In other words, when we begin to see the beauty and power of the Bible's story as a whole, we then begin to read each part of the Bible better."

"So you and I as readers need to ask, 'Do we understand how the story of the Bible develops? Do we understand the main themes that tie the whole Bible together? Do we understand how the different parts function to support the grand story of Scripture?' For instance, at times in the Old Testament, God intends an event, person, or institution to give us a picture, a foreshadowing if you will, of a greater event in the life of Christ. We call this 'typology,' and at many points when reading the Old Testament stories, we should ask, 'How does this story anticipate or lay the foundation for what God would do eventually in and through Christ?'"

I asked if he could give us an example. He did so by pointing to the story of the Passover in Exodus 12.

"When God brought His people, the Israelites, out of slavery in Egypt, the last plague had to do with the death of the firstborn son in each home. Yet the firstborn was spared if a lamb or young goat was sacrificed and the blood smeared on the door frame of the house. The death angel 'passed over' the home. God told the Israelites they were to celebrate this sacrificial meal every year in order to remember their deliverance from slavery.

"When Jesus comes on the scene more than one thousand years later, John the Baptist sees Jesus walking by and says, 'Look! The Lamb of God!' (John 1:36). Toward the end of John's Gospel, we are told that Jesus was crucified on the day of preparation for the Passover (John 19:14), and in 1 Corinthians 5:7 Paul says, 'For Christ our Passover has been sacrificed' (NIV). So the institution of the Passover meal in Exodus 12 is significant in and of itself, but it also anticipates a more significant sacrifice—the death of Jesus by which God's new covenant people would be liberated from sin and escape spiritual death. But you don't pick up on such important threads until you begin reading the whole story of the Bible as one story with one Author."

Conclusion: Our Part in the Story

As we moved toward wrapping up our time together, I thought of an important and obvious implication of our conversation. If

God is the ultimate Author of the Old Testament stories, if He still intends the stories to draw His people to a life of covenant faithfulness, then we should hear these stories as authoritative for our lives as we continue to live out God's story in the world. So I asked the professor, "Does this mean, then, that we are meant to take our place in the continuing story laid out by Scripture?"

Enthusiastically Professor Waltke responded, "You can think of the whole of God's work in the world as a series of 'acts.' You've been given the first acts in the Scriptures. You are in the next to the last act, which is still being written, and the final act begins in the future when the Lord returns. So you and I are in the next to the last act. You know the drama. You know the story. You know where it's going to end up. Now play it out. Play out your own role on the basis of what God has revealed in the Scriptures. It's sort of like an impromptu piece of jazz. You know the theme; pick it up and play it. In other words, live out the story in obedience to God."

I mentioned at the beginning of this chapter that one of my favorite stories is *Lord of the Rings*. Professor Waltke's words reminded me of a dialogue between Frodo and Samwise Gamgee near the end of the second book. Sam and Frodo are in a difficult spot in a dark world. As they travel toward Mount Doom, Sam says to Frodo,

> I wonder if we shall ever be put into songs or tales. We're in one, of course; but I mean: put into words you know, told by the fireside, or read out of a great big book with red and black letters, years and years afterwards. And people will say, "Let's hear about Frodo and the Ring!" And they'll say: "Yes, that's one of my favorite stories. Frodo was really brave, wasn't he, dad?" "Yes, my boy, the famousest of the hobbits. And that's saying a lot."
> Laughing, Frodo picks up the conversation,
> ". . . You've left out one of the chief characters: Samwise the Stouthearted. 'I want to hear

more about Sam, dad. . . . and Frodo wouldn't
have got far without Sam, would he, dad?'"

The humble Sam is embarrassed. "Now
Mr. Frodo, you shouldn't make fun; I was being
serious."

And Frodo answers, "So was I."[17]

As you think about the stories of the Old Testament, do you
hear God calling you to play out your part in His grand story for
the world, or have you left yourself out as a main character? As
we have heard from Bruce Waltke, we are called to enter God's
ongoing story, and the stories of the Old Testament are meant
to help us do just that. When we read them well, remembering
that God is both the main character and the supreme Author of
Scripture, we hear His authoritative call to follow Him down well-
worn paths of obedience, playing well our part in His story.

Summary & Application

Summation

- God is the main hero of the Old Testament stories.
- The Old Testament stories parallel our lives in many
  ways.
- The Old Testament stories have strategic tension
  crafted in.
- Through their stories, the Old Testament writers were
  writing history, reinforcing ideas about the covenant
  between God and people, and seeking to write
  beautifully.
- The Old Testament stories have a structure.
- Context is vitally important for understanding an Old
  Testament story.
- Sometimes Old Testament characters teach us what we
  should not do!

- The Old Testament stories should be read in light of God's grand story, and we should find our place in that story.

Conversation

1. What are your favorite Old Testament stories and why?
2. What are the keys to a story working well? What keys does Bruce Waltke point out that make the Old Testament stories effective?
3. With which Old Testament character do you most identify?
4. The story of David and Goliath, found in 1 Samuel 17, is one of the most loved stories of the Old Testament. Read that story now. How does your perspective on the story change when you read it, keeping in mind that God is the main hero of the story and the covenant with God is being reinforced?
5. According to Professor Waltke, how should we read the difficult stories of the Old Testament?
6. What principle or example from this chapter helped you the most?

Transformation

Over the next week, read the story about Joseph in Genesis 37–50, covering two or three chapters per day. Read the story in light of the main guidelines learned in this chapter, and write a summary of the fresh insights learned from the story. What personal applications might you draw from the story?

CHAPTER 6

Reading the Old Testament Laws

A Conversation with J. Daniel Hays

"Don't assume that I came to destroy the Law . . .
I did not come to destroy but to fulfill."

—Matthew 5:17

 If you have ever tried to read through the whole Bible, you know that when you first hit the parts dealing with the law, found in Exodus, Leviticus, Numbers, and Deuteronomy, it can be a bit challenging—like walking through a kiddie pool full of peanut butter. The beginning of Exodus—with Moses' birth, boot from Egypt, and burning bush—goes pretty well; and the exodus itself, with its striking plagues and dramatic getaway through the Red Sea, is impressive. But when slogging through the myriad of laws about priestly worship practices, the tabernacle, uncleanness, and primitive issues of justice, you may feel like the wheels are coming off your momentum.

Yet this part of Scripture is also God's gift to His people. Gems here are waiting to be unearthed from under the seemingly crusty surface, and those gems form a vital part of the foundation of the Bible's grand story. In an article in the *New Dictionary of Biblical Theology*, J. G. Millar writes:

> Much of the theological framework needed to
> understand the significance of Jesus' coming,

life and death was put in place by Moses in his
writing, and perhaps above all in Deuteronomy.
For it is here that the theology of blessing and
curse which lies at the heart of Jesus' sin-
bearing work is first articulated. It is here that
the hopelessness of humanity trapped in sin,
even when chosen by God, is exposed. It is here
that the prospect of a divine intervention so
radical that it changes people at the very core of
their being first appears.[18]

To help us grow in our appreciation of the Old Testament
laws and in our skill in reading them, I looked to my friend
Danny Hays. He is a laid back but disciplined student of the Old
Testament, having written articles and books on how to study
and interpret the Bible. Currently he serves as the dean of the
School of Christian Studies at Ouachita Baptist University in
Arkadelphia, Arkansas.

I caught up with Danny at the 2008 national meeting of the
Evangelical Theological Society in Providence, Rhode Island. On
the upper floor of the convention hall, with a wall of windows
on one side, a bank of meeting rooms on the other, and a small
café and concession area nearby, we pulled up a couple of chairs
for a conversation about how to read the law portions of the Old
Testament.

Is the Law Still Relevant?

I first wanted to explore whether the Old Testament law is
relevant for us today. "Danny, many Christians, when they think
of Old Testament law, think, *This is not really relevant for me anymore; we have the New Testament. After all, Jesus has established the* new
covenant. So talk to me first about the issue of relevance. Is Old
Testament law still relevant for Christians today?"

Danny glanced down at his Bible, found a passage he was
looking for, and said, "Most certainly it is, if we follow the lead
of the authors of the New Testament. In 2 Timothy 3:16–17 Paul

tells us that '*all* Scripture is God-breathed and is useful for teaching, rebuking, correcting and training in righteousness, so that the man of God may be thoroughly equipped for every good work' (NIV). Without a doubt Paul is including the Old Testament books of Exodus, Leviticus, Numbers, and Deuteronomy in his phrase 'all Scripture.' Remember that the Old Testament was Paul's Bible, and the first five books of the Old Testament were understood to be foundational for the rest of the Scriptures. So Paul seems to be stressing their relevance for us. These books that contain the Old Testament law (Exodus, Numbers, Leviticus, and Deuteronomy) are a critical part of God's revelation to us, and—as reaffirmed by Paul—they continue to reveal God to us, teach us about God's character, help us to understand the life and death of Jesus better, and also provide us with guidance in righteous living."

I asked, "Why, then, do many people have such a hard time engaging this part of Scripture?"

Danny gave a knowing grin and answered, "The problem is coming up with a consistent approach to reading the law. Most people have what I call a "willy-nilly" approach by which you open your Bible and just skim along. Maybe you're in Leviticus, for instance, and you're reading this law, and it doesn't make sense. You read the next one, and it doesn't make sense. You skip over this one because it seems weird. Then you land on one that makes sense to you, and you think, *Wow, this one's great!* Since it resonates with you, you underline it in your Bible. This is now a verse that serves as a guideline for your life, and then you skip over the next fifteen or twenty, maybe a chapter or two, because you are back to an 'I don't get it' group of verses!"

As Danny spoke, I thought about my daughter, Anna, who was twelve years old at the time, and her response to some of what she had been reading in sections of Old Testament law. I mentioned this to Danny. "My Anna has been reading through the Old Testament, and she keeps asking me questions about specific passages and saying, 'Dad, I just don't understand. This seems very strange. What do I do with this?' She is ministered to by a lot that is there, but she hits a lot of snags when she's dealing with these legal passages in the Old Testament."

Nodding his head in understanding, Danny responded, "She's not alone. I see people erring in two extremes in dealing with the Old Testament law. The first extreme is to ignore it and just say it isn't relevant—or at least to ignore parts of it—to write off large parts of the Old Testament law by labeling the different parts. This way of thinking points out that some laws are 'moral law,' and they apply to us; but part of the law is 'ceremonial law' (having to do with sacrifices, for instance), or 'civil law' (having to do with laws governing the social order of Israelite society), and those parts don't apply to us. The problem is that the Bible itself does not make those kinds of distinctions, and at times the lines between these areas seem to blur. For instance, when a person in ancient Israelite society was caught in adultery, was that addressed by a moral or a civil law? Really, adultery was both a moral and a civil issue. So putting the laws into rigid categories really is not helpful. That is one mistake we can make."

I responded, "So you are saying that if we think in these kinds of categories, it is easy to write off large portions of Scripture as completely irrelevant for us today."

"Right. So that part of the law is seen as having no applicability to us at all."

Danny leaned forward, placing his elbows on his knees, and continued. "Now on the other extreme are people who try to take the Old Testament law as applicable to us in exactly the same way as it was applicable to the Israelites. However, the situation for Israel was unique. God gave the law at that time for a specific purpose. The Israelites were headed into the promised land. These are the rules, the instructions for how they were to live in the promised land and be blessed. In that sense the law had a specific purpose for that time and that place.

"When we come to these Old Testament laws today, we're not in the same situation they were in. For instance, we're no longer under the old covenant that God had set up with the Israelites at Mount Sinai. The laws were the guidelines and parameters for how the people were to live out that particular covenant. In Galatians, Paul goes to great lengths to tell us not to put believers back under the law, back under this legal system. So what do you do? You don't want to respond by saying 'We need to follow the law just as they did!' Nor do you want to dismiss it, writing off this part of Scripture as irrelevant."

Continuity and Discontinuity

It seemed to me that Danny was moving us to an important point. One of the keys for reading the Old Testament laws must be to understand in what ways there is continuity between God's Word to the Israelites through the law and God's Word to us through the law, and in what ways there is discontinuity as we move from the old covenant era, in which the Israelites lived, to the new covenant era established by Jesus. There clearly is continuity, but what are the points of discontinuity? So I asked, "How should we think about the continuity and discontinuity between the Israelites' experience of these commands given by God and our experience of God's laws?"

Danny thought about the question for a second or two and then responded, "Of course the coming of Jesus Christ and the inauguration of the new covenant changed things. We are now under the new covenant and not under the old, Mosaic covenant, which was so profoundly oriented to the law. Paul makes this crystal clear in Romans and Galatians. The book of Hebrews likewise stresses the point that Christians are oriented to the new covenant, and now God's law is written on the hearts of His people (Heb. 8:7–13). God gave Israel the law in a specific historical context for specific reasons. The law (as contained in Exodus through Deuteronomy) defines the covenant relationship between Israel and God so that Israel could live in the promised land and be blessed as God lived in their midst.

"As Christians today, we are still God's people, and God still dwells in our midst, so there are lots of parallels. But we are not the nation of Israel, and the vast majority of Christians in the world do not live in the promised land. There are no Canaanites today to draw the people of God into the form of idolatry facing the Israelites. God lives in our midst now through the indwelling of the Spirit in His people, the church, and not by living in the tabernacle or the temple. We also approach God differently. Now we approach God through Jesus Christ and through His perfect and ultimate sacrifice rather than the old sacrificial system defined in the law."

What Danny had just described seems pretty clear from the New Testament. Like the light streaming through those massive windows to my left, the letters of the New Testament shine a great deal of light on how Paul and other New Testament writers understood the place of the law after Jesus had come. "What, then, are the areas that have continuity between the time during which the Old Testament laws were given and our time?" I asked.

Danny answered, "Some general principles stressed in the law are constant—God's commitment to His people, His holiness, and His demand for holiness ("be holy for I am holy"); the related connection between God's holiness, His presence, and power to do His will; God's concern for people and His demand that we also have concern for people; the seriousness of sin and the importance of dealing with it; and God's demand that His people be faithful—to Him, to their families, and to their neighbors. Jesus and His early followers specifically drive home the importance of the Ten Commandments, nine of which are reiterated in the New Testament (only the Sabbath command is not);[19] and, of course, we have the command to love God (Deut. 6:4–6), called the Shema, and the command to love others, taken from Leviticus 19:18. Jesus called these the two most important commandments."

As Danny mentioned this last point, I remembered doing a detailed study of James a number of years ago. James draws a number of the principles he wants to stress right from Leviticus 19. For instance, he tracks with Leviticus in calling for concern for the poor (James 2:5–9; Lev. 19:10), warning those who withhold wages from a worker (James 5:4; Lev. 19:13), exhorting believers not to favor the rich over the poor in a court of law (James 2:1–4; Lev. 19:15), and, of course, James quotes Leviticus 19:18 at 2:8. So James takes up a part of the law from Leviticus and uses it in exhorting the church. James did exactly what Danny was talking about—tapping key principles from the Old Testament law that still give dynamic guidance to Christian believers on how they should live.

How Should We Read the Laws of the Old Testament?

At this point I wanted to get into specifics, so I asked: "Danny, how should we read the laws of the Old Testament today? How do we get at the heart of what God was communicating to the Israelites and how the principles reflected in those laws might apply in our day? With some laws—several of the Ten Commandments or the commands to love God and our neighbor, for example—the step into our world seems direct. But what do we do with other laws that do not seem so directly applicable to us?"

In the distance I saw one of the people who worked at the convention center. Of course I did not know that person's spiritual situation, but I wondered, "How would a person 'off the street,' who had little experience with the Bible or the church, respond to much of what we find in Exodus or Leviticus?" It seemed to me that many people need practical help in moving from the strangeness of that ancient material to life in the modern world.

Danny shifted in his chair a bit, rearranged the notes he had in his hand, and continued. "First, we should realize that the Old Testament law is embedded in a narrative story. It is connected to the deliverance from Egypt, the establishment of the Mosaic Covenant, and life in the promised land. So we need to make sure that we don't just pull these laws out of context. We need to understand them as part of a larger story."

Keeping in mind the convention-center worker, I thought, *That's good. Most people can identify with stories. Beginning with the big-picture story would be a great place to start, and it would give the laws a meaningful context.*

"Second," Danny said, "as the New Testament makes clear, we should acknowledge that we are no longer under the Mosaic Covenant. Therefore, although the books of Exodus through Deuteronomy are still Scripture (God's powerful, inerrant, and infallible Word to us, to which we are to respond in obedience), they are no longer *law* for us. If someone breaks one of the laws today, they are not punished by the community as they were in ancient Israel. Thus we should read and apply the Old Testament legal material not as direct law but in a similar manner to how we would read the Old Testament narratives (stories) that contain the law. We need to understand the principles in the passages we are reading. What do they teach us about God? What do they teach us about human nature? What guidelines do we find here that can help us live for the Lord in the world today?"

A Process for Getting at the Principles

I wanted to push him a bit for a practical process to thinking through such principles, so I asked, "What then are steps we can follow to sort out the principles and how we might apply them?"

Danny started to click the steps off on his fingers, one by one:

"First, determine what the text meant to the biblical audience. What did it mean in their context?

"Second, determine the differences (for example, a different covenant, a different place, a different time) and the similarities (for example, God's holiness, the need to live for God in the world, the pressures that would fight against our living for God, sin) between the ancient biblical audience and those of us who are Christians today.

"Third, try to find a general theological principle within the intent of the law that applies both to the ancient audience and to us. Run this theological principle through the grid of New

Testament teaching. Does the New Testament address the same principle in some way?

"Fourth and finally, determine specific ways you can apply this principle in your own life."

I asked if he could give an example of how this might work with a specific passage. He laid out his example.

"OK, for instance, let's take a look at Deuteronomy 22:1–3. Here is what the text says, 'If you see your brother's ox or sheep straying, do not ignore it but be sure to take it back to him. If the brother does not live near you or if you do not know who he is, take it home with you and keep it until he comes looking for it. Then give it back to him. Do the same if you find your brother's donkey or his cloak or anything he loses. Do not ignore it.'

"What did it mean for them, in their day and time? Well, they lived in an agricultural society, and their livestock were important to them. God tells them that He expects them to look out for their neighbor's livestock and to be sure that lost animals get returned to their proper owners. But this law expands beyond that. Notice that it tells the Israelite farmers to get involved and help even if they do not know who the owner is (even for strangers). Likewise, the law is expanded to include things other than livestock, 'his cloak or anything he loses.'

"What are the differences and similarities between us and the original Israelite audience? Most of us do not live in an agricultural setting (although some do). I haven't come across any stray oxen, donkeys, or sheep in my neighborhood lately. Likewise, we are not under the old Mosaic Covenant, and this passage is no longer *law* for us. But we (the church) are still the people of God, and we still live in community with others.

"Identify the principles. God expects His people to take an active role in helping people and in looking out for their welfare. We cannot selfishly be concerned only with our own well-being, saying, 'I don't want to get involved; that is none of my business.'

"What does the New Testament say about this? Jesus Himself stresses the important place that the principle 'love your neighbor as yourself' should play in the life of God's people. Jesus

gives us the example of the Good Samaritan to illustrate how
He applies this principle to His contemporaries. Deuteronomy
22:1–3 is similar in principle to 'love your neighbor as yourself.' Thus Jesus reinforces the gist of this commandment from
Deuteronomy 22.

"How do we apply Deuteronomy 22:1–3 today? God expects
you and me to look outward and to be concerned with the welfare
of others. We cannot say, 'That is none of my business.' According
to Deuteronomy 22:1–3 (and numerous other Scriptures), helping others is our business. If someone in front of us accidentally
drops a ten-dollar bill and doesn't know it, our responsibility is to
pick it up and return it to him. If we come across a lost wallet or
purse (or anything else that has been lost), it is our responsibility
to see that it gets returned to its rightful owner, even if we do not
personally know the owner. So in a nutshell the application of
Deuteronomy 22:1–3 takes us from donkeys to dollars."

An Example from Real-life Ministry

That example was helpful. I wondered if Danny had sometimes put this process of interpretation to use in ministry. Danny
has had an interesting past. He was trained as an engineer and
spent a number of years on the mission field in Africa. So I asked,
"Can you remember a time in ministry when the law came up,
and you were able to draw on some of these principles you're talking about and help someone in his or her Christian life?"

He leaned back in his chair and responded, "A concrete
example comes from a time when we were missionaries in
Ethiopia a number of years back. The Marxist government had
taken over, and in our area they closed down the local churches
and said we could not meet on Sunday. The believers were struggling, asking, 'Should we go ahead and meet anyway and go to
prison? The Sabbath laws say we should keep the Sabbath holy.
Or is there another option?' This was a real, heartfelt question.
The believers wanted to be obedient to God's Word. At the heart

of their question was this key issue: how do we understand and live the Sabbath law?"

I commented, "So they were reading the Sabbath law as applying to Sunday?"

Danny nodded his head, "Right. I shared with them some of my thoughts saying, 'Don't go to jail for taking that as a legal obligation for us today. Let's meet on Tuesday night or some other time.' So the church just shifted to another night."

I noted, "The early church actually had changed their day of meeting from Saturday (which was the Sabbath) to Sunday because that was the day Jesus was resurrected. So they met on Sunday to recognize the resurrection of Jesus, but they still saw themselves as entering into worship, as having a day on which they focused on being together as believers, hearing the Word taught, and worshipping. So they fulfilled a number of principles built into the Sabbath commands of the Old Testament, but they fulfilled them on a different day of the week because of Jesus."

Danny responded, "Absolutely. When Jesus says, 'I didn't come to abolish the law but to fulfill it,' I think that's exactly what He means. He's not saying we're going to keep the law, every little part of it like the Israelites did in ancient Israel, but He says, 'I'm the ultimate fulfillment of the law.' So, in response to Jesus' resurrection on Sunday, we see a shift in how the Sabbath command from the law was understood. The church shifted the day on which they would meet for worship, fulfilling the spirit of the law in a way that is different from what Old Testament believers understood. I would say yes, absolutely, Jesus changes some of those laws because He is the fulfillment of them."

I thought through what we had discussed thus far. "OK, so what we've talked about thus far is that, when it comes to the Old Testament law, we want to understand the original context; we want to try to understand the principles inherent in those laws, as well as both the similarities and the differences between us and the original audience to whom the laws were written; and then we want to read the Old Testament laws in light of their fulfillment in the New Testament."

Danny leaned forward and nodded his head in agreement, "Right. For instance, we read, 'Don't commit adultery' in the Old Testament. What's the principle? Well, marriage is sacred. When you come to the New Testament, Jesus says, 'Yeah, don't commit adultery, but also don't think about sex with someone who is not your spouse' (Matt. 5:27–30). He actually draws out the heart and the intention of that law.'"

What about Those Weird Laws?

As we continued our discussion, I thought back to Leviticus again. Much is practical and straightforward like, "You must not steal, you must not act deceptively or lie" (Lev. 19:11), or "You are to have honest balances, honest weights" for measuring out grain that was to be sold (Lev. 19:36). Yet there is also strange stuff in that book! What are we supposed to do with passages that prohibit the mixing of different kinds of seeds or fabrics?

So I asked Danny, "What, specifically, do we do with those strange laws like 'Do not cook a young goat in its mother's milk?' or, 'Don't mix different kinds of seeds.' I have to say that neither has been a big temptation for me lately! So how do we deal with some of these laws that are kind of bizarre?"

Danny knew this question was going to come up. He smiled knowingly and answered, "On many texts like these, we struggle with the first step, 'Determine what the text meant to the biblical audience,' and it is important to do our best to understand *why* these laws were given at that time and that place. One of the most helpful tools a person can use at this point is a good, theologically sound commentary.[20]

"Let's put these laws in their story context. When God delivered the early Israelites out of Egypt, they had many strong pagan influences on their culture. Likewise, the idol-worshipping people in the promised land would exert a powerful, negative, cultural influence on the Israelites, drawing their hearts away from God. Some of the laws in Exodus through Deuteronomy are directed at prohibiting pagan practices. Sometimes scholars have enough background information on the pagan religious practices of Israel's neighbors to understand the biblical prohibition against them, and sometimes we just don't have enough background information to know the reason for the biblical prohibition. The law against cooking a 'young goat in its mother's milk' (Exod. 34:26) is probably prohibiting a Canaanite religious fertility practice, perhaps celebrated by the Canaanites on certain festival days. How would we apply this today? The unbelievers in our culture do not normally cook baby goats in the mother's milk, but some common practices in our culture have non-Christian religious overtones that we should avoid. What about horoscopes? Ouija boards? Certain aspects of Halloween? Perhaps the principle behind some of the strange laws in the Old Testament is, 'Don't mess with unhealthy spiritual influences from your culture.'

"As for the mixing of seeds, consider this. Think about the big picture. Back in the book of Exodus, God made the radical new declaration that He Himself was coming to live among the Israelites in His own tent (the tabernacle). The actual presence of the holy, awesome, powerful, and sovereign Lord in their midst *would change everything for them.* The book of Leviticus highlights the changes and explains how the Israelites were to live with the holy God in their midst and how they could approach Him and fellowship with Him. All of their daily life would change, now to be driven by the concepts of separation and holiness (so they wouldn't forget about God in their midst). In their day-to-day lives they had to keep numerous mundane commands that stressed separation across a gamut of activities: they couldn't mix two kinds of seeds together, they couldn't mix two kinds of cloth together either, etc. The activities of their daily lives (the continued focus on separateness in mundane everyday things) forced them *always* to keep in mind that with the holy, awesome God dwelling among them in their camp, there were now demands on their personal lives for separating from unholy things. That is, they were forced to live with a worldview consciousness of clean/unclean and holy/profane things.

"How much more should we as Christians today focus on the importance of holiness? We, who experience the presence of this same holy and awesome God through the indwelling of the Spirit, should be a holy people. God does not live across the camp from us in a tabernacle. The holy and awesome God dwells right within us, and through the new covenant He has put His laws in our hearts (Jer. 31:33; Heb. 8:10). We are no longer under the Levitical law, so we do not have to maintain the specifics of separation (cloth, seed, etc.). Yet God has written His laws on our hearts because He cares about holy living. Shouldn't we also be constantly conscious about what is clean and what is not clean in all details of our lives, now using the New Testament's teaching about what is clean and unclean? As 1 Peter 1:16 quotes from Leviticus, 'Be holy, because I am holy.' The law in Leviticus has helped me understand how the call to holy living should permeate all of the details of our lives."

Conclusion

We needed to wrap up our conversation, so I asked Danny, "If you could say one thing to people who are believers about how they should 'hear' the law of the Old Testament, what would you say?"

He concluded, "Don't become legalistic and apply the Old Testament legal material as a specific set of literal laws for you. Do read it as a profitable and valuable revelation about God and His character. Obey the broad universal principles reflected in the law as explained and refined in the New Testament revelation of Jesus Christ."

Summary & Application

Summation

- We should not ignore the Old Testament laws, which are God's Word to us.
- The Old Testament laws are not applicable to us in the same way as to the people of the Old Testament era.
- The Old Testament laws are applicable to us today in important ways.
- Read the Old Testament laws in light of the story in which they are given.
- The Old Testament laws are Scripture but not "law" for us.
- When dealing with the Old Testament laws, apply them to life with the following steps:

  - Determine what the text meant to the biblical audience.
  - Determine the differences and the similarities between the ancient biblical audience and those of us who are Christians today.
  - Try to find a general theological principle within the intent of the law that applies both to the ancient audience and to us. Run this theological principle through the grid of New Testament teaching.
  - Determine specific ways that you can apply this principle in your own life.

- Read the Old Testament laws in light of their literary and cultural contexts.

Conversation

1. In what ways do you think the Old Testament laws are relevant or "useful" as 2 Timothy 3:16–17 says?
2. According to Danny Hays, in what ways does a person's "new covenant" relationship with God through Jesus change his orientation to the Old Testament laws?

3. What are some ways Dr. Hays suggests the
   Old Testament laws are applicable to us today?
4. What does Danny mean when he says that the
   Old Testament laws are Scripture to us but not "laws"?
5. Read Leviticus 19:9–10, taking the passage through
   Hays's four steps for applying the laws to life.

Transformation

Over the next few days read Leviticus 19:1–18, and choose several of these laws to interpret in light of the insights gained from Danny Hays's guidelines on the law. How might you apply these laws to your life?

CHAPTER 7

Reading Psalms and Proverbs

A Conversation with David Howard

Help me understand the meaning of Your precepts
so that I can meditate on Your wonders.

—Psalm 119:27

 On a beautiful spring day with cool breezes blowing through an open window, I sat at a kitchen table and talked to my friend David Howard, professor of Old Testament at Bethel Seminary in Saint Paul, Minnesota. The night before we had taken in a San Francisco Giants baseball game at AT&T Park, had eaten San Francisco cuisine together on the Scoreboard Plaza, and, our bodies still adjusting to West Coast time, had made our way across the Golden Gate Bridge to Mill Valley, where we serve as affiliated faculty members in the Ph.D. program of Golden Gate Seminary.

David grew up on the mission field in Costa Rica and Colombia and has a wonderful family heritage. Prominent Christian author and speaker Elisabeth Elliot is "Aunt Betty" to David, sister to his dad. He has fond memories of Bible studies with his family and memorizing passages of Scripture as they traveled by car when at home on furloughs in the U.S. This grounding in the Scriptures led to a hunger to know more, and David eventually received a Ph.D. in Old Testament from the University of Michigan. In his ministry of scholarly speaking and writing, David mixes a breadth of knowledge about the Old Testament with a heart for the church. So, since we were going to be in California together, I asked David if I could interview him about how we should read Psalms and Proverbs. He graciously agreed.

Why Do We Love the Psalms?

I started by asking, "David, why are so many of us as Christians enamored with the psalms? Not only is Psalms at the center of our Bibles, but for many people they seem to serve as the most important part of the Old Testament for daily Christian living."

David smiled and responded. "I think it's because the psalms express human emotions in a way that is readily understood by people. Human nature hasn't really changed over the past three millennia. You can read some of the Bible stories, or more obscure parts of the Bible, and the words seem foreign to us in the twenty-first century. But the psalms don't seem foreign at all. For instance, when David speaks about people hating him without a cause, about feeling sick, or about despair in the face of other life challenges, we can identify with those experiences."

I added, "And on the other hand, the psalms give voice to the joy and hope we experience in our relationship with God. So the psalms give voice to our broad range of experiences and our emotions—both the good and bad."

David nodded in agreement. "Absolutely. They really express the whole range of our emotions from the highest highs of joy and thanksgiving to the lowest lows of depression and anger and everything in between. Sometimes in class I draw a line across the blackboard with a plus sign on one end and a minus sign on the other. I suggest we could plot the mood of every psalm somewhere along that line, from negative to positive. I think that's part of what gives the psalms their universal appeal.

"Another thing that is unique about the psalms is that they are the main place in Scripture where we find primarily human words *to God* or human words *about God*, instead of God's words to us. These are human words praising God, or lamenting some event or situation, or even questioning God in a reverent way. So the psalms draw us in because we recognize in them our own experiences and feelings, and they, in a sense, express for us those feelings about God or to God."

So the psalms often have a universal feel to them. I remember how much the psalms meant to me when I had started growing in my faith as a teenager. They certainly gave voice to many of my frustrations, my celebrations, and my experiences. Many of the psalms seemed as fresh and relevant as the morning newspaper.

Yet this part of God's Word was crafted in specific cultural contexts through which God gave the psalms to us. As we have discussed in other interviews, context is foundational for hearing the Scripture well. I wanted to understand more about that context. So I asked David how the psalms were used originally in ancient Israel.

Community Songs of Praise and Thanks

As a Weed Eater buzzed in the distance, just up the hill toward the seminary's main administration building, Howard rested his hands on his lap and answered. "As you know, roughly half the psalms were written by David, and the other half were written by other authors, some of whom we know, others we don't know. At some point most of them—not all of them, but most of them—were written for a corporate context, to be quoted or sung in large-group settings."

I interjected, "It strikes me that we most often use the psalms today for private devotions."

David responded, "Right. But if you look at the titles of the psalms, they'll say things like 'for the choirmaster, with stringed instruments.' Those would be instructions for the public use of these psalms. The congregation would come to the temple in Jerusalem and sing them. Maybe the priest or choirmaster would lead in an antiphonal way—the voices of two groups, or of an individual and a group, echoing back and forth. Psalm 136, for example, has a repeated line that says, 'For his steadfast love endures forever' (ESV). That line is repeated over and over throughout the whole psalm. It's easy to imagine the choirmaster leading, and the people responding with that line. Yet even the psalms that are written as individual psalms, expressing personal thoughts or emotions to God, were also used in corporate worship. This is similar to the way we use hymns or choruses today."

A thought hit me. When we think about how the hymns we sing came about—both the more traditional hymns and the modern praise choruses—those who wrote them were personally expressing worship to God, but often they also wrote the songs to minister to a larger group of God's people. So hymns or choruses work well, either in our personal devotions, or in large-group, corporate contexts. The psalms seem to have been driven by the same impulses, a mix of personal devotion and a desire to help the broader people of God worship Him.

I asked David if scholars use a label to speak of the corporate psalms of worship. He answered, "Scholars have different terms for them, but a common label is to call these psalms 'hymns.' They are, by definition, psalms that praise God for who He is and how He has revealed Himself to the world, and they are done in a corporate setting. The more individual psalms, where David or someone is speaking in the first person (e.g., "I thank you Lord for . . .") usually are called thanksgiving psalms. The psalmist mentions a problem in the past that has now been solved, or that God has answered some prayer, and then gives thanks to God. On one level, praise is speaking to God about who He is, and thanksgiving is more expressing appreciation for what He has done, but we want to be careful not to think of these two areas of worship as overly distinct. They really flow together. What God does flows from God's character, and we know God's character by what He has done.

"One scholar has proposed that psalms describing who God is should be called psalms of descriptive praise. He proposed that what we often call psalms of thanksgiving would be psalms of declarative praise since they declare what God has done. Sometimes these are called psalms of narrative praise since they tell (or narrate) the story of God's actions on behalf of His people. I think those are helpful distinctions."

I asked, "How would Psalm 106, which recounts the story of the exodus and the problems of the wilderness, fit in here?"

David shifted a bit in his seat, leaned forward, and said, "Actually, Psalms 105 and 106 together are kind of twin psalms, and they're sometimes called historical psalms because they look back and recite the history—or tell the story, if you will—of God's people. But they do so from different perspectives: Psalm 105 reviews Israel's history by telling what God had done for His people while Psalm 106 reviews Israel's history by emphasizing Israel's repeated stubbornness and rebellions and God's patience. But in the end both psalms are saying, 'Here's what God has done for us.'"

David's explanation of different kinds of psalms was helpful. Think about it this way. When we read the psalms, we can begin by asking, "What is this psalm doing, and what should I do in response?" If the psalm is *describing who God is*, then I can enter into praising God with the psalmist. If the psalm is *declaring what God has done*, I can use the psalm to thank God for similar things He has been doing in my life. If the psalm is *recounting a story* about what God has done among His people, I can celebrate that story as a backdrop to the story of my life, if I am a part of the people of God today.

Songs for Hard Times

These psalms of praise and thanksgiving point to who God is or wonderful things He has done. It is easy for me to embrace the message of these psalms on a beautiful day in California, as Canadian geese are flying onto the campus where we sit, landing in the grassy field across the road. But life is not all cool breezes and beautiful birds. I have spent time in the past few years in the hospital. Those times were frightening, frustrating, and financially burdensome. Thankfully, another side to the psalms gives expression to those experiences as well. In the lament psalms the psalmist cries out honestly to God about how difficult life is. So I asked David to speak to us about the laments.[21]

He picked up the conversation. "Laments are the psalms where David or the other psalmists are pouring out their hearts to God, being honest about the fact that life, at times, stinks! The psalmist has experienced some trouble, sickness, or the persecution of enemies. He may have people in his life who hate him. I think the church is greatly impoverished because we don't mine the lament psalms for the truths that are there and the way they can open up new avenues of approaching God in times of great stress and sadness in our lives."

As David spoke, I wondered how we in the church might come up with creative ways to incorporate the lament psalms into our worship. What if we helped people with cancer, for instance, or those who were struggling financially, give voice to their frustrations by using the psalms of lament? Would that be irreverent? No, it would be biblical since we have the pattern in the lament psalms. The wonderful thing about the laments is that they help people express what they are feeling, but then they move to confessions of faith about God, His character, and the hope we have in life because of God's character. They also often acknowledge that God is using our difficulties in various ways to grow us as people. The topic of God using our sorrows and turning them inside out seemed to hit a deep chord in David, who shared out of his own experience.

"Sometimes God will use the difficulties to form us and to train us and to show us parts of Himself that we never would have seen. One of the greatest crises Jan and I have had in our marriage was years ago when we were trying to start a family. We were not able to bear a child ourselves so we ended up adopting two daughters. Our girls are now grown, and they've been a great blessing to us. But trying to have a child was a time of deep darkness for us, a time of great disappointment. We would not have written the script of our lives that way, but as we look back, we realize that God opened areas of ministry and introduced us to people whom we never would have known apart from our own suffering. We've been blessed by that ministry, and now we wouldn't trade it for the world."

In a sense we can think of the psalms in terms of *reflection, response,* and *formation.* All the psalms help us *reflect* on who God is and what He has done. They call us to *respond* to who God is in worship, but they also *form us* as we learn from them how to respond to life and talk to God. The laments accomplish all three dynamics as they help us think about our frustrations with life and respond to God in the midst of those frustrations, but they also form us as we learn from them how to think about life and how to talk to God appropriately. They teach us how to hope in God based on His character. I mentioned this to David.

"That's a helpful point. The church has sometimes vacillated between two extremes. Sometimes there's the extreme that we need to have triumphal living and always be positive and looking up. Some leaders present a version of the Christian life that encourages people to say, 'Don't worry, be happy!' When we do this, we are missing an important spiritual opportunity to point people to the Lord in the midst of life's difficulties. On the other side, of course, in some branches of the church, or some approaches to counseling, for example, people are encouraged to wallow in their troubles, never really looking to the future with hope and never looking to God except perhaps to curse Him. I think the beauty of the psalms is that they are balanced, encouraging us to be honest about how hard life can be but also encouraging us to hope in God."

I asked David if he could give us an example.

He responded, "Psalm 42 is a great psalm of lament. 'As a deer pants for flowing streams, so pants my soul for you, O God. My soul thirsts for God, for the living God. . . . My tears have been my food day and night' (vv. 1–2 ESV). It's clearly a psalm of distress. But then verse 4 says, 'These things I remember, as I pour out my soul: how I would go with the throng and lead them in procession to the house of God with glad shouts and shouts of praise; a multitude keeping festival.' So it's clear that the psalmist has had in the past an experience with God where things were going well, and now he finds himself in a down time. Yet he uses that past experience as kind of a springboard for having hope. He goes on to say in verses 5 and 6, 'Why are you cast down, O my soul, and why are you in turmoil within me? Hope in God; for I shall again praise him, my salvation and my God.' So he thinks about the relationship he has had with God in the past and uses it as encouragement for the future. His problems do not cause him to question God's existence. (There are no atheists among the authors of the psalms!) But theologically and intellectually the psalmists experience tension at points, and I want to suggest that we struggle in the same way when life gets tough. So the psalms of lament give voice to our struggles."

I commented, "A lot of people in our contemporary context tend to approach that question of evil and suffering, saying that the bad things that happen to people are really an argument against the existence of God. Really, that's not reflected in the psalms at all. Bad things that happen to people are a part of life, and God is there ready to meet us in the midst of those experiences."

The Imprecatory Psalms

Of course another natural human response to suffering at the hands of another person is the impulse of revenge. I asked David about those psalms that express anger and judgment on the psalmist's enemies. At times, for instance, the psalmist says harsh things about his enemies; he wants their babies to be smashed against the rocks (not exactly the stuff of warm and fuzzy devotional reading!). I asked David how we should read and respond to such psalms.

He nodded his head knowingly. "These are called imprecatory psalms. At the root the psalmist is asking God to be faithful to a core promise that He's already made centuries earlier to Abraham: 'I will bless those who bless you, I will curse those who treat you with contempt' (Gen. 12:3). So in all these imprecatory psalms we see the psalmist saying in effect, 'God, I am Your person. Your enemies are persecuting me, but I believe Your promises. Do something!'

"The fuller context of Psalm 137, to which you were alluding, says, 'By the waters of Babylon, there we sat down and wept, when we remembered Zion. On the willows there we hung up our lyres. For there our captors required of us songs, and our tormenters, mirth, saying, 'Sing us one of the songs of Zion!' How shall we sing the LORD's song in a foreign land? If I forget you, O Jerusalem, let my right hand forget its skill' (vv. 1–5 ESV). And so it goes. Then the psalmist says, 'O Daughter of Babylon, doomed to be destroyed, blessed shall he be who repays you with what you have done to us. Blessed shall he be who takes your little ones and dashes them against the rocks' (vv. 8–9). So that's pretty intense. But understand, the psalmist is responding to the horrific devastation Babylon has brought on God's people. Their land has been destroyed, their family members wiped out, and the people of God have been transported hundreds of miles from home to live as refugees."

I commented, "So at this point the Israelites actually are in exile, hundreds of years after the time of David?"

"Right. This is not a psalm of David. It's a psalm from the exile, about the destruction of Jerusalem (see 2 Kings 24–25). The Babylonians did horrible things to the Jewish people. So in a sense the psalmist says, 'Lord, do to them what they have done to us because this is what You have *promised* You would do to those who attack Your people! This, ultimately, is an attack on *You!* Bring Your vengeance upon them for Your *own* name's sake.'

"David (and the other psalmists) never asked God to exact *personal* vengeance. David was a model in this: even though he knew he was God's intended, anointed king and that King Saul, who was seeking his life, was not, David nevertheless refused to take personal vengeance on two different occasions when he could have, when he had Saul's life in his hands (1 Samuel 24 and 26). So David is speaking in the imprecatory psalms with a consciousness that he is God's anointed—God's representative, really (see Pss. 2:7–9; 132:10–12, 17–18)—and that an attack on him was an attack on God's people and, ultimately, on God Himself."

I responded, "So in some ways these psalms are a confession that God will be faithful to His promises, faithful to His people, and faithful to His own agenda. Yet they also announce that judgment is coming for those who persecute God's people."

David nodded in agreement. "Right, and we need to remember that the psalms are expressing emotions, putting in words what the psalmist is feeling inside. These psalms show us that there is a legitimate place for righteous anger. Perhaps we haven't had our homes destroyed by an enemy, but we understand the frustration of having someone hurt us. So we can use even the imprecatory psalms, saying in effect, 'God, I am so angry with those people who are trying to hurt me! And in the end it's really *You* they're trying to hurt!' And yet, as we've said, the psalmists keep things in proper perspective; they don't ask for *personal* vengeance. For example, David, after saying incredibly harsh things about his enemies in Psalm 139 (v. 22 says, "I hate them with extreme hatred; I consider them my enemies"), goes on to put these things in proper perspective in the next two verses: 'Search me, God, and know my heart; test me and know my concerns. See if there is any offensive way in me; lead me in the everlasting way' (Ps. 139:23–24).

"The imprecations in the psalms don't sound much like Jesus' words about loving your enemies and praying for them (Matt. 5:43–48). But think about the fact that when the occasion demanded it, Jesus also harshly rebuked the ungodly (see Matt. 23) or spoke about God's harsh, eternal punishment for the wicked (Matt. 24:50–51; 25:31–46). On the other hand, the idea of treating your enemies with kindness and justice also finds a place in the Old Testament, in such passages as this one in Proverbs 25:21: 'If your enemy is hungry, give him food to eat, and if he is thirsty, give him water to drink.' So we need to read the imprecatory psalms in light of the whole counsel of God in the Scriptures. In the end these psalms teach us that sometimes it's OK to be angry about sin and injustice, but they also teach us to focus those thoughts and feelings along biblical lines and to leave vengeance to God who will deal with wicked, hurtful people in His own way and in His own time."

The Psalms as Poetry

As we talked, more geese came gliding onto the campus and landed on the athletic field across the street. Their song sounded like music, and their cupped wings cut through the air in a graceful dance as they joined the flock already on the grass. Set against a backdrop of huge pine trees and a hill that overlooks an inlet off San Francisco Bay, the sight was the substance of poetry, and I could imagine the psalmists drinking in such a scene and writing about the glories of God in creation. Much of Psalms, in fact, is poetry. So I asked David to tell me more about reading Psalms as poetic literature.

He was excited to take up the topic. "This is really important to understand if we are going to read the psalms well. We have different ways of reading poetry versus prose in essentially any language. One of the features of poetry is that it is much more emotional than narrative, and it is also much more oriented to using word pictures or figurative language. For example, consider two different accounts of David in distress. One is from a story account; the other is from one of the psalms. When David had an affair with Bathsheba, she became pregnant and had a child. The child became sick and eventually died. Before the child died, David was mourning, asking God to spare the child. Second Samuel 12:16 says, 'David therefore sought God on behalf of the child. And David fasted and went in and lay all night on the ground' (ESV). Clearly David is distressed about the situation. But it's kind of cold, kind of a 'newspaper' account of what's happening.

"Then over in Psalms, you have many examples of David in distress. I'm just picking one almost at random. In Psalm 69 he says, 'Save me, O God! For 'the waters have come up to my neck.' I sink in deep mire, where there is no foothold; I have come into deep waters, and the flood sweeps over me' (vv. 1–2 ESV). Now do we think David literally waded out into the Jordan River until the water came up to his neck, with his pen and scroll in hand? I don't think so. We understand that the water is a metaphor, a word picture, for how he feels in the middle of his distressing circumstances. We sometimes use a similar word picture when we say, 'I'm drowning right now!' We are not literally drowning in water, but emotionally we feel like we are sinking! In verse 4 David goes on to say, 'More in number than the hairs of my head are those who hate me without cause' (ESV). Has he actually gone out and counted the number of people who hate him and then counted the hairs on his head (as in, 'Wow, I have 2,105 hairs on my head and 2,500 enemies!')? Of course not. The word picture, however, is a wonderful way of saying, 'I feel like there are crowds of people out to get me!' Graphic language and sometimes exaggeration are used in the psalms to express feelings."

Making sure I understood the implications of this for how we read the psalms, I said, "OK, so we need to ask, as we're reading the psalms, what is this word picture expressing? I know different types of figures are used in Psalms, different types of word pictures. We probably don't have time right now to go into great detail there, but your point is, we need to learn more about how the figurative language works. We need to ask, 'What is this word picture expressing?'"

David agreed. "Usually, such a word picture or figurative language is pretty easy to detect. A good commentary can also help."

Another Important Aspect of Poetry

I also wanted to ask David about the extensive use of repetition we find in the psalms. So I asked him to discuss what scholars call "parallelism."

David gestured with his hands and said, "If you open most modern Bible versions today, you'll see that Psalms is written in poetic structure. There's more white space on the page because the poetic lines are presented in a structured format. The real thing we need to remember about Hebrew poetry is precisely what you just said: there is a parallel structure to the way it's laid out. One line will echo another in some way.

"Let me just give you an example of how that works. Psalm 1 is another kind of psalm, often referred to as a wisdom psalm because it celebrates a person who wisely builds life around God's Word. In fact, Psalm 1 is at the beginning of the Psalms because God's law is seen as the foundation of all the perspectives represented in Psalms."

I commented, "So God's law gives stability to all these emotions we have been talking about?"

David agreed. "Right. Psalm 1:1 reads,

> Blessed is the man who
> **walks** not in the counsel of the wicked, nor
> **stands** in the way of sinners, nor
> **sits** in the seat of scoffers (ESV)

"Do you see the words 'walks,' 'stands,' and 'sits'? Those verbs are parallel to one another. What we have here is a 'progressive' form of parallelism. The psalmist mentions three parallel actions—walking, standing, and sitting—but those actions progress from one to the other."

I asked, "What is the significance of that for how we read the psalm?"

David answered, "Notice that the person described is first walking, then coming to a standstill, and finally sitting. I think this represents a person who gets more and more deeply involved with evil and sin. The primary image is of a person who associates with those with whom he or she should not be associating, but there also is a progression that makes a person more and more entrenched in that pattern or lifestyle. The ultimate result is that such a person will not have a stable life and will not be accepted by God when judgment comes (Ps. 1:4–6)."

"Sometimes with parallelism a second line of poetry emphasizes the same basic truth mentioned in the first line. Sometimes the second line will express a contrast, and sometimes the second line will add new information. The key is to ask, 'How is the second (or sometimes the third or fourth) line in a parallel structure functioning? What is it adding to the author's poetic expression? Is it there to emphasize what has already been said, to present a contrast, or perhaps to add new information?'"

Messianic Psalms

Our discussion of Psalm 1 brought to mind Psalm 2, which I have studied a bit because of my work on the book of Hebrews. At Hebrews 1:5 the author quotes Psalm 2:7, where God the Father says to Jesus, "You are My Son." This psalm is filled with parallelism. For instance, it begins like this:

> Why do **the nations rebel**
> and **the peoples plot** in vain? (Ps. 2:1)

Do you see the parallelism? The second line reemphasizes the idea of the worldly leaders rebelling against God, but it also *adds* the idea that such rebellion is not going to accomplish anything.

David picked up the conversation by pointing out that Psalm 2 represents yet another type of psalm. "This psalm belongs to a whole category of what I would call royal/messianic psalms because even the ones that are speaking strictly of David as the king or Solomon as the king are prefiguring the great King, Jesus, who is to come. They're looking ahead, anticipating what God will do in Christ. So these psalms don't primarily express our emotions; they let us in on significant things God has planned for the world. This big, cosmic-sized picture of God in control and bringing all things to His desired end is an important aspect of the worldview represented by the psalms, but they especially emphasize God's appointed king as His coworker in ruling God's people. For us as Christians, this is realized through the rule of Jesus in our lives, and we can use these psalms as songs of worship, celebrating what God has accomplished in Christ."

Guidance through the Proverbs

At this point I felt we needed to move on to discuss Proverbs in our last few minutes together. We live in an age that has much information and little wisdom. We need the wisdom for living out what the Bible has to offer. That wisdom is expressed uniquely and concisely in the Old Testament book of Proverbs. So I said, "All right, let's shift gears just a little bit and talk about Proverbs. After Psalms, it is probably the next most popular book in the Old Testament. Why has Proverbs been popular with many people through the centuries?"

David answered, "I think it is because it is one of the most intensely practical books in the entire Bible. It speaks over and over again about practical dimensions of life. How do we get along with our neighbor? How do we treat others? How are we to act, live, and think? At the root of Proverbs and all of what we call the Wisdom Literature—Job, Proverbs, and Ecclesiastes—there is a running thread of continuity: the fear of the Lord, which means to have a proper reverence and respect for God. So at the beginning of Proverbs, a statement says, 'The fear of the Lord is the beginning of knowledge. Fools despise wisdom and instructions.'

What is wisdom? It's been defined in many different ways. I would define it as skill in living life in both its vertical (our relationship with God) and horizontal (our relationship with others) dimensions. Being wise means to know how relationships work and how to live accordingly."

I added, "But wisdom is not the same as intellect, is it?"

David answered, "Sometimes people equate wisdom with intellect. That's not the case at all in the Bible. Biblical wisdom has to do with relational skills, knowing the right way to live. You might have a person with an IQ of 70 who, from a biblical standpoint, would be wiser than a person with a Ph.D. who violates God's principles."

I added, "Wisdom also is not exactly the same as knowledge? I mean, I know they're related, but—"

David agreed. "It's not knowledge. It's not encyclopedic understanding. Wisdom has to do with knowing how to live. One scholar has defined *wisdom* as 'the discipline of applying truth to life in the light of experience.' Consider Proverbs 26:4–5. Verse 4 says, 'Answer not a fool according to his folly, lest you be like him yourself.' That's a practical guideline for life. Don't even answer the fool; don't sink to his level because you'll become like him. Sometimes in life it's not even worth engaging people who are foolish. Notice, however, that the next verse says, 'Answer a fool according to his folly, or he will be wise in his own eyes' (ESV). On its face, this verse directly contradicts the previous verse. But the point is, God's wisdom teaches us how to apply His truth to our lives in the light of our experiences. This proverb is also true because in some situations we're required to answer a fool. We need to confront him and show his foolishness for what it is. So the whole point is that wisdom says we respond to various life experiences in various ways, according to the need of the moment. Sometimes we respond to similar situations in different ways as we discern what is called for in that moment."

This brought to mind those proverbs that seem to give concrete promises for life. "OK, let me ask a related question. At times we see proverbs that sound an awful lot like promises. 'If a man lives righteously, then he is going to prosper in life' (see Prov. 21:21). 'Train up a child in the way he should go; even when he is old he will not depart from it' (Prov. 22:6). Those sound a lot like promises. Is that how we are to read them?"

David responded, "They are not really promises in the sense that we might think of a promise from God—"

I interjected, "In terms of ironclad assurances that what is described is guaranteed by God to happen. How then should we read them?"

David said, "They should not be read as promises but as guidelines, as principles for living. They show the way life works best 80 to 95 percent of the time. The Bible is clear throughout

Scripture: if you live a life oriented to God, you will tend to have a good life. And yet, of course, we read in the book of Job and the book of Ecclesiastes that sometimes life doesn't turn out that way. Job did all the right things, yet he still had difficulty and trouble."

This was an important point. I once knew a woman whose husband had left her, yet she had a "promise" from Proverbs that guaranteed her that her husband was going to come home. When he didn't, she became disillusioned with God. Part of the problem was that she was reading a proverb as a promise rather than as a general guideline for how life is best lived.

I added, "So the Proverbs give us guidelines for how life is supposed to be lived according to God's wisdom, but we also need to read them in light of God's broader revelation in Scripture. It's important to read Proverbs in light of other proverbs to begin with, the context of the book as a whole, so that we are getting the whole counsel of God about appropriate responses in different situations. But you're saying we need to read Proverbs in light of the whole Bible as well."

David said, "The book of Proverbs is a balanced book, and reading it cover to cover, from beginning to end, will get that balance. If we pull one verse out of context and make it a little plaque on our refrigerator or wall, there will be truth there, but sometimes it's not the whole picture."

I responded, "So that's why we can't read individual proverbs as proving an ironclad promise that works in every situation. A proverb is always true, but it is addressing various kinds of situations in life."

David leaned forward and said, "It'll always be true in certain circumstances, but the circumstances might be different in which there are other proverbs that come to bear, or other truths from Scripture. So again, part of the beauty of Proverbs is that it addresses such a spectrum of life experiences and says, 'This is how you respond in a wise way, in God's way.'"

Conclusion

I wrapped up our conversation by asking David to sum up what he wishes every believer could experience in interacting with Psalms and Proverbs.

He responded, "Years ago I heard Billy Graham speak in a Q&A session. Someone was asking about his own personal devotional life, and as I recall, he said that among everything else he did, he would read five psalms and one chapter of Proverbs every day, and that got him through both books in a month. He did that regularly, year after year after year."

I thought about the exemplary life and the powerful ministry of Billy Graham, one of my heroes of the faith. I commented to David that Psalms and Proverbs must have played an important part in grounding Billy Graham in life. Psalms must have given voice to his experiences and his worship before God, and Proverbs must have given him guidelines for how to live.

David agreed and concluded. "There you go. Psalms giving the voice and Proverbs giving the guidelines. So that's a great way to come at it. I would hope, that when we come to Scripture, we would approach it not as a chore or a duty or a textbook but as a source of delight. At times we should say, 'Wow! I've actually got the next half hour to read the Bible and talk to God!'"

The geese still grazed in the field across the street as we left for our meetings of the day. Later in the day I stood on the top of the hill overlooking the bay, and I thought about the gift of Psalms and Proverbs, giving us a great voice of worship and guidelines for living. Like the bay stretching out before me—just beautiful.

Summary & Application

Summation

- We identify easily with the psalms, and they express the whole range of human emotions.

- The psalms most often express human words to or about God.
- Most of the psalms were written to be sung in large-group contexts.
- There are different kinds of psalms, including hymns, thanksgiving psalms, psalms of descriptive praise, psalms of declarative praise, psalms of narrative praise, historical psalms, laments, imprecatory psalms, and royal/messianic psalms.
- The psalms help us reflect on who God is, respond to God, and think about God appropriately.
- Essentially, the imprecatory psalms are calling on God to be faithful to His promises to His people.
- The psalms are emotional, filled with figurative language, and use a poetic structure known as "parallelism."
- The book of Proverbs is practical, offering guidelines for how life is best lived.

Conversation

1. Which emotions in your life right now would you like to be able to express to God?
2. How are the psalms similar to most of the hymns and choruses we sing in church? How are they different?
3. Read Psalm 19. Based on the descriptions given by David Howard in this chapter, what kind of psalm do you think this is?
4. Look at Psalm 23. What truths about God is the psalmist trying to communicate through figurative language (word pictures)?
5. Read Proverbs 11:1–10. Which one of these guidelines for life is most applicable in your life at present?

Transformation

Write three emotions that you have experienced in the last few days. Now skim Psalms 1–15, find psalms that express each of those emotions, and turn to God in prayer, using those psalms.

Reading the Old Testament Prophets

A Conversation with Gary Smith

The word of the LORD came to me: I chose you before
I formed you in the womb; I set you apart before you were born.
I appointed you a prophet to the nations.

—Jeremiah 1:4–5

What comes to mind when you read the word *prophet*? People commonly use the term to speak of someone who can predict the future. My students might ask me, "Who do you think is going to win the ball game this weekend?" and I might respond, "Well, I am neither a prophet nor the son of a prophet, but . . ." and then go on to make a prediction. Although prophecies about the future play a vitally important role in the Bible, the prophets were much more than spiritual forecasters, and we need to understand their roles in Israelite history and society in order to read them well. Their literature is as varied as it is voluminous, as heartbreakingly beautiful as it is confounding at points. So, to sort out the prophets for us, I called on my friend and colleague Gary Smith.

Gary and I share a love of vegetable gardening, swapping practical tips, plants, produce, the joys of a really good tomato, and commiserating over the heat and humidity of our West Tennessee summers. Having come out of an upper-Midwest farming family, Gary strikes me as a solid man of the soil, as comfortable with herbs as he is Hebrew. Had they been born at the same point in history, he and the prophet Amos, himself a farmer, could have had a long talk about good soil and then turned to a discussion concerning how to craft a good book. Professor Smith has written a number of sound commentaries on the Old Testament prophets and has just finished an outstanding, two-volume walk through the sixty-six chapters of Isaiah—no small feat. So, on a day late in the spring of 2009, we sat down together on the campus of Union University for our talk about the Old Testament prophets.

The prophets offer us one of the richest repositories of cultural commentary, poetic power, and theological perspective in all of Scripture. Like the Old Testament stories, they sometimes contain narrative portions that give us details on the lives of these prophets. Like Psalms, their messages at times are presented in the form of poetry. So some of the skills we have been learning in earlier chapters of *Read the Bible for Life* will be relevant here too.

Yet digging around in the prophets without some orientation or guidance can feel like we are mining in the middle of a huge, rock-strewn maze; it is easy to get lost and discouraged quickly. So, wanting us to leave the maze and head down a road to an effective reading of this amazing part of Scripture, I asked Gary if he could give us an overview of the prophets.

An Overview of the Prophets

Gary began, "In terms of length, we have four longer prophetic books, often called 'the Major Prophets,' and we have twelve shorter prophets, referred to as 'the Minor Prophets.' So we have sixteen in all."

I commented, "It is no easy job to sort them out in terms of their main themes or to discern exactly where they fit historically in the flow of Old Testament events."

Gary smiled, leaned into the microphone, and responded. "They are kind of complicated. When you first start reading the prophets, they sound similar on the surface because they are all calling the nation of Israel to repent and follow God. But once you get to know a little bit more about the prophets, they all stand out as being distinct from one another, and it can be difficult to keep their various themes straight. They lived at different times, addressed a variety of problems, and each emphasized unique issues. This reminds me of when I was a boy living on a dairy farm. I knew the names and characteristics of each of our cows. My friends from the city thought they all looked the same, but to me they were all different with unique tendencies. The prophets are similar. Haggai is different from Obadiah, and Ezekiel is different from Jonah."

I laughed and said, "I guess it is a good idea to know which cow you are milking, and by analogy we need to know some details about a prophet if we are going to understand his concerns. Are there basic tools a person should have on hand as they begin to read the prophets?"

He pointed to some of the same ones suggested by other conversation partners in this book. "I encourage my students to buy a Bible dictionary and a good study Bible."

I interjected, "So for instance, if you're going to be reading through Micah, a logical beginning place would be to use a Bible dictionary, or perhaps the basic articles you find at the beginning of each book in a good study Bible, and read an overview of what is going on with that particular prophet."

Gary responded, "That's a wonderful place to begin as you start the process. Such articles will point out the time the prophet wrote, what is known about him, the main themes of the book, a general outline, and the historical situation of that prophet's time. A study Bible specifically will also provide cross-references, indicating where events or topics in the each book are discussed in Kings and Chronicles, or where similar themes are discussed in other prophetic books."

I suggested, however, that even with great introductory materials, understanding where the prophets fit in biblical history can be a bit confusing.

Gary agreed and continued, "Adding to the confusion, the prophets are not organized in chronological order. In fact not all of the prophets who wrote books of the Old Testament are mentioned in Kings or Chronicles so it is difficult to date some of the prophets in terms of their place in history. However, generally speaking the prophets can be divided into four main groups."

I interjected, "OK, what are the four groups?"

The Prophets Ministered during Four Stages of Old Testament History

Group 1: The Eighth-Century Prophets

"First we have the earliest group of prophets, who lived in the eighth century BC, over seven centuries before the time of Christ. These were the prophets Amos, Hosea, Jonah, Micah, and Isaiah."

I commented, "Didn't these eighth-century prophets write at a time when the nation of Assyria was on the move as a world power?" Even in the twenty-first century, we often think about the shifting currents of our world in terms of powerful political forces like China, Iran, Israel, or the United States. It was the same for the prophets, and the eighth-century prophets wrote with the Assyrian threat looming on the horizon or camped on the doorstep.

Gary picked up the conversation. "That's right. Assyria was the main problem at that time. In 722 BC the Assyrians destroyed the Northern Kingdom of Israel, and the eighth-century prophets pointed to that event as imminent."

Group 2: The Rise of the Babylon Empire

I said, "OK. Who is in the second group of prophets?"

He responded, "Next we have a group of prophets who prophesied in the decades prior to the fall of Jerusalem to the Babylonians in 587 BC, about six centuries prior to the time of Christ. The Babylonians supplanted the Assyrians as the top world power of the day, and so the Israelites had to deal with the Babylonians. In this group we have the prophets Jeremiah, Nahum, Zephaniah, Obadiah, Joel, and Habakkuk."

I commented, "So this group of prophets is writing when the Babylonians are on the move as a world power. They're the big world threat." Jeremiah, who sometimes is called "The Weeping Prophet" due to the openness with which he shares his emotions, experienced his call, recounted in Jeremiah 1, in 627 BC. In Jeremiah 5:15–17 the prophet speaks the Lord's words that He will bring a distant, powerful nation against the Israelites. That nation was Babylon.

Group 3: During the Babylonian Exile

We then moved on to discuss a third group of prophets.

"The third group is made up of the prophets who wrote during the Babylonian Exile," Gary explained. "The Babylonians conquered the Israelites and carried many of them hundreds of miles away to Babylon, located approximately where the country of Iraq is today. The exile lasted until 538 BC, when the Persians defeated the Babylonians, allowing the Israelites to return home. So the Israelites were in Babylon for much of the sixth-century BC, and there were prophets who ministered to them while they were in exile in Babylon. I would put Ezekiel and Daniel in that group."

It so happened that I had been reading Ezekiel that morning. I commented to Gary, "In Ezekiel you have interesting passages like the one where the Angel of the Lord comes and grabs Ezekiel by the hair and takes him in a vision back to Jerusalem (Ezek. 8). There he sees the horrible sins the leaders who were left in Jerusalem were committing."

Gary said, "One of the interesting things about Ezekiel is that he's actually in exile talking to people in exile, but a great deal of the book is about what is happening in Jerusalem. God in effect uses Ezekiel to correct faulty ideas the people had about God and His plan for Jerusalem."

Group 4: After the Babylonian Exile

I asked, "OK, what prophets make up the fourth group?"

"The final group consists of those prophets who wrote after the Babylonian Exile: Haggai, Zachariah, and Malachi. To give us a bit of historical perspective, these prophets wrote during the time of Ezra, Nehemiah, and Esther, each of whom played important roles in that period after the Persians had defeated the Babylonians and allowed the Jewish people to return to Palestine. Haggai and Zechariah encouraged God's people to get busy with rebuilding the temple, which had been destroyed by the Babylonians. The people had gotten caught up in building their own houses, rebuilding their own lives, and had neglected the building of God's temple. Malachi, on the other hand, writes about honoring God with the tithe, sacrifices, and through sound marriages. So these prophets who wrote after the exile have different concerns from the earlier prophets."

What was clear from our conversation thus far is that historical context is going to be vitally important for reading the prophets well. I mentioned this to Gary, and I asked why the world powers, like Assyria, Babylonia, and Persia, played such a large role in the developing history of Israel.

Gary answered, "Yes, understanding the historical context for each of the prophets is absolutely critical. We have to ask questions like, 'Who is the king at the time? Is the prophet writing to the Northern Kingdom of Israel or the Southern Kingdom of Judah at the time? Are the people following God or not? Is there a war going on, or is one imminent? What's the social situation at that time?' Once we begin to ask such questions, the message of each prophet begins to make more sense.

"As for why the world powers played such a large role in Israel's history, we have to remember that the Israelites lived (and still live today) on a narrow strip of land that averaged only about fifty miles from east to west. To the west was the Mediterranean Sea, and to the east was the desert. The Assyrians, Babylonians, and Persians had to travel through that little strip of land to confront the great nation of Egypt, which was to the south of Israel in northeast Africa. So Israel, though small, was significant geographically. At the same time, from a spiritual standpoint, God often used these great nations to bring judgment on the Israelites for their idolatry or, in the case of Persia, to deliver the Israelites from exile."

Aren't the Prophets Primarily Telling the Future?

As I mentioned in the introduction to this chapter, when we think about the prophets, what often comes to mind for many people is their ability to predict the future. I asked Gary what role looking into the future played in the writing of the Old Testament prophets.

Gary collected his thoughts and responded, "I think my first introduction to the prophets came when I was about thirteen or fourteen years old. Every so often the small country church I attended in Iowa had what they called a 'Prophecy Conference.' It was mostly about what God would do at the end of time, focusing on the prophecies of Ezekiel, Daniel, and the book of Revelation. The teachers that were invited to speak at these special meetings tried to explain some of the mysterious symbolism in these books. They gave us charts about what might happen in the future and encouraged us to be ready for the second coming because it could happen any day.

"Many years later, after I had finished my education and was teaching, I received an invitation to write the main article on 'Prophecy' for a major Bible encyclopedia, and that research was a key factor in heightening my interest in the lives of the prophets, their different roles in Israelite society, how to interpret their prophecies, and the significant influence the prophets had on the history of the nation of Israel. Through this research I found out that the prophets contained much more than just prophecies about end-time events.

"In short, we can think of the prophets as preachers of their day, addressing issues of their day, who sometimes pointed to what God would do in the future as a part of their message. Much of the prophetic literature does not involve prediction of the future, but prediction plays an important role in motivating the people to take seriously the prophet's message from God.

At times the prophet might be looking just a few years into the future, as when the prophet Amos says in effect, 'God is sending the Assyrians to bring judgment on you!' At the same time God sometimes uses the prophet to pull back the curtain on events far in the future, indicating God's greater plans for the world."

I interjected, "So are you thinking of passages like Isaiah 53, which pulls back that curtain to give a glimpse of the suffering of Christ?"

Gary answered, "That's right. Isaiah 53:5, written centuries before the birth of Christ, says, 'But He was pierced because of our transgressions, crushed because of our iniquities; punishment for our peace was on Him, and we are healed by His wounds.'"

Such prophesies are amazing in the specificity with which they point to the coming of Christ. I thought of passages like 1 Peter 1:10–11: "Concerning this salvation, the prophets who prophesied about the grace that would come to you searched and carefully investigated. They inquired into what time or what circumstances the Spirit of Christ within them was indicating when He testified in advance to the messianic sufferings and the glories that would follow."

The Prophets as Preachers: Three Key Themes

At the same time, Gary had noted that large portions of these prophetic books consisted of the prophet confronting the people of his day with strong messages from God. These messages had to do with how the people of Israel and Judah were to live for God in the world. I wanted to get at those messages and asked about the key themes the prophets seem to have in common. I thought that if we could have the key themes as a foundation, it might be easier to sort out the particular emphases of each prophet as we read through them. Gary began by pointing to a theme we have discussed before in earlier chapters of this book—God's covenant relationship with His people.

Theme 1: The Call to the Covenant

Gary responded, "To understand the glue that holds the prophets together, we have to go back to the first five books of the Bible, the Pentateuch (Genesis, Exodus, Leviticus, Numbers, and Deuteronomy) and focus on the covenants God made with His people. In the Pentateuch God made foundational covenants with the Israelites, first with Abraham, the father of the nation, and then with the whole nation after Moses had led them out of Egypt. He would be their God and live among them, and they were to follow the instructions for how to live under the covenant, living as a blessing to the nations. In addition God promised to give them the land of Canaan. This covenant relationship was based on God's love for them and their love for God, which was expressed by obedience to God's law."

Suddenly our conversation was sounding familiar. In my talks with Bruce Waltke about the Old Testament stories (chapter 5) and with Danny Hays about the law (chapter 6), both emphasized the need to read these parts of the Old Testament in light of the covenant relationship between God and His people. Now Gary was telling me that the covenants between God and the Israelites were at the heart of the prophetic literature as well. He explained that one of the prophets' concerns was that people during their day were focusing on the blessings of the covenants without giving attention to the specific instructions for living under the covenant.

Gary explained. "One of the criticisms the prophets have is that some of the people seem to have focused on the Abrahamic covenant or on the blessings of the Mosaic covenant. At times they also seem to focus on the Davidic covenant and its promise that a king from David's line would reign forever. So they latched onto these wonderful promises—this great future that God had planned, and how God was going to use His people. Consequently, when a prophet came and said, 'God's judgment is coming,' some of the people during his day said: 'That is impossible! We are the Jewish people whom God has blessed. We are the seed of Abraham, God's chosen! God will not let us be destroyed!' They said, 'The day of the Lord will come!' The day of the Lord was understood to be the day that God would show up and destroy His enemies. The Israelites said in effect, 'God will deliver us!' Yet the prophets responded, 'Yes, the day of the Lord is coming, but it is not what you expect!' In Amos 5, the prophet says:

> Woe to you who long for the Day of the LORD!
> What will the Day of the LORD be for you?
> It will be darkness and not light.
> It will be like a man who flees from a lion
> only to have a bear confront him.
> He goes home and rests his hand against the
>   wall
> only to have a snake bite him.
> Won't the Day of the LORD
> be darkness rather than light,
> even gloom without any brightness in it?
>   (vv. 18–20)

"In other words, the Day of the Lord would be a day of judgment on the Israelites themselves! Yet the Jewish people just flat out didn't believe judgment could happen; they had forgotten that God Himself said He would bring judgment, driving them out of the promised land, if the covenant was abandoned (Deut. 29:22–29)."

I interjected, "It reminds me of the people during the time of John the Baptist. According to Luke 3:7–9 many appealed to their relationship to Abraham as the reason they were OK with God. Yet John called them to repent."

Gary added, "To some extent this is even true today. People may depend on their family, their membership in a church, or even their American citizenship as validating their relationship with God. They might say, 'My parents were strong Christians in the church,' or 'I am a member of the church,' or even 'Of course I am a Christian—I was born in America!' Yet these relationships are not the basis for a healthy relationship with God."

I commented, "OK, so you have this theme of the covenant relationship that all the prophets share, pretty much."

Gary responded, "In essence, much of their message can be boiled down to: You are supposed to be living as God's covenant people. You are violating the covenant. If you don't repent, judgment is coming."

Much on God's judgment is found in the prophets. We need to read these words of judgment as expressions of God's holiness and His longing for a close relationship with His people. In broken relationships communication often means going into a "dark tunnel" of communication in order for restoration to take place. Yet such communication, although difficult, must be embraced as an act of love, grace, and hope.

I asked Gary, "Where does the idea of hope for the future come in?" It seems to me that we have beautiful, powerful words of hope interlaced throughout the prophets.

Theme 2: The Call of the Remnant and God's Eternal Kingdom

This led us to a discussion of "The Righteous Remnant." Gary commented, "Most of the prophets talk about the righteous remnant that God is going to save in spite of the coming judgment—the faithful few who continue to follow the ways of the Lord. For instance, Amos 9 speaks of God having a sieve, just like a farmer has a sieve when he separates the grain from the chaff. In verse 10 of that chapter, God says, 'All the sinners among My people who say: Disaster will never overtake or confront us, will die by the sword,' but in the next breath the Lord says, 'In that day I will restore the fallen booth of David: I will repair its gaps, restore its ruins' (v. 11). So even as God is pronouncing judgment, He also looks to a brighter future. This theme will be repeated again and again in the prophets, proclaiming God's salvation of the righteous but His judgment of the wicked."

I commented, "So at times God's people seem to give up on Him, but He refuses to give up on the vision of building a nation for Himself, one that will embody righteousness and be a light to the nations. God is always optimistic about the future because He is crafting a future for His people!"

Gary added, "In the future God is going to establish His ideal kingdom in which His people will live. It will be a kingdom of peace; there will be no more war. God will dwell among His people, and His people will live by His law in perfect harmony."

The prophets speak with resounding relevance for issues in the modern world, and no topic illustrates this better than the topic of peace. As Gary had mentioned, the prophets give a vision of the future, which consists of God's kingdom, His peaceful reign over the earth. As Christians, we know that God's peace comes in the lives of individuals and will eventually be worked out for the whole world through Jesus, the Prince of Peace. Perhaps you will recognize Isaiah 9:6, a verse often read at Christmastime:

> For a child will be born for us,
> a son will be given to us,
> and the government will be on His shoulders.
> He will be named
> Wonderful Counselor, Mighty God,
> Eternal Father, Prince of Peace.

Those words of Isaiah, written almost seven and a half centuries before the time of Christ, answer a deep longing in the hearts of all of us who live in such a violent world. Over the past few days, yet another suicide bomber shook the earth, shredding the lives of almost one hundred families in a Middle Eastern country. The resounding promise of peace still needs to be heard today; the prophets of the Old Testament have resonating messages the world still needs to hear.

Theme 3: The Call for Social Justice

Gary next pointed to another highly relevant topic for the modern world, the prophets' emphasis on social justice. To live for God means that we must value what God values, and the prophets proclaim powerfully that God values the poor and defenseless of the world. For God's people righteousness must be incarnated in the ways we care for "the least of these."

Gary explained, "We could go on for days on that issue! For instance, when you read the book of Amos, you realize that the society of Amos's day was divided sharply between the rich and the poor. It's a time of great wealth and prosperity. The Northern Kingdom of Israel to whom Amos was sent had a great deal of military strength prior to the onslaught of the Assyrians. It really was a golden age for the nation. Egypt was weak at that time, and Assyria was not yet threatening them. So Israel could pretty much do anything it wanted to do. The Israelites were successful in defeating the enemies immediately around them, expanding their own territory, and bringing in tribute money. In short, they became a wealthy, comfortable nation."

I interjected, "So they had a false sense of security because as they looked around, all the evidence pointed to God's blessing?"

Gary continued, "That's right. In fact, religion was booming. People were writing religious songs and bringing sacrifices to God. Yet the spiritual poverty of the nation was seen in the way they treated the poor and the injustice in the court systems, which favored the rich and powerful. People lived in luxury while the poor among them struggled to survive. Again the Israelites were ignoring many of the specific instructions God had given in the law. Leviticus 19, for instance, gives clear instructions on caring for the poor. Yet the Israelites seemed to think that since they were religious, they did not have to be righteous. God hates such empty religion."

I remembered the striking passage from Amos 5:21–24, where God says:

> I hate, I despise your feasts!
> I can't stand the stench
> of your solemn assemblies.
> Even if you offer Me
> your burnt offerings and grain offerings,
> I will not accept them;

> I will have no regard
> for your fellowship offerings of fattened cattle.
> Take away from Me the noise of your songs!
> I will not listen to the music of your harps.
> But let justice flow like water,
> and righteousness, like an unfailing stream.

If you remember, during the Civil Rights movement in the United States, Dr. Martin Luther King Jr. quoted that last sentence in a powerful plea for justice for blacks, illustrating just how universal some of the messages we find in the prophets really are.

Gary agreed. He talked about how the social and religious dynamics in Amos serve as a cautionary tale for those of us in the modern, Western church; without careful attention to God's Word, we can be oblivious to the needs, the desperate situations of the world's poorest people. "Most people have not gone overseas. I was in Egypt a few years back, and I was amazed at the poverty. Thousands of people lived on a huge garbage dump, searching for food. That was their job; that was the only job they had. They lived in unbelievable squalor. So the prophets call us to deal straightforwardly with how we are responding to the poor of our day."

Issues like the need for covenant faithfulness, peace in a world of violence, and the need for giving in a world of social injustice provide a taste of what the prophets have to offer as relevant guides to God's values in a fallen world. In our conversation we had discussed several points for reading the prophets well. We need to understand each prophet's historical context. We need to understand orienting themes, especially the call to covenant faithfulness, the judgment that falls on the unrepentant, and the hope of a wonderful future for God's remnant. Yet the prophets make up a large part of the Old Testament, and learning to read them well will take time, developing certain skills and learning to use helpful tools.

Digging Deeper into the World of the Prophets with Good Tools

I asked Gary if there were other tools beyond a Bible dictionary and a good study Bible that could help us read the prophets more effectively.

He answered, "For someone who is a Sunday school teacher, I would encourage them to buy a commentary or two on the book they are reading or studying."

With a smile I shot back, "Especially commentaries by Gary Smith on the prophets!"

With a laugh Gary nodded his head in agreement, "That would be wise!"

I continued, "I say that jokingly but, seriously, we really are blessed with wonderful resources that have been produced over the last thirty years in evangelicalism. A lot of wonderful commentaries are available on every book of the Bible."

Gary said, "That's right. I think some laypeople and some pastors feel intimidated by commentaries. But I would encourage people to go to their local bookstore, or if there is a Christian college in the neighborhood, to check out what commentaries are available in the library. I think particularly in the Old Testament when people feel a little bit uncomfortable with 'What does this mean and how do I apply it to today?' you can get some real help from a good commentary."

To return to my references to gardening in the beginning, I know that both Gary and I have found that having the right tools at hand really can make all the difference in growing a healthy garden. It makes life a lot easier if I have the tools I need when I need them. Commentaries, a good Bible dictionary, and a good study Bible are basic tools to help in reading the prophets well.

Conclusion

As we concluded our conversation, I thought about how pertinent the prophets are for the world into which we all have been born. The movement of world powers; the longing for peace; the need for social justice; the vapidity of an empty, smug religion that assumes God's blessings without careful attention to the loving demands for obedience; God's ongoing work of building a remnant people to live in His eternal kingdom. The prophets, though two and one-half millennia old, really seem a playbook for our times; and Gary Smith had given us several helpful suggestions for taking that playbook in hand, opening its pages, and beginning to read it more carefully.

Summary & Application

Summation

- The prophets did more than forecast the future. They also were the preachers of their day, calling people to covenant faithfulness.
- There are sixteen prophetic books in the Old Testament, four longer books and twelve shorter. These prophets can be grouped into four historical periods: the eighth-century prophets, those who ministered during the rise of the Babylonian Empire, those of the Babylonian Exile, and the prophets who ministered after the exile.
- Use a Bible dictionary or study Bible to get a good introduction on a prophet's historical context before you begin reading the book. Buying a good commentary on a prophetic book can really help as well.
- The prophets focus on faithfulness to God's covenants and coming judgment if people do not repent.
- The prophets tell of a faithful remnant of God's people and of God's eternal kingdom.
- The prophets call for social justice.

Conversation

1. In your own words, how would you define the term *prophet?*

2. Is there anyone in our culture whom you consider to have a prophet-like ministry? Why does that person(s) strike you as "prophetic"?

3. With which of the Old Testament prophets are you most familiar? What do you remember about that prophet's message?

4. As the chapter suggests, the prophets call the people of God to covenant faithfulness. What does covenant faithfulness look like today?

5. The prophets preach against idolatry and lack of concern for social issues like fairness in court and poverty. How should the church today address such issues? How do those issues relate to love for God?

6. How were aspects of the prophets' messages fulfilled in the person and work of Jesus?

Transformation

In a Bible dictionary or a study Bible, read an introduction on the book of Amos. Now read Amos 5 carefully and identify parallels with our culture. What warning in this chapter is most applicable to your life at present?

PART THREE

Reading the New Testament

CHAPTER 9

Reading the New Testament Stories
A Conversation with Darrell Bock

Many have undertaken to compile a narrative about the events that have been fulfilled among us, just as the original eyewitnesses and servants of the word handed them down to us.

—Luke 1:1–2

 In our chapter on "Reading the Old Testament Stories" (chapter 5), I wrote about how much I love a good story. A cozy winter's evening by the fire with Dickens can be profoundly renewing for me, charging my emotional batteries and helping me see the world with fresh eyes. Yet some stories are so significant, so foundational for who we are as people, they really belong in a category all to themselves. Such stories are life orienting, providing perspective on how our days should be lived and why they should be lived that way. Such are the stories we find in the Gospels and Acts of the New Testament.

To talk to us about the power-packed storytelling of the earliest Christians, I tapped a friend and evangelical scholar who has been visible in the media over the past decade. Darrell Bock serves as research professor of New Testament Studies and Professor of Spiritual Development and Culture at Dallas Theological Seminary. As a scholar who has spent his life focused on studying the life of Jesus, the four Gospels, and the narrative of Acts, he has played a significant role in the past few years defending a biblical view of Jesus as the Son of God in venues such as major newspapers, ABC News, *20/20*, and universities around the world. At the same time Darrell has written numerous articles, commentaries, and other helpful books that guide pastors and laypeople to a deeper understanding of how to read the stories of the New Testament in a way that is life changing. So with thunderstorms rumbling over the city of Dallas, Texas, we sat down this past April in a small conference room on the seminary campus to talk about how to read these stories more effectively.

Why Four Gospels?

I began our conversation by asking Dr. Bock why we have four Gospels in the New Testament.

Darrell has a big voice and a bigger laugh that certainly could be heard down the hall during our conversation. He jumped right into the question, with the energy of the highly engaged teacher he is. "I tell my students that we have four Gospels on purpose, each providing a nuanced perspective on who Jesus is and what He came to accomplish. Altogether they provide us with a full and consistent picture of Jesus.

"Three of the Gospels work the same way, and one of them works a different way. The three that work the same way are Matthew, Mark, and Luke, often called the Synoptic Gospels (*synoptic* means "to see together"). The one that does its own thing is John. Now, in the history of the church, the problem has been that we naturally gravitate to the Gospel of John because John does all the heavy theological lifting for us. From the beginning of his Gospel, Jesus' identity is presented with twenty-twenty vision. John tells the story from the perspective of heaven down."

I interjected, "So are you saying that John begins with crystal clarity on Jesus' identity as the Lord of the universe?"

Bock continued, "Exactly right. So John starts off the prologue with (Bock speaking in a deep, booming voice), 'In the beginning was the Word, and the Word was with God, and the Word was God—this is CNN!'"

We both laughed.

Bock added, "John starts us there, moves immediately to the incarnation, and then walks through the gospel, all the while making statements like, 'Behold the Lamb of God!' In other words, right from the beginning John affirms what we as Christians have come to believe about Jesus, and that makes it an easy Gospel for us to read. He highlights those moments in which Jesus' identity was made clear and adds his 'cosmic perspective' commentary so the reader can't miss the point. The Gospel of John is wonderful and plays an important role in presenting Jesus as both completely human and completely divine. We see Jesus more clearly by the way John presents his Gospel.

"But here's the kicker—and this is one of the things I love about the Gospels!—three of them don't take that approach. Matthew, Mark, and Luke tell the story of Jesus from what I call 'the earth up,' allowing the reader to discover who Jesus is as the story unfolds. As you read, you start asking, 'OK, what kind of a person is Jesus? What is going on here?'"

Reading as a Process of Discovery

I said, "Darrell, you obviously think this is important for the way we read the Gospel stories. Why is that?"

He explained, "What we as Christians tend to forget is this: gradual discovery is how almost everybody experiences Jesus. No one being confronted with Jesus' identity immediately 'gets it' completely. No one came out of the womb, received the swat of life on the backside, and then cried, 'Jesus! He is God! The second person in the Trinity! Waa waa waa!'"

We both laughed out loud, Darrell's laughter mixing with the booming thunder that lightly shook the building.

He continued: "No one starts out there. Everyone at some point has had someone sit down and lead him or her to a deeper understanding of Jesus. This is true even for those people who hear the gospel and respond to it immediately. They then have to be taken deeper into what the identity of Jesus is all about.

Gradually we grasp the fact that Jesus is different from any other person who has ever lived, and this is how Matthew, Mark, and Luke tell the story of Jesus. They gradually unfold His identity. Like John, they know who Jesus is, but many of their first readers don't, and they are leading them to a deeper understanding of Jesus."

"But," I suggested, "because we as Christians know Jesus' true identity, that can be frustrating for us if we don't understand what Matthew, Mark, and Luke are doing. It can make it difficult for us to enter wholeheartedly into the developing story because we know the ending so well."

Darrell agreed. "As a result, when we come into the Synoptic Gospels after walking in the clear sunshine of John's Gospel, we're struggling. All of a sudden the sky has clouded over because these Gospels aren't saying everything the way we would say it and the way we're used to hearing it. We might ask, 'Why are the disciples being so dense?' But being clueless was their experience at points, as they gradually understood who Jesus really was. That is why many people find Matthew, Mark, and Luke intriguing, interesting, fascinating, but oddly foreign."

I added, "Which really parallels the disciples' experience of Jesus" and noted that Ben Witherington actually calls the disciples in Mark's Gospel the 'duh-sciples'! We need to remember that they were in completely uncharted territory. No one had had the experience of walking around Palestine with the Son of God before. They were in a process of discovery that shifted their categories and their expectations of what God might be up to in the world.

Darrell added, "That's part of the story, to tell the disciples' story of discovery. This is important for us as we read the Gospels, but it is also a key for how we read the Gospels with people who have yet to believe the gospel message. What we've got to do is learn to read the Gospels on the Gospels' terms."

I interjected, "To enter the story with fresh eyes, like a person who is in the process of discovery."

Bock continued excitedly, his forearms resting on the table, but his hands gesturing as he made his points. His passion for helping non-Christians read the Gospels really came through. "That's right. We need to recover the ability to read with fresh eyes and to lead others through the conversation the Gospels are initiating, as opposed to just flipping to the end of the story. We have to walk with people through a process. We have to understand that when we say that Jesus is unique, that Jesus is the only way to God, we are going against the grain of our culture, which says, 'There are lots of ways to God.' So how do we help people get there? I think we should let the Gospels tell the story, uncovering the identity of Jesus a step at a time. That's what the Synoptic Gospels attempt to do, and they do it, in part, through the way the disciples are coming to realize who Jesus is as they hang out with Him."

An Example: Peter's Confession of Jesus

I asked Darrell if he could give us an example of this in the Gospels, and he pointed to Peter's confession in Luke 9:18–22. "A good example is Peter's confession of Jesus as the Christ at Caesarea Philippi. This is an important step in the story. People generally were saying, 'Jesus is one of the prophets, one of the crowd.' Peter confesses that Jesus is the Christ, God's Anointed One, the Messiah, which means He is unique. Jesus responds in effect by saying, 'OK. Now I can work with you. You understand that I have a unique role in the plan of God.'

"But then Jesus throws the disciples a curve ball: 'The Son of Man is going to suffer.' That is quite a juxtaposition if you think about it. The Son of Man, mentioned in Daniel 7, is an exalted figure in the Old Testament, one who rides the clouds, which is something only gods do; He comes up to the Ancient of Days to receive dominion, an everlasting kingdom. That is the kind of Messiah the disciples are looking for—one who would wipe out the Romans. They could get behind that kind of Messiah!

"But Jesus says something they don't associate with a conquering Messiah: 'I am going to suffer.' So Peter responds in effect, 'That's a disconnect.' He pulls Jesus aside and begins to have a friendly, theological conversation with Him: 'Well, wait a minute now. I buy that you're the Messiah, but this suffering thing—that can't be part of God's plan.' Jesus turns around and says, 'Get behind me, Satan!' I'm sure when Peter heard that he blinked—it was a two-by-four between the eyes. Jesus had changed the categories, changed how they were to understand God's Messiah."

So the main point is that the disciples were in a process of discovery, and we have to enter into these stories at a deeper level, walking with the disciples in their experience of discovery, if we are going to read the Gospels well.

What about Acts?

I asked Darrell if this perspective changes as we consider how to read the book of Acts. Is discovery still in play, or is there another foundational guideline for how we should read that book?

He thought for a moment, rested his hands on the conference table, and then answered. "If John tells the gospel story from heaven down and the synoptics tell the gospel story from earth up, Acts—in an exciting way—is somewhat a combination of the two. You remember that Acts is volume 2 of the Gospel of Luke, and Luke starts Acts by referring back to the third Gospel: 'I wrote the first narrative, Theophilus, about all that Jesus began to do and teach' (Acts 1:1). So Acts, rather than moving on from the story of Jesus, continues it. Here's the rest of the story. So Acts is kind of the Paul Harvey volume of the canon. Only now Jesus' identity is clear. After the ascension in Acts 1, Jesus is seated at the right hand of God the Father in heaven. He pours out the Holy Spirit in Acts 2. He confronts Paul on the road to Damascus in chapter 9. Whereas the synoptics are gradually unfolding Jesus' identity, by the time we get to Acts, the curtain has been pulled back all the way. Jesus has died for the sins of the world and been resurrected, shown to be God's Messiah, the Son of God. As the exalted, unique One, Jesus has given the promised Spirit, who in turn gives Christ's followers a relationship with God and completes the promise John the Baptist said was coming as a result of Jesus' ministry (Luke 3:16). The experience transforms the disciples from distraught, disillusioned followers to leaders of a movement that would shake the world, and they follow the lead of the Lord Jesus, who now works through the Holy Spirit in the church. Acts works from heaven down in that sense."

I asked Bock how Acts reflects a perspective that is also from "the earth-up."

He responded, "Acts still is working from the earth up from the standpoint of the church. There is still discovery going on, only what is unfolding now is God's mission, His agenda in the world, which has as its reference point the identity of Jesus and the implications of His death and resurrection. There still is struggle going on as the first followers of Jesus try to figure out how to live under Jesus' lordship in the world. There were no seminaries, church buildings, church-growth materials, or missions agencies. And there are still plenty of surprises in Acts, like that fact that God really cares about people who aren't Jewish. We have a hard time grasping what a shocker that was. In the beginning Christianity was a Jewish movement. Period. No one looked like people from the West, and these Jews just saw themselves as the true fulfillment of Judaism, inheriting the covenant promises of Israel. So Acts is working from the earth up in the sense that God unfolds His will for the church step-by-step, and that makes the story exciting."

I commented, "And that is also what makes the Christian life and mission exciting today. We struggle and discover and try to follow God under the lordship of Jesus. Lots of struggle, but being on mission is exciting." Darrell agreed wholeheartedly.

From what we had discussed thus far, the identity of Jesus clearly stands at the heart of the four Gospels and Acts and serves as a foundational reference point for reading the big-picture, developing story of the Gospels and Acts. But I wanted to get down to nuts and bolts for reading the many individual stories we find in these books. Bock said we need to begin with asking an important question.

What Does This Story Tell Me about Jesus?

"The first thing we have got to do is ask, 'What does this story tell me about Jesus, the unique Promised One?' which from the Gospels' perspective is the same as asking, 'What does this story tell me about God?'" He explained, "The most foundational question for reading the Bible well is to ask, 'What does this tell me about God?' Period. I don't care where you are, whether you are in the Gospels or somewhere else. He is the orienting point of the story. As I get properly oriented to Him, I not only get the story right; I get my life right. Sometimes people come to the Bible and ask, 'What does this passage say about me?' and they bypass the God part."

If you remember, in our conversation with Bruce Waltke about the Old Testament stories, he said exactly the same thing: God is the main actor of Scripture, and we have to begin by asking the "God" question. It turns out this insight played a significant role in Darrell's coming to the Christian faith.

He explained. "When I was in college, before I was a believer, someone handed me a Bible and said, 'Look, you're smart. You can read. Just read this and ask one question: how central is Jesus to what is happening?' That person really had their act together because that really is the point. They said to me, 'Start with Matthew, and yes, we know that you'll hit the genealogies, but just keep reading.' So I read, and it became clear to me as I was reading that Jesus was at the center of the story. There was no way to get to the story of God without dealing deeply with the story of Jesus. The two were like a piece of DNA, a double helix, all wrapped up together. Before I knew it, I was struggling with questions like, Who is this Jesus, and How does He fit into a relationship with God? Why are people reacting to Him the way they are? So asking the right questions about Jesus led me to Him and laid a solid foundation for my relationship with God."

I asked Darrell if he could give us an example of how to read a passage, asking, "What does this passage tell me about Jesus?" He gladly agreed and pointed to the story of a paralyzed man being dropped down through a hole in the roof.

An Example: A Paralytic Drops In on Jesus

"Let's think about the story of the paralytic in Mark 2:1–12. This guy literally drops in on Jesus while Jesus is at a home in Capernaum. So many people were crammed together in the house, the guy's friends couldn't get him close to Jesus, so they made a hole in the roof and lowered him down to land right in front of the Healer. Imagine when the dust and bits of roof started falling on the crowd. They must have cleared a spot quickly! So there he is, suddenly lying on his mat in front of Jesus. What is the first thing Jesus says to him? 'Son, your sins are forgiven' (v. 5). Think about it. You're the paralytic and Jesus says to you, 'Your sins are forgiven.' What are you thinking when Jesus says that to you? Well, you probably are thinking, *That's not why I dropped in on You and crashed this party!*"

I asked, "So what's going on? How is this pointing to Jesus?"

Bock continued. "For a clue, notice the thoughts of the theologians in the room. The Jewish teachers are thinking, *Why is he saying that? He's blaspheming! Only God can forgive sins.* And Mark goes, 'Bing bing bing bing! Right answer!'

"Also, notice Jesus' question (it is another important clue): 'Which is easier: to say, "Your sins are forgiven," or to say, "Get up, pick up your stretcher, and walk"?' It's a great question because the one thing you can see and the other thing you can't, but God is the only one who can accomplish either. So Jesus ties the two together. He says, 'In order that you might know that the Son of Man has authority in heaven and on earth to forgive sins (the thing you can't see), I say to you, Get up and walk.' So when the paralytic gets up and walks, his walking (again, the thing they could see) *says something about Jesus*: 'The Son of Man has authority on earth to forgive sins' (v. 10). The key is Jesus' authority, which is one with God's authority. The response was immediate: 'They were all astounded and gave glory to God' (v. 12).

"Now most people read that story and say, 'Well that's nice. The guy who couldn't walk can walk now, and his sins were forgiven.' And they might follow with, 'What are my needs that I want Jesus to address? What sins do I need forgiven?' Good questions, but you get to those questions by first reading the story on its own terms. To read the story well we have to think about the staggering theological implications of the story. How in the world could Jesus, a human being, exercise that kind of authority, authority that belongs in the hands of God alone? That is the question Mark wants us to ask."

The "God" Question in Acts

I asked Darrell how the "God question" shifts as we turn to the book of Acts.

"The question is the same question. I still am asking, 'What is God doing here?' But now the question is, 'What are the implications of Jesus' lordship for the mission God has given the church in the world? How is the Holy Spirit directing the church? How does all this express the heart of God the Father?' Ultimately each story of Acts challenges us to ask, 'How does the church carry out God's mission today?'"

Wow. Clearly we gain perspective by beginning to read the Gospels and Acts by asking, 'What do these stories tell us about Jesus?,' or 'What is God doing here?' We would return to specific examples from the book of Acts later, but I wanted to press on to other helpful guidelines. I asked Professor Bock what other insights he had on how we could read the Gospels and Acts more effectively. He pointed in a direction we have been pointed before, a consideration of the cultural backdrop of the Bible.

Understand the Cultural Context

"You are never going to understand what these stories in the Gospels and Acts are doing without learning more about the culture of first-century Judaism. It is just not going to happen. If we simply read the stories without taking that step, we will superimpose our cultural scripts on the stories and change them into something they were never intended to be."

By "cultural scripts" Bock was referring to patterns of life, like food, standards of behavior, attitudes, and clothing, but more important, ideas about God, religious practices, and the Jewish Scriptures, just to give a few examples. People in first-century Palestine had their cultural scripts, just as we do today.

Bock offered an illustration, one of our twenty-first-century cultural scripts in the United States—NFL football. "If I say to you, 'The Cowboys are going to the frozen tundra to melt the Cheeseheads,' most any American will know that I am talking about NFL football. Nowhere in that sentence did I refer to the NFL. Yet you're so embedded in the culture that you catch the references to Cowboys and Cheeseheads. But if I put that sentence in writing and handed it to a person living in Saudi Arabia, who spoke English but was not at all familiar with American sports, it would make no sense to them, even if they understood every English word in the sentence, because the gap in understanding is cultural.

"The Bible is loaded with those kinds of cultural scripts. They run throughout the Gospels and Acts. Even if we understand the words on the surface, we might be missing vitally important things God wants to say to us if we don't understand those cultural ways of thinking. So another important aspect of reading the Bible well has to do with learning those cultural scripts, those ways of thinking that would have been common to a Jew of the first century."

The Example of Jesus Cleansing the Temple

Again, I asked Darrell if he would give us an example, and he leaned forward into the microphone as rain now drove hard against the window. "Think about the time when Jesus marched in and cleansed the temple. What are some of the cultural scripts we need to understand to read this story better?"

Matthew's version of the story reads, "Jesus went into the temple complex and drove out all those buying and selling in the temple. He overturned the money changers' tables and the chairs of those selling doves. And He said to them, 'It is written,

My house will be called a house of prayer. But you are making it a den of thieves!'" (Matt. 21:12–13).

"First," Darrell suggested, "we need to understand how important the temple was for a Jew of the first century. There was no more important place on earth, the most sacred spot on the globe. The temple was at the heart of worship and was the crown jewel of Judaism. It was even more important to many Jews than the White House or Capitol dome would be to many Americans. So when Jesus, who was not a local and had no position of authority, walked in and started cleaning house, He was dealing with the heart of Judaism of the day. He was dealing in an unprecedented manner with the most sacred space on the planet. It would have been seen as an audacious act, to say the least."

In chapter 2 on "Reading the Bible in Context," Andreas Köstenberger also pointed to the tremendous significance of the temple in the first century.

Second, Bock pointed to cultural views about the Messiah, who He was expected to be and what He was expected to do when He came on the scene. The Messiah was the anticipated Jewish King, who many hoped would restore Israel's kingdom and drive out the Romans.

Bock pointed out, however, that among some teachers of the day the Messiah was expected to deal with the temple. "In Jewish theology, one of the main things the Messiah would do is put things right with the temple, restoring proper worship. A work written in the century before Jesus' birth, *Psalms of Solomon* 17–18 tells us of this expectation. In the religious and political system in place in first-century Jerusalem, the chief priests were the ones who had authority over the temple. So by His act of cleansing the temple, Jesus really is setting up a showdown with the Jewish leaders."

That is why Matthew also writes, "When He entered Jerusalem, the whole city was shaken, saying, 'Who is this?'" (Matt. 21:10). They were asking the key question the Gospels raise, as we have discussed. And there was tension about His identity and authority. Even as He entered the city with many praising Him as a king, others in the crowd saw Him as merely a prophet (Matt. 21:11) and others as a deceiver. Jesus coming to Jerusalem was an unsettling event that constituted a political and religious threat to the establishment.

Darrell added, "This brings us to a third cultural script behind this story—the political and religious authority of the Sanhedrin. The Sanhedrin, the official Jewish court, who held their authority by permission of the Roman government, had been co-opted by the Romans. Messiah figures brought political crisis because they were seen as a jab in the eye of Rome, leading political opposition to the Roman government. Further, the temple was the seat of the Sanhedrin's power, their headquarters. That is why a little later in the chapter, the Jewish leaders challenge Jesus with, 'By what authority are You doing these things? Who gave You this authority?'"

I said, "So we are back to the issue of Jesus' authority."

Darrell responded, "That's exactly right! I love this event! When the Jewish leaders say to Jesus, 'Who gave You the authority to do these things?' what they are thinking is, 'We didn't, and this is our temple. We're in charge of this place. God gave us as priests this place to care for. The Romans let us do our business here in this complex *as long as we successfully keep the peace.* So, who do You think you are? Where'd you get the authority to say who can or can't do anything here?'

"Jesus understands the question, so He puts a question to them. He says, 'OK, let's talk about authority. John the Baptist, was he from God?' So the religious leaders go and do what all great leaders do whenever they get themselves in a corner; they form a committee. They have this committee meeting and say to one another, 'Well, we can't say he didn't come from God. That won't fly with the populace, so we'd better not say that. But answer number two, that he was from God, won't work either because we didn't believe him. This is not a good situation.' So they do what all self-interested political leaders do when they can't come up with a good answer; they punt. They go back to Jesus and say,

'We're not going to answer that question.' And Jesus says, 'Then I am not going to answer your question.'

"The reader who understands the cultural dynamics in the story knows exactly what Jesus just did. John the Baptist spoke with God's authority. Jesus, who was associated with John's ministry, also is acting and speaking by God's authority, even though the Jewish leadership is not willing to recognize it. So Jesus doesn't need the Sanhedrin's permission to deal with the temple because it's God's temple. Who has the right to walk in to the temple and cleanse it? God's Messiah does because He acts with God's authority. The Sanhedrin did not see things that way, and that is what led to Jesus' crucifixion."

Conclusion: Reading the Crucifixion and Resurrection as the Climax of the Story

As we think about how to read the stories of the New Testament, there is no more important part of the story than the crucifixion and resurrection of Jesus. All of the Gospels come to a climax with these twin events, and they really function as a primary climax of the whole story of the Bible. All four Gospels build to this point, and Acts launches from this point and develops with these twin events as a primary reference point. Yet, for many of us, this old, old story has become the oh-so-familiar story we yawn our way through. I asked Darrell if he could give us his thoughts on the ways we should approach reading about the crucifixion and resurrection with "fresh eyes."

He responded, "Well, first of all, several of the guidelines we have already talked about are still in play. Obviously the disciples still are very much in a process of discovery. They pretty much are in the dark until the resurrected Jesus explains what is going on. So again we need to try to enter their process of discovery, using our imagination to do so. Think through what they would have been feeling at this point in the story."

I thought about the fact that even when we get to the crucifixion story in the Gospels, the disciples don't understand

Jesus' suffering. They are devastated by Jesus' arrest and crucifixion, driven into hiding, and fearful of the future. We tend to pass
right over that part of the story.

Bock commented on this. "I tell my classes, when you read
the Gospel accounts of the announcements of the resurrection,
the disciples do a brilliant job of reacting to news of the resurrection just like modern people: 'You've got to be kidding!' In
response to the witness of the women at the tomb, who proclaimed that Jesus had risen, the disciples say in effect, 'You
ladies have had a rough weekend!' So the story still is unfolding
for them. Even after the resurrection Jesus is teaching them how
to read the Old Testament in a fresh way and pointing to the
future. Entering the story more deeply can help us read the story
in a fresh way."

As we talked, I wondered how we might do this more effectively, for instance, as we celebrate Easter each spring. But that
was a conversation for another day.

"Second," Bock continued, "lots of cultural scripts still need
attention. Details about crucifixion, the respective roles of the
different political powers in Jerusalem, burial practices, the backdrop of the Old Testament sacrificial system, and ideas about
resurrection in Judaism play important roles in providing a backdrop for the story."

Darrell continued by moving to the "God" question that had
been such a significant part of our conversation.

"Third, God still is at the heart of what is going on, and Jesus'
identity has everything to do with what God is bringing about.
In fact, almost everyone else in the story drops away from Jesus
at this point, and He is alone on the cross. It is almost as if the
spotlight of the whole universe is focused right there."

I commented, "One of my professors liked to say, 'The day
Jesus was crucified was the darkest and brightest day of human
history.'"

Darrell responded, "That is right to an extent because we
know the implications of Jesus' sacrificial death. But actually the
following Sunday was the brightest day, because Jesus' death was

shown to be more than just the killing of a Jewish peasant. Lots of people were crucified by the Romans in the first century. But the resurrection pulled the curtain back all the way on Jesus' identity and the implications of His death. When that tomb goes empty, the point isn't merely that we will live one day because He lives. That's telling the story with us at the center of orientation. If you want to tell the story with God at the center of orientation, the story becomes this: God has raised this Jesus and brought Him to His right hand in His very presence in heaven to share His throne. Jesus has been vindicated as God's Son, the Messiah, the Lord and center of the whole universe, and He has an offer for you—receive the forgiveness of your sins and a new way of relating to God—a completely new kind of life, life to be lived as it was designed by God to be lived. Bow to Him as your Lord and join in His mission for the world. That's the punch line in the story and sums up the point of all the stories in the Gospels and Acts."

Having given this summary, and as the storm outside came to an end and the sunshine began to break through the scattered clouds, Darrell closed with a final question.

"The key question every reader of these books needs to ask is this: 'What are the implications of this story for my life?' If you have yet to respond to the gospel, you need to grapple with the implications of Jesus' identity for your life. If you are already a Christ follower, you need to allow yourself to be led to deeper levels of discovering who Jesus is and how you can live out His mission faithfully in the world. Ultimately, if we are really reading the stories of the New Testament well, really reading them on their terms, that is the path they take us down."

Summary & Application

Summation

- The four Gospels together give us a full and consistent picture of Jesus.

- Matthew, Mark, and Luke approach the story of Jesus from "earth up," leading a reader to a discovery of Jesus' identity. John, on the other hand, approaches the story from "heaven down," focusing on the identity of Jesus as the Lord of the cosmos from the beginning.
- Acts combines an "earth up" with a "heaven down" approach. Jesus is the exalted Lord who directs the church (heaven down), and the church is in a process of discovering how to live under the lordship of Jesus in the world (earth up).
- A key to interpreting stories in the Gospels is to ask, "What does this story tell me about Jesus?"
- A key question for interpreting Acts is, "What are the implications of Jesus' lordship for the mission God has given the church?"
- We cannot understand the stories of the Gospels and Acts without understanding the cultural contexts of these stories.
- We should read the crucifixion and resurrection as the climax of the New Testament story, indeed the climax of the whole Bible!
- We should ask, "What are the implications of these stories for my life?"

Conversation

1. What are your two favorite stories from the life of Jesus? Why are these your favorite stories?
2. Darrell Bock suggests that understanding the "earth up" approach of Matthew, Mark, and Luke can help us in sharing the gospel with people who have no background in the church. How might we practically use the Gospels in this way? How does that perspective change the way you read these Gospels?
3. Read Mark 5:1–20. Notice to whom Jesus says yes in the story and to whom He says no. What does this story tell us about Jesus? How does its picture of Jesus relate to our lives today?

4. Acts 13:1–3 tells the story of Paul and Barnabas's call to the first mission trip. In relation to this story, how would you answer the question, What are the implications of Jesus' lordship for the mission of the church? How does this relate directly to your church?

5. Read Acts 10:1–16. What are the cultural scripts we need to investigate to be able to read this story well?

6. According to Darrell Bock, how do we read the crucifixion and resurrection stories with God at the center? What are the implications for us as we read this climax of the Bible's story in this way?

Transformation

Read Luke 2 and ask, "What do these stories tell me about Jesus?" Write down as many insights as possible.

CHAPTER 10

Reading the Teachings of Jesus
A Conversation with Craig Blomberg

When Jesus had finished this sermon, the crowds were astonished at His teaching, because He was teaching them like one who had authority, and not like their scribes.

—Matthew 7:28–29

 I flew into Denver, Colorado, on a snowy evening in April. There was so much snow that my flight was turned away from the airport twice, refueled in Texas, and finally allowed to land about eight hours after our scheduled arrival time. When we finally touched down, a former student picked me up at the airport in a dog sled (really it was a rugged truck that fit my mountain man of a student well), and we slid to his house for a late supper, a short night's sleep, and then a slip-sliding drive over to Denver Seminary, where I met my friend Craig Blomberg.

Craig looks and lives the part of a scholar—tall, lanky, tousled hair, glasses, and a sparse but neatly trimmed beard. He brings to his work a razor-sharp mind and an amazing ability to digest, dissect, and disseminate large amounts of material. A professor at Denver Seminary who has written numerous books and is known for his skill in the classroom, Craig also travels throughout the country and around the world, speaking to issues related to New Testament studies in general and the study of Jesus in particular. In recent years numerous secular scholars have called into question traditional understandings of Jesus' identity and mission, as well as the historical veracity of the Gospels. Blomberg insists that we can trust the Gospel witnesses about Jesus, and he has written much that can help the church answer such objections.

At the same time Craig Blomberg challenges those of us in the church to take Jesus and His teachings more seriously. I wanted to discuss with him how we can do just that by learning how to read Jesus' teaching more responsibly. So we made our way to his office and, surrounded by hundreds of scholarly books, with snow gently settling onto the parking lot outside the window, our conversation got right down to business. "Professor Blomberg, take us back to the context of the first century. How did Jesus' teaching parallel the teaching that was going on in the broader culture of the day, and how was His teaching unique?"

Jesus and the Kingdom

Craig confidently leaned forward and answered with a practiced precision, "At the risk of stating the obvious, the first thing we have to remember is that Jesus was Jewish! The label 'Christian' was not yet a religious option; the word would not even be invented for perhaps another twenty years. So we need to understand some things about Judaism of the first century, especially how Jewish teachers taught and the themes they addressed.

"For instance, as we look more closely at Judaism, we discover that Jesus' teaching has many themes in common with other Jewish teachers of His era. Questions about the Roman occupation of Palestine were in the air. How was God going to deal with this seemingly unbiblical and often intolerable plight—Israelites living in the land that God had promised them in perpetuity and yet under the thumb of Rome?! The Romans taxed the Jews mercilessly and often brutalized them. So teachers of the day were asking, 'Why is God letting this happen? What do we need to do about it? When will the kingdom of Israel be restored?'"

Craig had hit on a vitally important issue—understanding the historical and cultural context of the biblical literature. We simply cannot understand Jesus and His teaching apart from His context; it would be like trying to understand George Washington or John Adams without any reference to the American Revolution and the political winds blowing during that time. To attempt to read the teaching of Jesus apart from His context causes us to twist the Scriptures as we superimpose the way we see and understand the world onto the world of Jesus. I noticed that Craig had numerous books on the history and culture of Judaism in first-century Palestine, so he is immersed in the topic.

He continued, speaking about the Jews' longing for God's kingdom and how Jesus would have been heard by the people of His day. "So, when Jesus comes and speaks about God's kingdom, people sit up and listen! Jesus announces that the kingdom of God, God's rule on Earth, has in fact arrived. Some naturally raised questions concerning whether Jesus understood Himself to be God's anointed king, the Messiah (the Christ), who would put things right in the political situation with Rome. Would He be the one to vanquish the oppressors?

"And yet Jesus announces the coming of the kingdom without a call to arms, without amassing the troops to rebel against Rome, without apparently being all that concerned that Rome is occupying the land, which creates tension in people's minds. How can God's kingdom be arriving if the Romans aren't leaving? And Jesus answers: God's kingdom is different and offers a new kind of freedom, the kind of freedom that is most crucial for people, a spiritual freedom that requires God's people to repent of their sin and enter into a different kind of relationship with God."

I wanted to make sure I understood Craig's point, so I asked, "You're saying, first of all, that when Jesus started His ministry of teaching, He was answering hot-button questions that were in the air; He just wasn't answering the questions the way people were expecting the Messiah to answer the questions."

Craig nodded his head, agreeing, "That's well put."

This made me wonder if we at times read Jesus' words, looking to His teaching for direction on hot topics of our day, but finding that He doesn't always answer in a way that fits our pre-conceived ideas about how God works in the world.

Jesus' Teaching about the Law

As I thought about Jesus' countercultural teaching on the kingdom, it brought to mind another theme in Jesus' teaching that seemed to unsettle people—the law. In Jesus' day, the Pharisees especially focused on how the Jewish people were to live out the law, and their discussions with Jesus on the matter often degenerated into heated disagreement and even dangerous conflict. So I asked Craig about how we should read and understand Jesus' teaching on the law found in the Old Testament.

As the snow continued to fall outside, Craig rested his fingers lightly on the table in front of him. He responded, measuring his words carefully. "If you go to the Sermon on the Mount, Jesus addresses that question most clearly in Matthew 5:17–20. This comes at a stage in His ministry when He already has been countercultural enough that people are asking, 'Is this man in some way overturning the authority of God's holy, perfect, eternal, and unchangeable law?' So Jesus begins by saying, 'Don't think I've come to abolish the law and the prophets'; but then He says, 'I've come to fulfill them' (instead of using words that would be the natural opposite of 'abolish,' like 'preserve without change'). In the Bible the word *fulfill* normally is used with reference to prophecy. Here Jesus uses the word *fulfill* to speak about the law. He goes on to say that none of the law will pass away until everything is accomplished, and with some of the categories of Jewish laws, His ministry clearly brought about the fulfillment of specific laws. For instance, He fulfilled the laws about sacrifice for sins, since, by His death on the cross, He served as the once-for-all sacrifice for the sins of humanity. There is no need to bring bulls and goats and sheep and pigeons to church so we can butcher them as a sacrifice for sins."

Blomberg continued, "The law does not remain unchanged; neither is it abolished; it is fulfilled by Jesus. So we dare not quote

any of the 613 commandments of the Hebrew Scriptures and simply assume that they will apply to New Testament-era Christians
the way they did to Jews in the Old Testament. We will have to
study the New Testament revelation and see what, if anything,
has been changed by Jesus."

I asked Craig, in light of the teachings of Jesus on the matter,
what other missteps we need to avoid when reading the law.

He responded, "In general, once we have identified those
laws that the New Testament clearly says were fulfilled by Jesus,
we need to avoid two big mistakes in dealing with the other
Old Testament laws. First, we should not suggest that, unless
clearly transformed or set aside by the New Testament, a law
remains in force. By that logic, for instance, we would have to follow Old Testament laws like, 'Do not wear clothes made with two
different kinds of fabric,' or 'Allow newlyweds a year to enjoy each
other without going to work (or to war),' or 'Give 23 ¹/₃ percent of
your income to the annual "triple tithe."'

"But, second, neither is it appropriate to write off as insig-
nificant everything in the law that is not explicitly dealt with
in the New Testament. That approach would lead us to declare
divination and sorcery as acceptable practices; it would permit
us to marry a close relative. These are among the Old Testament
laws, but they are not addressed in the New Testament! Such
Old Testament laws speak to us about God's priorities and values.
This too is God's Word to us! I think the key is to understand
the principles they embody, understanding those principles as
an aspect of God's will for us.

"So we need to ask how we might read the Old Testament
laws without falling into one of these two extremes."

I asked Craig to give us an example of the principles we
might derive from laws that have been fulfilled by Jesus or are
not mentioned in the New Testament.

He graciously responded, "For instance, we can learn much
from studying the ancient sacrificial system (see the New
Testament book of Hebrews) even though we do not replicate
those sacrifices as believers. The same is true with the dietary

laws. The practice of those laws has been abolished in view of Acts 10 and Peter's vision of unclean food that God commanded him to eat. However, we can learn from principles inherent in those dietary laws of the Old Testament.

"So we have to proceed on a case-by-case and category-by-category basis and see how each kind of law is fulfilled in Christ. Basic moral principles or commands (such as 'Do not commit adultery') are regularly reaffirmed in the New Testament, though often internalized in ways that get at the heart of God's intention for that law. But in other cases we have to look for larger principles that led to the Old Testament Law in the first place and find contemporary equivalents that would accomplish the same thing. For example, leaving grain unharvested around the perimeters of our farms would not help the poor today; most wouldn't live close enough to the fields to glean even if they wanted to! But setting up a thrift store in urban centers where even the homeless could afford to buy clothes, where everyone had to pay at least something to make a purchase, would replicate the spirit of the gleaning laws, in which the poor had to give something, but something they were in fact able to give (their work) in order to acquire basic foodstuffs."

The Methods Jesus Used and How to Read Them

As I looked over Craig's shoulder at the parking lot outside, a lone goose waddled its way across the icy asphalt. I could imagine how much a maverick Jesus must have seemed to some in His teaching on the kingdom or the law. In some ways He was very much out of sync with other teachers of the time. I wanted to probe whether the way He taught was also out of step, so I continued, "How about His teaching methods? Was Jesus' style of teaching also unexpected?"

Craig explained that, just as with the topics He addressed, Jesus' teaching methods had much in common with other teachers of the day, but also significant differences should be noted. "Almost all of the teaching methods used by Jesus were well known and used in Israel, especially by other rabbis. Jesus uses parables, controversial pronouncements against those tagged as out of step with God's will, long speeches, dialogues, proverbs, riddles, and the like. When He is not speaking in parables, He is likely to be using short, proverb-like sentences, either by themselves or in clusters. One thinks, for example, of the Beatitudes in the Sermon on the Mount.

"There are times, particularly in the Gospel of John, when we see Jesus offering more lengthy sermons. These often seem to be structured similarly to ways that rabbis gave sermons or homilies. He also asks rhetorical questions, challenging people to answer questions that He knows the answer to, prompting them to think in particular ways about themselves and God's kingdom. He appeals to object lessons, illustrations from common, everyday life. He may use a vine or a lamp or salt as a word picture meant to teach people clearly about some aspect of God and His agenda for life."

I thought about the various methods I try to use when I teach my university students. Jesus had an arsenal of teaching techniques at His disposal! When I think about the art of teaching, I tend to think primarily in terms of creativity and clarity; I want people to get the message of my teaching. Certainly Jesus was seen as bringing a profound freshness and clarity to His teaching by using a wide variety of methods, but some of these methods are not familiar to us as modern people. So the question is, How can we read the various forms of Jesus' teaching more effectively, making sure we understand the point? I put the question to Craig.

He responded by giving several examples, beginning with Jesus' longer discourses. "With Jesus' longer sermons, like the ones we have in Matthew, or in John's Gospel, the best approach is to look for the key themes that join sections of these discourses together. For instance, in Matthew 24:45–25:30 we find Jesus' teaching about a slave put in charge of a household (24:45–51), His parable about ten virgins (25:1–13), and the parable of the talents (25:14–30). The common themes in these three units of material are (1) a key figure (representing Jesus) being away, (2) the faithfulness or unfaithfulness of those left with certain responsibilities, and (3) their accountability to the key figure when he returns. Further, these teachings are set in a context that deals with the end of the age (24:3–8) and Jesus' second coming (24:29–31). So, in reading this portion of Matthew, we see the importance of Jesus' followers remaining faithful even though His return has been delayed."

That made a great deal of sense. As we track key themes across broad stretches of Jesus' sermons, the purpose of the various sections of those sermons begin to make more sense.

I asked next about the short, pithy sayings that Jesus so often used, like, "A student is not greater than his teacher," which appears twice in the Gospels (Matt. 10:24; Luke 6:40). Blomberg responded, "Crucial to understanding proverbs is to recognize them as general principles or guidelines for how life works, not truths for which there never is an exception. Furthermore, Jesus spoke most proverbs in a specific context or situation, and it is important to clue into that situation. For example, we should read Jesus' words about the student not being greater than his or her teacher in context; this is not meant to be an ironclad rule for every situation in life. Many students outdo their teachers in academic accomplishments! However, in Matthew 10:24 Jesus is speaking about persecution; if a teacher (Jesus Himself) is being persecuted and students (the disciples) are loyal followers, chances are good that they will be persecuted as well. This is the point of the proverb as Jesus used it in that context."

These examples Craig provided were helpful. How many of us read the Gospels in a rather flat way, treating every passage the same, approaching proverbs and parables and pithy sayings pretty much the same way? It sounded as if we need to treat Jesus' various teaching methods with respect, discerning how each method works and what we need to do to respond to them. I asked if he could also comment on Jesus' use of figures of speech.

"Jesus' teaching is somewhere between 80 percent and 90 percent poetic in style, so we should not be surprised that it is filled with various kinds of figures of speech. His injunction to those who lust to cut out their eyes if necessary (Matt. 5:29) cannot be intended literally because blind people can lust, too, especially those who once had sight and have good memories! Rather, Jesus' words refer to taking drastic action, if necessary, to remove oneself from stimuli that produce lust. This is a figure of speech called 'hyperbole.' The application of that teaching of Jesus might be to get rid of Internet access in our home (if we are struggling with online pornography) or to set up strong accountability with friends from our church.

"Also, Jesus often used object lessons or other kinds of comparison. You might remember from high school literature class that a simile is a comparison using *like* or *as*, and a metaphor is a comparison not using *like* or *as*. Jesus uses simile when He says, 'The kingdom of God is like a mustard seed.' He is using metaphor when He says, 'I am the door of the sheep.' The point of the mustard seed simile is that the kingdom of God grows dynamically, out of all proportion to what would be expected. The point of Jesus' metaphor comparing Himself to the door is to proclaim that He is the way people get into the kingdom. So with these types of figures of speech, as well as many of His object lessons, the key is to think through the main parallel between the figure and the spiritual truth Jesus is wanting to communicate."

What about the Tension in Jesus' Teaching?

Jesus was a master of clear, vibrant communication. His teaching often throws living pictures into our minds as we read the Gospels. Yet it seems to me this is only part of the story. Jesus often said things that were obscure, that people misunderstood. He sometimes taught in a way that freaked people out or made them angry! At the end of John 6, Jesus said, "Unless you eat My flesh and drink My blood, you can't be My disciple." This not only confused people; it repelled them. Many of those who had been following Him left! I raised this issue with Craig, asking about the balance in Jesus' teaching between creativity and clarity on the one hand and, on the other, a sense of tension as He said things that unsettled people. He agreed that this was an important aspect of Jesus' teaching.

"For instance, the Jewish leaders of the day—not all of them, but a good handful—regularly come under fire for misinterpreting Jesus' teachings and/or for simply not obeying that teaching. So while Jesus typically makes His point clearly enough, He sometimes creates a good bit of tension through His responses to these leaders. Often Jesus' succinct statements come as climactic and controversial pronouncements at the end of such a passage. Such statements typically are the keys to understanding the passages in which they appear.

"For example, at the end of the parable of the wicked tenants (Mark 12:1–12), Jesus concludes with the statement, 'He will come and destroy the farmers and give the vineyard to others' (12:9). In response to this statement, the Jewish leaders went away plotting to destroy Him because they recognized, Mark says, that He told the parable against them. They understood that He was equating them with the wicked tenants in the story, and they didn't like it one bit! The tension is created because His message challenges the status quo. When we read such a story, we need to look for the punch line and ask what attitudes or actions Jesus is condemning. We also need to ask whether we are guilty of those attitudes or actions."

Reading with Fresh Eyes

When we engage the Scriptures today, I know my tendency is to rush over these familiar but difficult stories or the familiar sayings of Jesus. It is easy for me to read in such a way that I never really enter the story. I don't allow myself to be confronted. I don't hear the teaching of Jesus in a way that is fresh. So I asked Craig, "How do we read the teachings of Jesus with fresh eyes, if you will, with fresh hearts—hearts that are open to hear what God is saying to us?"

Craig nodded knowingly, "One good approach is to stop and ask who in our world or in our little subcultures most correspond

to the characters with whom Jesus interacts, or who most corresponds to the fictional characters in Jesus' parables. We also need
to ask: 'How do I correspond to these characters?'"

I knew exactly what Craig was talking about. When I met
with Craig, I recently had read Tim Keller's book *The Prodigal
God*, which is about the prodigal son story in Luke 15:11–32.
I was challenged that at times I resemble the elder brother more
than I do anyone else in the story. That was unsettling for me
in a good and important way. "So what you are saying, Craig, is
that we need to allow ourselves to be pulled into the story Jesus is
teaching, and we need to use our imaginations to see where the
real parallels are with our world. We have a tendency to think in
terms of insiders and outsiders. We say to ourselves, 'We're obviously the insiders with God, and those Pharisees are the outsiders.' Therefore if we're not careful, we can skip right over a lot of
relevant material in the teaching of Jesus, just assuming it doesn't
have anything to do with us."

Blomberg agreed that this fallacious rut is all too easy for us
to fall into in our reading of the Gospels, and we need, rather,
to enter the stories of Jesus ourselves in order to apply them to
our lives.

Reading the Parables

Blomberg then picked up the conversation and wanted to
talk more about the parables, the most dominant form of Jesus'
teaching in Matthew, Mark, and Luke. He explained that later
rabbis also used parables but used them to teach about the law.
Jesus, by contrast, used parables to teach about God's kingdom.
Since Craig is one of the leading experts in the world on the
parables, I was excited to hear more from him on the subject.

"There are several key principles to keep in mind as we read
and interpret the parables. The stories employ a few key characters to represent God and various ways of responding to Him
and His kingdom. In about two-thirds of the parables, one can
identify a master figure (a king, father, slave owner, landlord,

shepherd, etc.) whose actions in some way mirror God's actions. So, for instance, in the parable of the prodigal, the father represents the love of God as seen in the ministry of Christ."

I asked, "How does the picture of the father in the parable give us a picture of God's love?"

Craig answered, "Kenneth Bailey, who has written several helpful books that deal with historical and cultural details behind the parables in Luke, points out that for a well-to-do Middle Eastern head of household to be seen in public running down the road, as we're told this father does when he sees his son at a distance, would have been considered undignified. Respectable fathers simply would not have done such a thing. It's a little point, but it simply adds that much more poignancy to how the father is throwing his reputation to the winds. He cares only about his son coming home, and if people think he is acting in an undignified way, then so what? This gives us a beautiful picture of God's love for the lost person who repents."

"So," summing up this first guideline for reading the parables I said, "the central character of a parable often represents God."

Craig nodded in agreement and continued. "In the parables we also find pairs or groups of contrasting subordinates: a good son and a wicked son, a good servant and a wicked servant, lost sheep and sheep that aren't lost. Not always but more often than not, the category of son or servant or subordinate who turns out to be the good example is not the one anyone would have suspected at the beginning of the story. And the person we would have expected to be the good model turns out to be the one who has to be rebuked in some way. The prodigal comes home and is welcomed back; apparently he has repented. The older brother, who seems to have been so faithful all along, has the serious problem of begrudging God's generosity to the wayward. And if we are placing ourselves in the roles of the characters in Jesus' story, we may suddenly discover that we are more like the older brother, just as you suggested a moment ago."

I interjected, clicking off the points on my fingers, "So a

main figure normally represents God, and two subordinate characters or groups normally represent other spiritual dynamics."

He nodded in agreement. "From the actions of the main characters, we can learn the main lessons of the parable, and we should be convicted when our lives or attitudes line up with the wrong character or characters in the story! So the key to reading a parable is to understand who the main characters represent."

I asked if there are ways we can seriously misread the parables, and Blomberg jumped on the question. "We must not allegorize the remaining details—the pig food, the ring, the robe, the fatted calf, and so on, ascribing to them hidden spiritual meanings that would have been nonsense to the original audience! This has been done at times in the history of the church, and it obscures Jesus' intention for the parables. Such elements are typically realistic details, meant to provide color and to drive home the main points of the parable. When we read that the prodigal desired to eat pig's food, or that the father ordered a ring to be put on the finger of the son, these aspects of the story work to support the main points concerning how far a person can fall in life and how lavish is God's love for those who are down and out."

Conclusion: Reading as Disciples of Jesus

We were moving toward wrapping up the conversation. From our discussion it seemed clear that we face certain challenges in reading the teaching of Jesus in fresh ways. We face the challenge that we really don't know the culture. Jesus uses some forms in His teaching that we may not understand. So we need to learn something about how those forms work. Craig had given us helpful guidelines to that effect. It seems that one of the greatest struggles we have is that we also are embedded in a culture ourselves, and our culture gives us certain blinders in terms of what we are able to hear from Jesus' teaching.

I asked Craig, "What would be your desire for those people out there in the churches who really want to honor God, who want to engage the teaching of Jesus well? What would be your hope for them as they learn to read the Gospels with fresh eyes and hearts that are open to hearing what Jesus would say?"

Craig leaned back in his chair and responded, "I think I'd have two hopes, one related to the first century and one related to the twenty-first century. It can't be stressed often enough that as we read any part of the Bible, unless we consciously make the effort to think otherwise, we will by default lapse into the mode of assuming the people and the culture and the language and the customs we find in the biblical text are simply like the people, the language, and the customs of our own culture. Sometimes they are, but often they are not. I have long since lost count of the number of times I have heard even well-trained Christian leaders say, 'Well, this isn't the way I would do such-and-such.' And they're absolutely right; but that's irrelevant because we're reading the Bible, and God chose that place and that time and that culture in which to reveal truth. Therefore, I want to challenge us to study the Gospels seriously, learning about first-century Palestine and how Judaism of the day worked.

"Second, my hope would be that we as Christians today would never assume that we have arrived—that we never become complacent or satisfied with the status quo of our own culture's embodiment of Christianity. No matter how long we have been involved with the Christian movement, we need to be challenged in fresh ways by Jesus and His teaching. Many of us need to live in a much more countercultural way, more in line with Jesus' teachings and less in line with the values of our own culture. When we take Jesus' vision of life seriously, we will be called to spend much less on ourselves, as individuals, families, and churches. We might be convicted about spending so much on fancy houses and fancy church buildings that gobble up huge amounts of mortgage money. We would be much more committed to small groups and a personal, community-oriented form of discipleship, and a holy, sacrificial love of our fellow believers would be clear to the rest of the world. Leadership would be much more servant oriented and much less CEO and celebrity oriented. The ministry of our churches would focus on the physical and spiritual needs of those who are lost, without Christ, and many of our lost friends would be open to hear the gospel because they see and sense such authenticity in the church. Thinking about Jesus' love for and ministry to the outsider, without condoning homosexual practice, we'd be known as the people who went out of our way to be kind toward those who claim gay and lesbian orientation instead of being known (rightly or wrongly) as those who are often most hostile to them.

"Our preaching and teaching would be a lot more focused on the beauty and grace and holiness and majesty of God than on specific how-to lists that become a new law for people. In short, if we took Jesus' teachings seriously, most of us would have to alter some aspects of the way we do life and church. Our vision of what it means to follow Jesus would be challenged and changed in healthy ways."

As I packed up to leave, Craig and I said our good-byes. The snow had stopped falling, but I still had a forty-five-minute drive back to the airport (which, by the way, was an exercise in faith, as my mountain-man former student careened through the slide and slush obstacle course of a freeway). Through our interview it had become clear that we have a lot of work to do if we are to read the teachings of Jesus more effectively. We need to learn more about Jesus' context and how to interpret His methods of teaching. But just as important, we need to grow in reading our own culture and contexts in light of Jesus' teachings. In some ways such an endeavor feels as hazardous as my drive to the airport; but it also seems as faith building and exciting. Only God knows what might be accomplished in us and through us if we became radically committed to living out Jesus' vision for kingdom life.

Summary & Application

Summation

- To understand the teachings of Jesus, we must take His Jewish context seriously.
- Jesus came to fulfill the Old Testament law. We should not assume that all of the Old Testament laws are directly applicable for Christians today. Neither should we assume that the Old Testament laws are irrelevant for Christians today; many principles found there give us insight into God and how to live for Him in the world.
- Jesus used a wide variety of methods in His teaching, including long sermons, rhetorical questions, object lessons, proverbial sayings, dialogue, riddles, and parables.
- We need to look for key themes in Jesus' longer discourses.
- Jesus' proverbs should be understood as general principles or guidelines for life and need to be read in light of the context in which Jesus gives them.
- Eighty to 90 percent of Jesus' teaching is poetic in style and thus uses many figures of speech, including exaggeration (hyperbole) and various types of comparison.
- Jesus also taught in such a way that tension developed in those who heard.
- When reading the parables, we should not allegorize the parables (finding hidden spiritual meaning in all the details of the story), and we need to remember that God often is represented by a main character in the parable. Two subordinate characters or groups normally represent other spiritual dynamics.

Conversation

1. Which of the guidelines in this chapter for reading the teachings of Jesus most surprised you? Most helped you?

2. If you had to describe your attitude toward the Old Testament law, would you say that you are: (1) uninformed, (2) not interested, (3) intrigued, (4) blessed, (5) overwhelmed. Why did you give that answer?

3. Which of the teaching methods of Jesus do you find easiest to understand? Hardest to understand? Why?

4. Read the parable of the good Samaritan in Luke 10:29–37. How does the literary context affect your understanding of this parable? Read a Bible dictionary article on "Samaritans" and answer, "How does cultural context affect your understanding of this parable?" Whom do the main characters in this parable represent? Why is God not represented by a main character here?

5. What is one thing you can do to learn more about the teachings of Jesus? What is one thing you can do to live out the teachings of Jesus?

Transformation

Read Mark 4:1–20 carefully. As Jesus explains, the parable is about various ways people respond to God's Word. How would you describe the condition of your heart at present in terms of openness to God's Word? Which seed and soil best parallel your life? What do you need to do to become more open to God's Word?

CHAPTER 11

Reading the New Testament Letters

A Conversation with Douglas Moo

I charge you by the Lord that this letter be read to all the brothers.

—1 Thessalonians 5:27

In our home's gathering room, we have a memorials table—a low, square-shaped coffee table with drawers and a glass top, which sits in front of the fireplace, right in the middle of the room. The glass top reveals numerous items in the top drawer—a piece of brick, a small matchbox truck, an old German Bible, a property deed that dates back to 1923, pictures of Joshua and Anna's baptisms, and a newborn's hospital bracelet, among many others. Each item serves as a memorial, a reminder of some work God has done in, through, or on behalf of our family. The memorials table also holds two letters, one the original correspondence between me and a mentor who has now gone to be with the Lord and the other a note to Pat from author Elisabeth Elliot, which came at a time when my wife needed greatly the encouragement it offered. God worked in us through personal correspondence.

We live in a world of many communication options. You can e-mail, call on a landline or a mobile phone, tweet, Skype, post a note on Facebook, fax, message someone, or (if you absolutely must) print out a typed letter. Few people still write handwritten letters. In the ancient world there were primarily two options for long-distance communication: letters or a messenger, and messages often were sent via a combination of the two. In God's wisdom twenty of the twenty-seven books of the New Testament are letters, and to help us think through how we might read them more effectively, I flew to West Chicago, Illinois, for a conversation with Professor Douglas Moo, the Blanchard Professor of New Testament at Wheaton College.

Doug's commentaries on the letters of the New Testament are seen as a masterful integration of clear thinking, careful scholarship, and sound application. I had Professor Moo as a teacher and advisor at Trinity Evangelical Divinity School in the mid-1980s and had the privilege of being in his home for meals (and Ping-Pong!) with Doug, his wife Jenny, and their five children (now all grown). The Moos authentically seek to live out God's Word, and Doug has grappled extensively not only with the meaning of nouns and verbs, sentence structure, and Paul's use of the Old Testament, but also with the implications of the New Testament writings for everyday life. So, after Jenny had served us a wonderful lunch, Doug and I sat at the kitchen table in the Moos' lovely home and talked about reading the letters of the New Testament.

Why the Letters of the New Testament Appeal to Us

Many Christians I know would name a letter in the New Testament as their favorite book of the Bible, and often teachers in the church focus on these letters in their Bible studies and sermon series. So I started our conversation by asking, "What about the letters appeals to us?"

Without hesitation Doug answered, "Immediacy. The writers of the New Testament letters often seem to be writing directly to us. They talk about many of the same issues and challenges we face as believers today. So the translation from the culture and situation of the early church to our own culture and context—at least when it comes to certain issues—seems fairly straightforward. Therefore, as we read the letters of the New Testament, we should ask questions like, 'What does this letter tell me about how I should live for Christ in the world?' or 'What guidelines are here for how we should work together and worship God as Christ's church?'

"Another reason we tend to favor the New Testament letters is their importance in teaching foundational Christian truth. If you think about it, this is the only group of books of the Bible written to encourage and instruct Christians in a wide variety of issues related to church life or personal life. All of God's Word, of course, is valuable for teaching us about God, His purposes, and our place in His plan. But the letters of the New Testament arguably contain the most direct and fundamental teaching for Christians on how to think about and live the Christian life. Just take the letters out of the Bible, and imagine how impoverished our understanding of Christianity would be.

"Finally, the letter is also a form that we are familiar with. Even though e-mails and Facebook postings are quickly taking the place of letter writing, most of us still write and receive letters. In that sense we know how letters work, and so letters might seem more familiar to us than a psalm or a book of prophecy."

Letter Writing in the First Century

As Doug mentioned, since most of us have written letters, we might feel we intuitively have some sense of how the letters of the New Testament were produced and were meant to communicate. Yet letter writing was a bit more involved than we might imagine. So I asked Doug to speak to us about how letter writing was done in the first century.

He explained, "In the first-century world, of course, writing wasn't as easy or as common as it is now. Writing materials were valuable and sometimes scarce, so a letter could be a costly investment."

I asked, "What types of materials were used?"

Moo continued, "A wide variety of materials were used in the ancient world, including animal skins, but often people used papyrus, a paper-like material made from the stem of a plant. Most letters were not as long as Paul's. In fact, even Philemon, one of our shortest letters in the New Testament, is a bit longer than letters commonly were in the first century. For longer letters, however, sheets of papyrus could be glued end-on-end and then rolled up to make a scroll. Writing was done with ink, at times made by mixing soot, oil, and gum."

I interjected, "And a person often hired a trained scribe to write out the letter."

Moo continued. "That's right. Often the person doing the actual writing of a letter was a trained scribe, sometimes referred to as an *amanuensis*, a secretary. That's why in the New Testament letters we have references in several places to people who did the actual writing down of what the author was dictating to that person. An example would be Tertius, mentioned at Romans 16:22: 'I Tertius, who wrote this letter, greet you in the Lord.' People of education often employed a scribe for the physical task of writing a letter so that they could focus on thinking about what they wanted to say, and the physical task was not as easy as we might think. A scribe could not go to Walmart in Jerusalem and buy bulk paper. Scribes had to cut their own papyrus into sheets, mix their own ink, and cut their own reed pens. On a wax tablet or a reusable 'notebook,' the scribe would take down notes or dictation from the person sending the letter and then write the letter out in a clear, often beautiful script (think calligraphy). Scribes normally were used because they could write small, neat, carefully crafted letters and make the best use of the scroll."

I jokingly told Doug that he had mentored me in writing notes on my students' exams and papers—often they can't read what I have written! Both of us lamented that we at times cannot even read our own handwriting when a student asks for clarification. Clearly a literate person does not necessarily produce legible handwriting!

Professor Moo had mentioned that letter writing could be a costly venture, and with a process as involved as the one he described, you can see why. Randy Richards, in his book on first-century letter writing, estimates that in today's dollars, because of its length, 1 Corinthians would have cost approximately $2,100 if produced by a professional scribe![20]

I commented to Doug, "So the image we have of Paul sitting down and quickly jotting out a letter and sending it off probably isn't the way it happened in the first-century world."

Shaking his head slightly, he remarked, "I don't think so. I picture Paul walking around a room, pacing, thinking, pausing. Some of the letters were long enough that he probably dictated them over the course of two or three days rather than in one sitting."

What all this means is that a great deal of care went into crafting Paul's letters. It also took a great deal of effort to deliver a letter, as Professor Moo explained next.

You've Got Mail: The First-Century Postal System

He continued. "Not only were letters produced differently than we produce them today, but they were delivered in a way that is somewhat foreign to us. Today we write a letter, put it in the mailbox, and the postal service delivers it. But in the first century there was no postal service. Letters were delivered in person, perhaps by someone who knew the sender of the letter. Also, the letter carrier often was a person who was familiar with the contents of the letter and could interpret those contents for the letter's recipients."

I commented, "So you had to arrange for someone to take your letter and deliver it in person?"

Doug continued, "That's exactly right. You might hunt around for someone who was making a trip from Corinth to Rome, for instance, and entrust that carrier with a letter to a particular person or, in Paul's case, to a congregation. Then that person would be there as a representative of the sender not only to read the letter but also to interpret, apply it, and answer questions. Also, most reading in the ancient world, even reading in private, was done out loud. So originally the New Testament letters were meant to be *heard* in one sitting, by a congregation or an individual, with the reader offering interpretation of what was being read."

These were interesting points to think about in light of how we conceive of Bible reading today. When we think about a Bible reading plan, for instance, we tend to think of individuals reading the Bible alone and quietly. You have your time with the Lord in the morning, you sit down, and you silently do your Bible reading for the day—and this is a good thing; we need more people reading the Bible individually! Yet with individual reading alone you may or may not discuss what you are reading with somebody else.

By contrast most people in an early Christian congregation would not have a personal copy of the Scriptures; again, it was cost prohibitive. And many people could not read. So reading the Bible was a community event. Doug commented on the contrast.

"Obviously we are blessed to have the production of the Scriptures so that each of us in our own homes can have our own copy of the Bible, and we should not take that for granted. The opportunity to read, think about, and learn from the Bible on a daily basis is a great gift. But we also need to be in a community where we can read the Scriptures with other people because we learn so much from one another when we read together. Other people have insights we don't have. They raise questions we didn't even think of. Gifted teachers can help us understand what is being read, and we are accountable for how we are reading and living God's Word. The Scripture becomes so much deeper and richer to us when we read it in that community context."

So reading the letters of the New Testament, as well as the Bible generally, will be enriched as we balance our personal reading with reading in Christian community. Having laid this insightful foundation, I wanted to press on to other specifics on how we might read the New Testament letters more effectively.

Take a Hike but Take a Map

My wife, Pat, and I know Jonathan and Stacy, Doug's son and daughter-in-law, who for the past few years have lived in Cambridge, England, where Jon has been completing a Ph.D. in New Testament at the University of Cambridge. While on a recent visit to Cambridge, Pat and I stayed with Jon and Stacy, who, from the pictures scattered throughout their apartment, obviously have a passion both for photography and for hiking. Beautiful vistas, rock-strewn trails, hiking boots, walking sticks, and lots of smiles adorned their walls and tables. Since Doug and Jenny are in many of the hiking photos, I mentioned to him, "Your family seems to enjoy getting out in the wild and hiking," and I asked if he could draw an analogy between hiking and how we read the letters of the New Testament.

Doug responded, "Sure. You're right about my family loving to hike. I think comparing reading the New Testament letters to hiking is an interesting analogy in several respects. When you hike, you usually have a map. You need some idea of where you're going and what the landmarks are. Without a map you can quickly start wandering aimlessly, or get lost, and even get in a dangerous situation. In reading the letters of the New Testament, likewise, a person can simply plunge in and start reading at any point, and I'm sure God blesses that at times, but we're going to do a lot better in reading the letters of the New Testament if we have an overview of a book as we start out. If we understand how a book is organized and how it develops, our reading will be much more productive."

I thought about my trip to Chicago that day. Since the Moos live about thirty minutes away from Chicago O'Hare International Airport, I had printed out MapQuest directions in preparation for the trip. The map led me step-by-step through the twists and turns of Chicagoland's complex roadways. My schedule was somewhat tight that day, so it was important that I not get lost, and Map Quest took me right to the Moos' door. In the same way, knowing an overview of a book can help direct us as we read the New Testament letters.

I asked Professor Moo if he could give us an example of how knowing something about the structure of a book can help us read it better.

"Certainly. The first seventeen verses of Romans are the letter's opening statement. Up until verse 16, Paul writes to the Romans about his ministry and his desire to come visit them, but with verse 16 there is a decisive shift, the apostle now focusing on the theme of *the gospel* with red-hot intensity. In Romans 1:16–17 he writes, 'For I am not ashamed of the gospel, because it is God's power for salvation to everyone who believes, first to the Jew, and also to the Greek. For in it God's righteousness is revealed from faith to faith, just as it is written: The righteous will live by faith.' These two verses are important. They present the theme of the letter and the point from which Paul launches into an extensive treatment of the nature of the gospel in the following chapters. If we understand that, we will read those chapters asking, 'How am I to understand the gospel?' So grasping the role of Romans 1:16–17, which really is an important hinge between the opening and the main body of the letter, can help us read Romans better."

I asked Doug how we can access a "map" or overview of these letters. He rested his hands on the table, at times drumming his fingers lightly on the table's surface. "Sometimes it's best to skim the letter first to get an idea of what the main landmarks are so that you don't get lost as you do more detailed reading. Most New Testament letters have an opening, an introductory thanksgiving or blessing, a body, and then a closing, so we can learn to recognize these movements of a normal letter from the first century. The paragraph or chapter headings that most Bibles have can help with this. Also, a good study Bible, a Bible dictionary, or a good commentary will include outlines of each book of the New Testament, and these outlines can really help us get a sense of how a book is developing."

If you remember in our conversation with Andreas Köstenberger, we talked about using such tools to discern the literary context of passages in the Bible, and I was glad to hear Doug echoing Andreas's thoughts at this point.

The Importance of Historical Background

In many of our interviews we have heard time and again about the importance of historical background. God revealed truth in specific ways, at specific moments in time, to specific people, who were in specific circumstances. Reading the Bible well often demands that we work at understanding the historical situation reflected in a book. Professor Moo next emphasized that this is vitally important as we read the letters of the New Testament because they often were written to address specific situations in the life of a church or group of churches.

Doug commented, "A second main point for reading the New Testament letters well is this: we have to have a good idea of the background behind these letters. Again to play off of our hiking analogy, historical knowledge of a place can be very helpful. If I am hiking around Mount St. Helens and notice the devastation in the landscape, knowing what happened there some years ago will enhance my understanding and experience.

"Yet, if I could just shift to another analogy, I often think that reading a letter in the New Testament is like listening to one side of a phone conversation. We've all had that experience when we hear someone on the telephone—all too often these days in Starbucks with someone on their cell phone talking way too loudly—and it's fascinating listening, trying to figure out what the person on the other end is saying.

"As we read the letters of the New Testament, we are hearing one end of the telephone conversation. We have Paul responding to situations or answering questions a church has asked, but often we don't know what those situations or questions were. We need to read the New Testament letters with an ear open to the questions or historical situations being addressed. So when we read and study New Testament letters, we need to find out what we can about their context. Who wrote them? When? Why? To whom? In what circumstances? Also, as we run into material we don't understand in a particular passage, is there important information from the culture at that time that can help us understand what is going on?"

Again I asked Doug if he could give us an example and he responded: "The New Testament has a lot of good examples, of course. One passage that is debated to this day is 1 Corinthians 11, where Paul talks about the importance of head coverings for women in the church. This is in a section of the letter in which Paul addresses problems that had come up in worship. We're not even sure exactly what he means, whether it's a head covering like a veil or whether it's a particular way of wearing the hair, but obviously something was going on in that culture that made the covering of the head of the woman significant. It had a certain symbolic importance then that a lot of us just aren't familiar with. To understand that passage as we read it, we need to dig and find out what was significant about a woman's head being covered. We might find, for instance, that married women in that culture kept their hair 'done up' rather than loose and flowing, which in some circles was a sign of singleness or (in a Jewish context) even that a woman had been suspected of adultery. Some pagan women 'let their hair down' when involved in worship of the gods. Another possibility is that some of the women were wearing their hair cut short, almost shaved off, which again could be a symbol of someone convicted of adultery or a sign in the broader culture of a woman being involved in lesbianism. The point is that Paul was concerned about the signals being sent by a woman not having her head covered in the Christian worship service.

"By analogy, I might say to my daughter, 'I don't think I want you to get a naval ring.' Can you imagine someone five centuries from now reading that statement and thinking, *Naval rings? What is that all about? Was it symbolically or religiously significant? Why shouldn't a person have one, or why would someone want one?* You would have to do some digging in our culture to try to figure it out. So often we have to do that kind of digging when we're reading the New Testament as well."

I continued by asking Doug what tools might help us get at that kind of background information. I commented, "I know everyone doesn't have time to go out and get a degree in archeology or first-century culture. So how can a person who is reading through the letters of the New Testament get at such background information, or even basic information on introductory issues like authorship, date, or purpose, behind each of the New Testament letters?"

Moo leaned forward a bit and answered, "We are fortunate indeed to have so many resources readily available to us. First we need to get a good study Bible, which we have already mentioned. Most of the major English versions now have produced substantial study Bibles with footnotes that provide a lot of helpful information."

Doug continued, "In addition, Bible dictionaries have entries that give us some idea about the world of the Bible, and good commentaries often clarify the situations behind a New Testament letter. So, a lot of resources are accessible for people. All of the tools we just mentioned were written for people with no advanced training in the Bible."

How to Bridge the Gaps

Another issue as we read the New Testament letters has to do with bridging the gap between the specific cultural situations faced by the earliest Christians and our situations today. Professor Moo had mentioned that there are many parallels, but as we saw in his example of head coverings in 1 Corinthians 11, there also are significant differences at points. So I asked, "How can we make the jump from issues like 'meat offered to idols' in 1 Corinthians 8 or 'head coverings' in 1 Corinthians 11, to our world of Internet cafes and more casual approaches to church attire?"

Jenny and Christy, one of the Moos' daughters, were walking around in the backyard, allowing the Moos' new golden retriever puppy, Paxson, to romp in the grass. The picture of modern suburban life in America, framed by the glass door, seemed light-years away from the dusty streets of ancient Corinth. "Perhaps the first thing that needs to be said is that, for all our modern technology and our modern contexts, we humans are not really any different from the humans of the first century. People have not fundamentally changed; nor, of course, has God. Many of the issues dealt with in the New Testament letters are as equally and clearly applicable to us today as to the first-century recipients of the letters. What are human beings basically like? What is the fundamental human problem? What is God like? What has He accomplished through His Son, Jesus Christ? These and many other similar questions lie at the heart of the New Testament letters.

"But, as you pointed out, there are, of course, many other issues the first-century readers of the letters were facing that we don't and many issues we face that they did not."

I interjected, "I haven't struggled much with whether I should eat food offered to idols this week! And a Christian in first-century Corinth never was tempted to throw a computer out the window!"

"Right! So how do we make the New Testament letters relevant for us on such matters? One important approach is to consider the principles on which the New Testament letter writers are basing their specific advice. We may not face the question of whether to buy meat that has been sacrificed to idols in our local grocery store, but the principles Paul uses to address this issue in 1 Corinthians 8–10 are terribly relevant: act in love toward those who differ with you, don't become so arrogant that you let yourself get entangled in un-Christian forms of spirituality, etc. As the New Testament writers deal with these first-century issues, they usually tell their readers why they are to do something or not to do something. And in these explanations are found fundamental principles that are relevant for a host of issues that we face today."

If you remember, in chapter 4 on "Reading the Bible for Transformation," we talked about tuning into the principles behind the passages in the Bible, and it was good to have Doug mention the importance of principles for applying material from the letters. In this way, then, we can validly use the New Testament letters to address issues today that the writers of those letters never imagined. Doug noted, "There is a kind of generic similarity to issues across the centuries. The kind of issues treated in the New Testament letters often have a close counterpart in problems we face today."

Conclusion: Reading the Letters as an Adventure

What we had discussed thus far was helpful, reiterating guidance we had heard at times from other conversation partners but also pointing to the uniqueness of the New Testament letters and the need to think carefully about how we read them. Yet, as we moved to the close of our discussion, I wanted also to push to issues of the heart. Reading the Bible is more than just a science; it has much to do with relationship, our relationship with God, our relationship with fellow brothers and sisters in the church, and our relationship with nonbelievers around us in the world. So I asked Doug what role matters of the heart, dynamics like the joy or humility, play in reading this part of the Bible.

"Again, if I could return to our hiking analogy, when we hike, we may have a map, but there is no substitute for the actual on-the-ground experience, and often you run into surprises. Suddenly you're confronted with a mountain or a creek you didn't realize was going to be there. Or you crest a hill and a beautiful vista you didn't expect suddenly is right there in front of you. Those kinds of surprises make hiking a lot of fun and very fulfilling.

"In the same way, I think as we read the letters of the New Testament, we have to be open to surprises. We have to go where the letter takes us and not be so locked into what we expect to find that we don't see what's really there. In short, we have to be open to change. As we talked about earlier, we can start with a map—guidance from others—but nothing can replace reading the Bible carefully for ourselves, and we need to read with a sense of wonder and adventure, expecting God to speak to us in fresh ways. So one of the keys to reading the letters well is simply to liberate the letters from our own presuppositions, to let them speak and have their way with us."

I added, "And that means we are going to have to read with humility and a heart open to change."

Doug agreed. "I think that is so important. I confess that one of the frustrations I have often had over the years in teaching classes and churches has to do with people coming to class with their minds already made up concerning what a passage of the New Testament means. They've come with a preexisting interpretation, and they don't seem willing even to question their own thinking or patterns of life. Part of living under the authority of Scripture has to do with always being willing to hear God's Word in a fresh way and let it change our mind or our actions. That's what the authority of Scripture is all about. If I'm reading a New Testament letter, and I'm not willing to let God change my mind as I read it, then I'm not reading it in a way that honors that Word and honors God. I am not suggesting that we throw out good teaching or a solid background that a lot of us do have. Nevertheless, being excited about what God might have to say to me next is one of the most important foundations for reading the New Testament letters well."

And on that note our conversation concluded. I told Doug and Jenny good-bye and thanked her again for a lovely lunch. My MapQuest directions in hand, I climbed back into my rental car and made my way through West Chicago back to the airport for the flight home.

Summary & Application

Summation

- The New Testament letters are popular with Christians today because of their immediacy (they are obviously relevant to our situations in life) and role in providing doctrinal foundations for the church. The letter form also seems more familiar than some other forms of literature in the Bible.

- In New Testament times letter writing was often done by a trained scribe on a paper-like substance called papyrus. The process was expensive.
- Since there was no postal system, letters were delivered in person by a representative of the person sending the letter, and the reading of the letter often was a community event.
- When reading a New Testament letter, it helps to have an outline of the book in front of us, and such an outline can be found in a good study Bible or Bible dictionary.
- When reading a New Testament letter, we need to tune in to any historical and cultural background information that we have available to us.
- We should move from the first-century cultural context to our own by asking, "What is the principle behind this teaching or exhortation?"
- Read the New Testament letters as an adventure in which we discover what God wants to say to us as members of the church today.

Conversation

1. With which of the New Testament letters are you most familiar? Why that one?
2. What aspects of ancient letter writing described in this chapter surprised you the most? What are the implications of that aspect of letter writing for how we think about the New Testament letters?
3. What is the most difficult aspect of reading the New Testament letters well? What one thing might you do to grow in reading the New Testament letters well?
4. What tool have you used that helped you get at the historical and cultural background behind a New Testament letter?
5. Read 1 Corinthians 8. What are the main principles in this chapter? How might we apply those principles today?

Transformation

Read Colossians 3:1–17. In a study Bible or Bible dictionary, find an article on Colossians, investigating the historical situation of the letter and an outline of the letter. How does this passage fit in the developing message of the book (literary context)? How does this passage address the historical situation? What three principles from the passage are most relevant to you at this point?

CHAPTER 12

Reading Revelation

A Conversation with J. Scott Duvall

The revelation of Jesus Christ that God gave Him
to show His slaves what must quickly take place.

—Revelation 1:1

As I write, yet another apocalyptic blockbuster has been released so that moviegoers can spend a couple of happy hours contemplating the cataclysmic, brutally violent end of the world as we know it. Such movies paint a dark picture of a future in which the world has become a wasteland and human beings have been turned into either animals or soldier-survivors. People seem to be fascinated with a peek at the final page of Earth's history.

If you asked most Christians, "Where does the Bible speak about the end of the world?" most probably would reply, "The book of Revelation." Yet, if we are honest, few actually spend time reading it, in spite of the fact that here is a book of the Bible that comes with an amazing promise: "The one who reads this is blessed, and those who hear the words of this prophecy and keep what is written in it are blessed" (Rev. 1:3). Perhaps the reason most of us do not read Revelation is that it is just plain difficult. From the start we are met with bizarre images, obscure allusions to the Old Testament, and historical references that make no sense to us. Yet, as we will see, Revelation has so much to offer those who are willing to enter its pages and learn to read this most unread of New Testament documents. So, to help us crack the code of Revelation, I turned to J. Scott Duvall, the J. C. and Mae Fuller Professor of Biblical Studies at Ouachita Baptist University in Arkadelphia, Arkansas.

One of my dearest friends, Scott and I met and got to know each other well while in seminary, and our lives have been on parallel tracks ever since. We both have taught for the last two decades at academically strong, Baptist, liberal arts universities in the South. We both love teaching university students but have also done administrative work. We have published books (one of them together) and helped plant new churches in our respective towns. Our wives, also close friends, both love blue-and-white dishes, tea parties, and all things British; and our children—Scott's three and my two—just happen to be five of the greatest kids on the planet. For the past few years Scott has developed a keen interest in the book of Revelation, and I knew he would be a good person to help us unravel its mysteries. We met for our conversation at the Sheraton Hotel in New Orleans, Louisiana, during the annual meeting of the Evangelical Theological Society.

"Scott Duvall, you and I have been friends for a long time, and I appreciate you taking a few minutes to talk to me today about the book of Revelation—a nice, easy topic!" I said jokingly.

He laughed. "I appreciate you putting me on the spot like this! No, I am glad to be here, and Revelation really is a great book and an important one for us to read and apply to our lives."

Why Is Revelation So Difficult to Understand?

I started by asking, "Revelation seems so different from other books of the New Testament. Why is that, and why is it so intimidating?"

Scott answered, "Well it is different. Most people make it through the first three chapters, maybe chapters 4 and 5, and then . . . (a pause)"

I interjected, "And then the wheels come off!"

Scott agreed. "And then the wheels come off. One of the main reasons Revelation is difficult to read is that it combines three different types of writing."

I asked, "OK. What are those?"

"First, Revelation is a *letter*. The book opens and closes like a typical New Testament letter (1:4–5; 22:21). In fact, the whole book of Revelation should be seen as a single document meant to be passed around seven churches in Asia Minor in the first century: Ephesus, Smyrna, Pergamum, Thyatira, Sardis, Philadelphia, and Laodicea. If you look at a map of that area, you will see that the churches are named in the order in which a letter carrier would visit them starting from Patmos (where John is in exile at the time of writing) and moving in a circle through the heart of Asia Minor."

I interjected, "So, an ancient postal route."

"That's right," Scott said. "We don't normally classify Revelation as a letter, but it does have some characteristics of the letter form."

I said, "So Revelation includes some material we would expect to find in a letter. What else?"

He continued. "Second, Revelation also claims to be a *prophecy* (1:3; 22:6–7, 10, 18–19). Bible prophecy includes both prediction of God's plans for the future and proclamation of God's truth for the present."

I echoed, "So prophecy involves the prediction of events—"

Scott replied, "—which is how most people think of prophecy; but it also involves the delivering of a message from God for people at a particular time, who are dealing with a particular situation. Although we might want to focus on prediction because it's fascinating, most biblical prophecy actually emphasizes proclamation of a message. In the places where Revelation is described as a prophecy, the readers are exhorted to 'keep' it (1:3; 22:7). It's hard to 'keep' a prediction but perfectly natural to think of keeping or obeying a message. This means that Revelation is not just about the future, although it does point to events that will take place at the end of time, when Christ returns to Earth. It's primarily about how God wants His people to live right now in the present."

I prompted Scott, asking for the third type of literature found in this enigmatic book.

He answered, "Well the third is the most complex and the most difficult for us to deal with. It is called 'apocalyptic.' In Revelation 1:1 we are told that the book is a 'revelation' (*apokalypsis* in Greek) that comes from God through Jesus Christ, an angel, and John to the servants of God. Many scholars believe that apocalyptic literature grew out of Hebrew prophecy during an especially intense time of difficulty for God's people. If you've ever read Daniel, Ezekiel, or Zechariah, you have encountered apocalyptic literature. This type of writing includes God's revelation to a well-known person (like John or Daniel) in which God promises to intervene in the course of history and to overthrow evil empires, setting up His kingdom. So apocalyptic literature has to do with heaven breaking into Earth in some significant way."

I added, "I can see how the combination of these different types of literature makes reading the book a bit challenging."

Scott answered, "We are used to reading various types of literature in our culture—a phone bill, a textbook, a novel, a love letter—but we normally don't see those woven together in one place, and we are not used to dealing with prophecy and apocalyptic. So the mix becomes confusing."

Can You Paint Me a Picture? Revelation's Use of Symbols

One of the things that makes apocalyptic literature so challenging is the use of symbolic language, often bizarre images that make little sense on a surface reading of the book. So I asked Professor Duvall about Revelation's use of symbolism, noting that these strange symbols in the book seem to throw most people for a loop.

Scott gestured with hands, emphasizing his points as he continued. "Right from the start, in Revelation 1:1, John hints that he is going to be using symbols in this book. There it says that God sent the revelation 'and signified it through His angel to His slave John.' Here the word 'signified' means to 'make known through symbols.'"

Someone has drawn an analogy between the symbolism of Revelation and political cartoons in our culture, in which pictures represent a reality. They are not to be taken literally, but they are to be taken as pointing to a reality. I mentioned this to Scott, explaining how I use the analogy when talking to my students about Revelation. "So, for instance, I ask my students to imagine a political cartoon in which there is a wagon full of money with ropes tied to both ends of the wagon. An elephant is pulling in one direction, and a donkey is pulling in another. I ask them, 'Who in the room thinks that somewhere in America there is a literal elephant and a literal donkey fighting over a wagon full of money?' No one does, and I ask them, 'What does this represent?' and they all know exactly what it represents because they are familiar with Republicans and Democrats in our political system. The picture is symbolic, but it points to a real situation in the world. So how would Revelation's use of symbols be similar?"

Scott remarked, "That is a great illustration. Similarly, Revelation is not saying the events being portrayed never happened in history or will never happen in history. In fact, the presupposition behind Revelation is that realities are being represented."

I added, "So when we say that these word pictures are not literal, we are not saying that they are not literally true."

Scott said, "That's right. We should take the symbols seriously, even though we don't take them literally. Let me give you an example. We are told in this book that we as Christians are the bride of Christ: 'Let us be glad, rejoice, and give Him glory, because the marriage of the Lamb has come, and His wife has prepared herself. She was given fine linen to wear, bright and pure' (Rev. 19:7–8). Well, I am not a bride; I am a husband; I wore a tux at my wedding; I have never worn a dress, much less a linen one. I am not a bride . . . but I am a bride! I am part of the bride of Christ, the church."

I added, "And the symbol there represents intimacy of relationship between Christ and His people, as well as the purity of God's people."

Scott responded, "That's right."

I continued, "And the symbol works better than just a straight forward statement of fact. The author could have simply said, 'God's people are pure and in close relationship with Jesus,' but that would not have been as effective."

Scott added, "Symbols are powerful. They charge the imagination and help us see and connect with greater realities in a way that can change the way we think and live. For instance, on my wedding day, when my wife, Judy, was standing at the back of the church, I did not think, *O, there is a beautiful woman in a white dress.* That would have been true factually but not very romantic! My thoughts were more along the lines of, *There she stands, bathed in the sun, wrapped in a blanket of pure snow, beauty crowning her head, the center of my universe!* That sounds a bit sappy, but you get the point. Symbols magnify the reality."

I commented, "It is a way of expressing the glory of the reality."

"Absolutely," he replied, "in a way plain language does not equal."

Word Pictures for Hard Times

I asked, "Weren't the symbols in Revelation also meant to be a code language for those being persecuted by the Roman government?"

Scott answered, "Yes. Most scholars think Revelation was written either in the 60s during the time of the emperor Nero, or in the 90s under the emperor Domitian, but persecution of Christians took place under both. The use of symbolic language was a way of talking about the persecutors without pointing a finger and naming them. So, for instance, many scholars believe that references to 'the beast' in Revelation refer to the Roman

READING THE NEW TESTAMENT

emperor. The 'mark of the beast' that one had to have if they were going to buy something, may be a reference to Roman coins, many of which had the image of the emperor stamped on them."

I interjected, "So they used a word picture that would represent the emperor, and that was safer than coming out and saying, 'Stand strong against the emperor.'"

Scott replied, "For believers in Asia Minor to whom this book was originally written, the worship of the emperor was a powerful force in their communities. For instance, Domitian wanted people to address him as *dominus et deus noster* (Our Lord and God). There were festivals and parades and places to worship the emperor, and at times, if you did not participate, you lost your job. So Christians faced economic persecution or worse. Of course, the confession of Caesar as Lord conflicted with the confession, 'Jesus is Lord.'"

I commented, "Revelation is saying, 'Jesus is the real King, the real Caesar.'"

Scott answered, "That's right. That confession is at the heart of the book of Revelation. He is the one sitting on the eternal throne of the universe (Rev. 5), not just the temporary throne of the Roman Empire."

An Example: The Dragon of Revelation 12

As we continued the conversation, I thought it might be helpful for us to discuss a prominent symbol of the book, the dragon in Revelation 12. I asked Scott if he would read part of chapter 12 and talk to us about that symbol.

He responded, "I would be glad to." He read, "'Then another sign appeared in heaven: There was a great fiery red dragon having seven heads and 10 horns, and on his heads were seven diadems. His tail swept away a third of the stars in heaven and hurled them to the earth. And the dragon stood in front of the woman who was about to give birth, so that when she did give birth he might devour her child'" (Rev. 12:3–4).

Scott commented, "This really presents us with a graphic symbol of Satan."

I added, "Which John himself tells us later in that chapter in verse 9, calling the dragon, 'the ancient serpent, who is called the Devil and Satan, the one who deceives the whole world' (Rev. 12:9)."

Scott responded, "That's right. The significance of the dragon symbol really hit home to me when our school took a biblical studies trip to Asia Minor in 2006 and visited the ruins of the city of Pergamum, which of course John refers to in Revelation 2:12–17. In that passage Jesus says to believers who live there, 'I know where you live—where Satan's throne is! And you are holding on to My name and did not deny your faith in Me' (2:13).

"While in Pergamum we saw where archaeologists say that throne was. Actually, 'the throne of Satan' itself is now in the Berlin Museum, and on the base of the throne are carved huge serpents that are attacking people. So for the people in Asia Minor in the first century, the serpent was a powerful symbol of evil personified. When John uses that symbol, he is saying to the early Christians and to us, 'We are not primarily up against political forces; your real enemy is a spiritual force. We are engaged in spiritual warfare.'"

I added, "Which really dovetails nicely with the biblical imagery in the rest of the Bible, where Satan often is depicted as a serpent."

"Absolutely right, the first example being the story of the fall in Genesis 3. And Revelation's message, which stands in a beautiful bookends relationship with the first chapters of Genesis, is that Christ has now defeated Satan. In Revelation 12 we read:

> Then I heard a loud voice in heaven say:
> The salvation and the power and the kingdom
>   of our God
> and the authority of His Messiah have now
>   come,
> because the accuser of our brothers has been
>   thrown out:

> the one who accuses them before our God day
>   and night.
> They conquered him by the blood of the Lamb
> and by the word of their testimony,
> for they did not love their lives in the face of
>   death. (vv. 10–11)

"So believers are given strong encouragement to hold to the gospel ('the blood of the Lamb') and to their testimony, even in the face of death."

I asked Scott how this symbolically packaged message fits with John's purpose for writing the book.

Scott became animated and summed up John's purpose as follows. "The overall purpose of Revelation is to challenge believers to think and live a certain way in response to these strange images and symbols. These images create a symbolic world into which readers can enter as they hear the book read aloud. It would be like us putting on a virtual-reality helmet and goggles and entering another world. As the readers (or hearers) enter this symbolic world, what they see affects them deeply and changes their perception of the world in which they live."

I interjected, "In other words, they are given fresh eyes to interpret the circumstances in which they find themselves?"

He responded, "That's absolutely right. What they read or hear in Revelation allows them to see reality from a heavenly perspective. What they see there is that God is more powerful than evil. No matter how much it looks like evil is winning in the world around them, Revelation tells them that in the end God will win. For believers in the first century, who were living in a hostile environment, that was great news. As they hear the book read over and over, they are continually reminded that what they believe is not crazy but is completely true and accurate from God's point of view. This would give them hope and great encouragement to remain faithful to God."

Other Guidelines for Reading Revelation Well

Our discussion of Revelation's symbolic language had been helpful, so I wanted to push on to other guidelines for reading the book. I asked Professor Duvall, "Can you help us think through other key principles that can help us interpret Revelation appropriately?" He gladly agreed to do so, and he clicked through a number of helpful guidelines.

Pray for Insight

"First of all," Scott said, "we are told that Revelation is 'an open book.' So we need to remember that the Lord wants us to understand this book. We should pray, asking the Holy Spirit for insight and discernment as we read, even as we are putting forth effort to study and understand it."

That is an excellent point and one we haven't focused on too much in the book thus far. Reading the Bible is not just a "science" or even just an "art." Reading the Bible, including its oh-so-challenging last book, constitutes a spiritual discipline, and we need the Spirit to illumine—shine His light on—our reading. This does not replace the hard work of study and interpretation, but it is a vitally important spiritual foundation for reading well.

Read with Humility

Scott continued. "Second, we should read Revelation with humility. As we have already discussed, Revelation is not an easy book and thus demands that we approach it with a humble spirit rather than with arrogance. People who insist that they understand the book perfectly are probably reading into Revelation things that are not there."

I remember a time years ago when I had a student who condemned anyone who disagreed with him on Revelation's interpretation as "liberal" theology. That's the kind of arrogant spirit Scott was talking about.

He reflected, "We should be cautious about experts who claim to have all the answers. We should be willing to change our interpretations when the evidence points in a different direction. This does not mean we can't land on firm inter-pretations; it simply means that we need to read with joy and excitement and a sense of discovery but also with humility, acknowledging that we do not have all the answers and at points the answers are not easy to come by."

Read in Light of the Original Audience

At many points in *Read the Bible for Life*, we have talked about the importance of historical background information. This foundation stone of interpretation is still in place as we read Revelation, and Scott affirmed it with his third point. We need to try to discern what a book would have meant to the original readers of the document. God's Word to original readers was God's Word for us from the very beginning. Yet God provided it for us by giving it to them.

Accordingly, Scott emphasized, "We should begin by trying to understand what Revelation was saying to the original readers since God chose them as the original recipients of the book." He suggested, "The best place to begin is with the question, What was John trying to communicate to his audience? If our inter-pretation makes no sense for the first readers, we have probably missed the point of the passage. Our tendency will be to skip past the first Christians and jump directly to God's message for us. Revelation certainly has something to say to us, but it first had something to say to them. We need to understand what it *meant* in John's day in order to understand what it *means* today."

Don't Try to Find a Historical Chronology

In a related vein Scott offered a fourth suggestion. "We shouldn't expect Revelation to give us a precise chronological map of future events, which some interpreters in the history of the church have suggested. Unlike a typical letter of Paul, for instance, don't expect Revelation to move forward in a neat, linear fashion from point A to point B. For example, there are three series of seven judgments in the book (the seals, trumpets, and bowls). But at the end of each series, the reader is taken to the end of the age. Revelation 19–22 provides the most detailed picture of the end of the world as we know it, but this is not the first time the reader has been transported to the end of time. The book is filled with visions, the chief purpose of which is to make a dramatic impact on the reader. Rather than searching for a detailed, chronological map of future events in Revelation, it's much more important to grasp the main message in each vision, and that vision often is given to encourage believers to obey God in the present, in spite of intense persecution. So the book does point to certain events that will take place at the end of the world as we know it, but it does not give us a timetable or a schedule leading up to that time."

Pay Attention When John Interprets a Symbol for Us

As a fifth guideline, Scott underscored the need to pay attention when John identifies or interprets an image for us. "John will occasionally identify or define an image for his readers, as we saw with the case of the dragon in chapter 12. When he does this, we should pay special attention. For example, in Revelation 1:17–18, John tells us the Son of Man is Christ; in 1:20 the golden lampstands are the churches; in 5:5–6 the Lion is the Lamb (who is Jesus); and in 21:9–10 the heavenly Jerusalem is the wife of the Lamb, the church. When images that John has identified are repeated later in the book, we should assume that they probably refer to the same things. For example, the lampstands in Revelation 1:20 represent the churches. The image is used again in 11:3–6 with reference to the 'two witnesses.' This probably means that the two witnesses of Revelation in some way represent the witnessing church as the church stands over against the power structures of the world. Sometimes John uses the same image (like a woman or stars) to refer to different things, but when he specifically identifies an image, we should pay attention."

Read in Light of the Old Testament

That was helpful. Scott had pointed to the two witnesses in Revelation 11:3–6. In that passage verse 6 reads, "These men have the power to close the sky so that it does not rain during the days of their prophecy. They also have power over the waters to turn them into blood, and to strike the earth with every plague whenever they want." If you are familiar with the stories of the Old Testament, "the power to close the sky so that it does not rain" and "power over the waters to turn them into blood" sound a lot like allusions to the ministries of Elijah and Moses respectively. I asked Scott about the allusions.

"Well, George, you are picking up on an important dynamic in the book. We really need to look to the Old Testament for help understanding the images and symbols in Revelation since Revelation contains more Old Testament references than any other New Testament book with the exception, perhaps, of Hebrews. It is full of them. For instance, you are exactly right about the allusions in 11:6. 'The power to close the sky' alludes to 1 Kings 17:1; 18:41–46 and the story in which Elijah announces God's judgment against the nation of Israel during the time of King Ahab when the worship of Baal was prevalent. Also, as one of the plagues against the Egyptians, Moses turned the waters in Egypt to blood. We see that story in Exodus 7:14–24; 8:1–11:10."

I asked Scott how those images were being used here in Revelation. He responded, "One interpretation is that two witnesses, like Moses and Elijah, stand against the enemies of God; but in 11:7 we see that the beast makes war against them, and it is hard to see how war can be made against two individuals. So another interpretation, which I mentioned a moment ago, is to understand the two witnesses as the witnessing church, perhaps especially the preachers and teachers of the church, who, like Moses and Elijah, combat God's enemies with the powerful, prophetic Word of God. Prominent evangelical scholars such as Robert Mounce, Craig Keener, and Greg Beale present this interpretation in their commentaries on the book. This interpretation suggests that the church, as it bears witness to God's Word, has at its disposal resources just as great as the supernatural power displayed by two of the greatest figures of the Old Testament. That is strong encouragement!"

Discerning allusions made to the Old Testament in Revelation can become challenging, so you may need the help of a good commentary on Revelation, like the ones Scott mentioned, and a good study Bible can help immensely. Yet Scott pointed out that the habit of reading through the story of the Bible on an annual basis can lay an important foundation for reading Revelation well.

He suggested, "As you read the whole story of the Bible through the years, you begin to understand more and more of what John is doing in this book."

Conclusion: The Relevance of Revelation for the Church Today

As our conversation drew to a close, there was so much more we could cover, but our time was slipping away. To wrap up, I wanted to be sure to address the issue of the *relevance* of Revelation for Christ's church today. Everyone knows Revelation is a difficult book to read, and features like symbolic language and allusions to the Old Testament can give the false impression that the book is far removed from us and our concerns. Nothing could be farther from the truth. Life in this age between the cross of Christ and the second coming can be hard, the kind of hard that beats relentlessly against one's faith and perspective. Jesus really is Lord of the universe, but many of His enemies still walk the earth, and they can be brutal. Whether we are battling cancer, persevering under persecution by a political regime, or simply trying to live counterculturally in a world that shouts loudly against the Bible's message, we need the stability and encouragement Revelation offers.

I asked Professor Duvall how Revelation encourages believers in the face of life's harsh realities. He pointed to the theme of "overcoming" as central to the book. "This idea of overcoming provides an important application for us today. At the beginning of Revelation, we are challenged to overcome. In each of the messages to the seven churches in Revelation 2–3, Christ promises rewards to those who overcome (2:7, 11, 17, 26–29; 3:5–6, 12–13,

21–22). Revelation 12 constitutes the heart of the book, and there we are told that true believers 'conquered [overcame Satan] by the blood of the Lamb and by the word of their testimony, for they did not love their lives in the face of death' (v. 11). Then at the end of the book, we read the promise that the 'victor' [overcomer] will inherit all God has to offer, and God says, 'I will be his God, and he will be My son' (21:7). If you want to read a book of the Bible about overcoming or staying faithful to the Lord until the end, this is your book!"

I added, "And we are able to overcome because we know that God wins."

Scott responded, "It really is foundational for our perseverance. The knowledge that God wins gives you perspective and strength and hope to persevere in the present. If you've ever read about people who have suffered persecution, they will tell you that one of the most important things to hang onto is hope. If people lose hope, they just give up altogether, but if they can hang on to hope, then they can continue to persevere. So Revelation says, 'Hang in there! Don't lose hope. God wins in the end. Caesar is not lord; Jesus is Lord! God will judge the evil people who are hurting you.'"

"Isn't it true," I interjected, "that at the center of God's victory is the gospel?"

Scott agreed wholeheartedly. "Look at the images of Jesus in Revelation 5. He is a conquering lion who 'has been victorious' (v. 5). The image of the lion is an image of royalty. But how has He conquered? Through sacrifice. The other image of Jesus in that chapter is the image of a slaughtered lamb (v. 6). He is powerful enough to accomplish the purposes of God: 'Because You were slaughtered, and You redeemed people for God by Your blood from every tribe and language and people and nation. You made them a kingdom and priests to our God, and they will reign on the earth' (vv. 9–10). So power comes through sacrifice."

I added, "And the gospel also opens the way for us to live in face-to-face relationship with God, which is where the book of Revelation—and the Bible—ends."

"George, I might get a bit excited here. When you look at Genesis 1–2, think of the garden of Eden, not as a small flower garden in your backyard but as bigger and more grand than a huge, glorious, national park, and God is walking through the park with these human beings. They are experiencing His presence. Then in Genesis 3 something terrible happens, and in judgment they are driven out of God's presence. Revelation shows the complete reversal of that judgment. At the end of Revelation we read:

> I also saw the Holy City, new Jerusalem, coming
>   down out of heaven from God, prepared like
>   a bride adorned for her husband.
> Then I heard a loud voice from the throne:
> Look! God's dwelling is with humanity,
> and He will live with them.
> They will be His people,
> and God Himself will be with them and be their
>   God.
> He will wipe away every tear from their eyes.
> Death will exist no longer;
> grief, crying, and pain will exist no longer,
> because the previous things have passed away.
>   (Rev. 21:2–4)

"The story of the Bible really is about God getting us back into His presence. You see this in the covenants. You see it in the tabernacle and in the temple. You see it in Jesus' incarnation and in the coming of the Holy Spirit in Acts to indwell the church. Now in Revelation 21–22, the temple of God has come down to earth, and the Bible ends where it started, with God walking with people. I can't fathom what that will be like, but God says to us, 'I want to be with you.' That is a happy ending to the story."

As I thought about it, that is an apocalyptic blockbuster we can look forward to.

Our conversation ended, and we said good-bye. I asked Scott to greet Judy and the girls for me, and he in turn sent Judy's greetings to Pat. We made our way out of the room and into a hurting world that desperately needs to hear the message of hope found in Revelation.

Summary & Application

Summation

- Revelation is difficult to understand because it combines three types of literature: letter, prophecy, and apocalyptic.
- One thing that makes apocalyptic literature challenging is its use of symbolism. Like political cartoons, symbolism uses images to communicate truths about reality. Although the symbols are not to be taken literally, they should be understood as literally true.
- Revelation was written at a time when the Roman emperor was persecuting Christians in the early church and was written as a message of hope. It gives hope by pointing to cosmic realities.
- When reading Revelation, pray for insight and read with humility.
- Read Revelation in light of the original audience, and don't try to find a chronology of history in its pages.
- Pay attention when John, the author of Revelation, interprets a symbol for us, and read in light of allusions to the Old Testament.
- As we face evil forces in the world today, Revelation is wonderfully relevant for Christians, especially for those facing harsh persecution.

Conversation

1. Which of the following best describes your experience of Revelation in the past? Why? (1) fulfilling, (2) confusing, (3) terrifying, (4) mixed, (5) other

2. In this chapter an analogy was made between the
    symbols of Revelation and political cartoons in
    our culture. In what ways are these two forms of
    communication similar? How are they different?
3. Which of the guidelines given in this chapter for
    reading Revelation was most helpful to you? Why?
4. Read Revelation 21:1–8. In what ways does this passage
    offer hope for believers struggling with an evil world?

Transformation

Read Revelation 5. Use a study Bible to understand better the symbolism in this chapter. What do you learn about the Lamb (Jesus) in this chapter? How might you use this chapter in worship?

PART FOUR

Reading the Bible in Modern Contexts

CHAPTER 13

Reading the Bible
for Personal Devotion

A Conversation with Donald S. Whitney

Like newborn infants, desire the pure spiritual milk,
so that you may grow by it for your salvation.

—1 Peter 2:2

 A few years ago I traveled to China and taught the New Testament books of Hebrews and James to a group of ministers from across the country. While there, my wife, who was at home in the U.S., got sick and was struggling spiritually. Her thyroid had been radiated weeks earlier (essentially killing it), and she had gone "hypo-thyroid" while I was half a world away. With hypothyroidism, the body does not get the hormones it needs, and the condition wreaks havoc on various systems of the body.

I called Pat on a Tuesday evening, and she told me about her illness, but she was also experiencing a deep sense of spiritual oppression, a dark cloud of anxiety and disorientation. Although such emotions could have been due to her physical condition, we both felt spiritual dynamics were involved, possibly related to my ministry in China. I went the next morning to the twenty-five or so brothers and sisters in my class, most of whom were from western China. I asked them if they would pray for my wife. Immediately they all stood up, and one after another, for the next thirty-five minutes, they prayed powerful, passionate prayers for Pat. It sounded to me like they were bombarding the gates of heaven! Since I do not speak Chinese, I asked the interpreter what they were praying, and she said their prayers were almost pure Scripture. Within twenty-four hours both the physical effects of Pat's illness, which could not have been corrected that quickly by medication, and the sense of horrible spiritual pressure lifted from her.

Our brothers and sisters in China are saturated with God's Word, and the Word is brought to bear on a wide variety of situations in life via powerful, Scripture-infused prayer. The house churches in China do not have buildings or resources or training like we have in the West. Yet they know God, they know how to pray, and they know and live God's Word. I came back from China longing to be a person who knows the Scriptures more deeply and talks to God in prayer more faithfully. I want to challenge you, my reader, to join me in that adventure.

To lead us in a discussion concerning how we might interact more meaningfully with God's Word and integrate our reading of the Word with a more dynamic life of prayer, I tapped Donald S. Whitney, associate professor of biblical spirituality at Southern Seminary in Louisville, Kentucky. Don has written extensively on what have been called "the spiritual disciplines" and offers practical, down-to-earth suggestions for building a life of devotion to Christ. In April 2009 Don came to speak in chapel at Union University, so it gave us an opportunity to sit down for a conversation. Sitting across from each other in a podcast booth at Union, we talked about the spiritual disciplines of Bible reading and prayer.

I opened our discussion with, "Don, Scripture seems clear that God's people are to orient their lives to God's Word and communicate with God through prayer. In almost every book of the Bible, these two practices show up as normal, regular, foundational parts of a spiritual life well lived. We all struggle with consistency—I know I do! So why is it so hard for us to be consistent in our commitments to these spiritual disciplines?"

Delighting in God's Word

Don, gesturing with his hands, answered, "Let's begin by talking about our time in God's Word. I think in most cases we struggle with consistency due to our methodology. Most people *merely read* the Bible, checking off the requirement for the day. Reading gives us *exposure* to Scripture, and that is where we need to start, but most of us want to enjoy our time in God's Word, and we want to be changed by it. The key to delight and transformation is *meditation*. Meditation helps us to absorb Scripture, to take it into the depths of who we are as people, so we can live it out in our lives. I would venture to say that if you ask most people, 'When was the last time your Bible reading changed your life?' they would have to admit that it's been awhile."

If you remember, in the introduction of this book I pointed out that a recent poll by LifeWay Research found that only 37 percent of those who attend church regularly said that reading and studying the Bible had made a significant difference in the way they live their lives. That statistic seems to support Don's assumption.

Whitney continued, "We might be tempted to think of consistent Bible reading as for the spiritually elite. Yet God wants all of His people to enjoy His Word, so joy in the Word must be possible for ordinary people, and I think the answer is meditation— thinking deeply about what we are reading. Most people simply read the Bible, close it, and then if pressed, would have to admit what, George?"

I answered, "That they have forgotten what they had just read." I thought of many times that I had done my Bible reading and then could not remember the particulars of what I had just read! Don had nailed an all-too-common experience for me.

Don smiled, "Right. 'I don't remember a single thing I've just read. But I've done my Bible reading for the day and can get on with life!' That does little good."

I added, "That is what I would call a 'checklist' approach— just getting my reading done so I can check off the reading for the day." I've benefited from ministries that have given me a Bible

reading plan to go by, and I have been developing Bible reading
plans to help others (two of which are in the appendix of this
book!). But what Don was saying is that we've got to move beyond
a checklist approach that says, "That's that. I've done my bit." We
need to meditate on the Word.

So I continued, "Talk to us about what we mean by 'meditation.' For a lot of folks, meditation is unfamiliar territory.
Meditation has to do with 'mentally chewing' on a passage, right?
Talk to us about how you meditate because I can imagine some
people are thinking, *Am I supposed to go into a yoga position?*"

How to Meditate on Scripture

Whitney smiled, shaking his head from side to side as he said,
"No, no, no, that's not what we mean. First, let's remember that
meditation is biblical and an activity that God blesses! Psalm 1,
strategically placed at the beginning of the Bible's songbook, says
that a person is blessed whose 'delight is in the LORD's instruc-
tion,' who 'meditates on it day and night' (v. 2). So meditation
is more than just a good idea. Scripture strongly encourages it."

I asked, "OK, so how do we meditate?"

Don became more animated; meditation clearly is something
he feels passionate about. "When we talk about meditation, we
mean deep thinking—whatever deep thinking is for you. For
instance, consider the following psalms and notice the ideas that
parallel the act of meditating:

> I will reflect on all You have done
> and meditate on Your actions. (Ps. 77:12)

> I will meditate on Your precepts
> and think about Your ways. (Ps. 119:15)

"In these psalms, the idea of meditation parallels *reflecting*
on what God has done and *thinking* about God's ways. Usually
the Scriptures speak of meditating on God's Word or commands
(see Ps. 119:27, 48, 78, 148), although the Bible does speak of
meditating on God's actions, for instance, or God's creation.

"One way we can think deeply about what we are reading is to think through questions about a passage or to write out questions about the passage in the margins of our Bibles. Probe the passage you are reading, asking who, what, when, where, why, and how? Ask questions like: 'Who is saying this? Why did that person respond to God in that way? Where is this taking place? What is important about this part of the passage? etc.'

"We also can meditate by taking a verse and thinking deeply about it one word at a time. For example, in the 'water to wine' story in John 2, Mary told the head steward, 'Do whatever He (Jesus) tells you' (v. 5). Think about that verse carefully, emphasizing one word at a time. Pause for a minute and say, '*Do* whatever He tells you.' 'Do *whatever* He tells you.' 'Do whatever *He* tells you.' 'Do whatever He *tells* you.' 'Do whatever He tells *you*.' Squeeze every one of those inspired words. That causes you to linger over the verse, and you begin to see nuances in what is written. Such an approach causes us to slow down and think about what we are reading."

What about Those of Us Who Are "Too Busy"?

I mentioned to Don that I could imagine certain people listening to or reading our discussion and saying, "That might be great for a monk or a retired person, but I don't have time to meditate on that level!"

Don laughed and responded, "I have had people say to me, 'Well, meditation sounds like a wonderful idea in an idyllic world, but I'm always in a hurry to get somewhere! Look, I'm working two jobs. I'm a single mom. I'm fortunate if I get six hours of sleep. There are days when the best I can do is chisel out ten minutes of my day to read the Bible. Now you are saying I need to add meditation on top of that?! Get real!'"

I interjected, "What advice would you give to that single mom?"

Whitney continued: "What I would say to such a person is, 'OK, you only have ten minutes. Let's transform those ten minutes. Don't read for ten minutes; read for five minutes, and then meditate for five minutes. That will help you hear from God. Then meditate on the passage as you work through your day. The reality is, many of us do live hectic lives. There are times you shouldn't stop. You have deadlines to meet, so you need to get busy. But I want to argue that we also need times to slow down in life, even if it is just for a few minutes. We might need to work at scheduling our 'slow down' times. 'Pay careful attention, then, to how you walk—not as unwise people but as wise—making the most of the time, because the days are evil' (Eph. 5:15–16). I'm just saying it is appropriate to make time each day to stop and see something in God's Word that you won't see if you are always going sixty-five miles per hour through life."

As we talked, I thought of something I wanted to try. I live about fifteen minutes from where I work. Maybe what I can do is have my time of Bible reading in the morning and then pick out one verse I want to think about on my way to work. If you are reading this book and you are saying, "I only have ten to fifteen minutes in the morning, and then I have to dash out the door!" why not pick one verse from your Bible reading and spend some time as you're driving to work meditating on that verse?

I asked Don what he thought about the idea. He answered, "I think that's a great use of time. I would also encourage people, so their minds don't wander, to pick out some things along their commute, maybe a billboard that always gets your attention, or another particular landmark that always attracts your attention—have two or three of those that are prompts to say, 'Am I meditating on the Scripture? Has my mind wandered?' That will prompt you to go back to that text that you said you wanted to meditate on as you're driving."

Balancing Meditation and "Big Picture" Reading of the Bible

We had talked a lot about the micro-reading of the text, getting down to the details, thinking carefully about the pieces. Yet, as I have pointed out at numerous places in *Read the Bible for Life*, I think we often forget what we've read because we're not reading the Bible in the context of Scripture's developing story. So

I asked Don, "How can we incorporate the big picture into our devotional reading, balancing meditation on the details with getting the grand sweep of the Bible's story?"

He answered, "To use a word picture, reading several chapters of the Bible a day is like going across a lake in a speedboat. Meditation is going across that same lake in a glass-bottomed boat. We need to do both. You might say, 'I'm going to read through the Bible this year. I'll read three chapters today.' When you read in this way, you see the 'lake' in terms of the big picture. There are rocks on this side of the lake and trees on that side. There's a beach straight ahead. The lake narrows here. You need the big picture.

"However, you also need meditation, a 'glass-bottomed boat' approach. Every day you need to slow down and read parts carefully, focusing on the beauty in the details. You'll see depth and clarity and insights you'll never see if all you do is speed through your daily Bible reading. On the other hand, if all you do is meditation, you won't see the big picture of Scripture. So that's why I encourage people to read a chapter or three chapters (that's the big picture) a day, and then choose a few verses out of those chapters for meditation."

I asked, "Does it matter how a person reads through the Bible?"

Whitney responded, "I think a systematic reading of Scripture is vitally important. Instead of saying, 'I think I'll read Colossians 3 today, and tomorrow I'll read Habakkuk 2,' we need an approach that is going to expose us to all of God's Word over time. Reading in light of a developing context in a book helps us understand the book. You get the flow. In fact, I want to make a case for regularly reading through the Bible systematically. Jesus said, 'Man does not live on bread alone but on every word that comes from the mouth of God.' How are you going to live on every word if you've never read every word? I encourage people to read regularly through the Word of God, whether it takes them one year, two years, or three years.

"Now some people will say, 'I tried. Genesis was OK, but then I got into the second part of Exodus and Leviticus, and frankly

I just couldn't keep it up.' I advocate a plan of reading from multiple starting places. I'll give you two. The one I typically do in the start of the year when I'm reading through Scripture is to start in five places. I start in Genesis, which is the beginning of the Law. I start in Joshua, which begins the History. Job begins the Wisdom or Poetry literature. Isaiah begins the Prophets. Matthew begins the New Testament. For some people reading five different chapters a day is too many. So they could start in three places: Genesis, Job, and Matthew. Read roughly equal amounts in those passages, and you'll finish them all about the same time. When people find themselves bogged down in some sections of Scripture, they can think, *Well in a minute I'll be over in the Psalms, and that's a lot easier reading. In a minute I'll be in the New Testament, and that's easier to follow.* I've found that helps people keep the momentum if they read in multiple places."

In the appendix of this book are two Bible reading plans, the first a 'chronological' plan that will lead you in reading through the Bible according to the developing story of Scripture. Since our books of the Bible are not organized in historical order, this can help you learn a great deal about how the different parts of the Bible fit historically. The other plan, like the ones Don mentions above, has you read from multiple places in the Bible each day.

Integrating Meditation and Prayer

One of the most helpful parts of our conversation had to do with using deeper meditation on Scripture as a basis for a more fulfilling prayer life, and I want to encourage you to pay special attention to this next part of the chapter. As I talk to many Christ followers, the organization and practice of daily prayer seems to stupefy most. Helpfully Don pointed to a deep meditation on Scripture as providing an appropriate framework for our prayer lives as well.

Whitney explained: "One of the best ways to meditate on Scripture is by praying through a passage, and, correspondingly, one of the best ways to pray is for Scripture to guide us as we bring our needs and the needs of others before the Lord. When they pray, most people say the same old things about the same old things. George, that's boring. And when it's boring, it's hard to make yourself pray. And when you do pray, your mind is wandering half the time, and you feel like a failure."

In my own prayer life I have kept a prayer list in various ways, using a notebook for instance, or a set of index cards. Yet I, too, had found that my detailed prayers, whether for myself or for others, tend to bog down after awhile, returning again and again to certain basic issues on my list. So I said to Don, "Even for those of us who keep a prayer list, it's easy for such a list to turn into a rut in which we pray the same things over and over. You're saying that such an approach to prayer can work itself into a dead end after awhile."

Don answered, "Yeah, if you pray the same thing enough times, it becomes so routine that it's boring. Even though you love the people for whom you are praying, and you love the God you're talking to, the method makes it boring to you.

"Now, you might use the ACTS acrostic (Adoration, Confession, Thanksgiving, and Supplication) to give structure to your prayer life, working through each of these areas of prayer. So you pray and say, 'OK, I'm going to use the ACTS today. I want to start with Adoration. How am I going to adore the Lord today? I guess I'll adore Him the way I did yesterday.' Most people don't have the time or creative energy in their personal devotional life to talk about the same things every day in a different way. To pray about the same old things is normal. Our lives tend to consist pretty much of the same old things. Your job doesn't change that much from day to day. Your family doesn't change every day. Our lives tend to consist of mainly the same old things. That's not the problem; the problem is that we say the same old things in prayer. That method quickly becomes boring."

This discussion hit home. I have been using the ACTS acrostic for the past thirty years or so, and I have to admit that, as I mentioned a moment ago, I get in a rut sometimes. So I asked Don, "OK, how do we keep from getting in a rut?"

From Drudgery to Delight in Your Prayer Life

Whitney rested his hands on the desk in front of him. "When we pray, we can pray through a passage of Scripture. After reading a chapter or several chapters in your Bible reading, go back and pick one verse, perhaps a verse that stood out to you. Or you can pick a verse or passage you believe is a theme verse or a key passage in the section you have just read. Then pause over that verse and pray through it."

I asked Don if he could give us an example.

He responded, "Sure. Let's say that you are reading through the psalms in your daily Bible reading, and you come to Psalm 23. You decide that you are going to meditate on and pray through Psalm 23:1: 'The LORD is my shepherd; there is nothing I lack.' If you spend just sixty seconds praying over that verse, that's thirty times longer than you normally would spend simply reading that verse—*thirty times!*—and it is a much deeper, much more meaningful way to interact with God's Word.

"Think for a minute about Psalm 23, and let's allow it to prompt us to pray in certain ways. We read the first line: 'The LORD is my shepherd.' We can pause and think about the idea of shepherding. I might pray, 'Lord, You really are a good Shepherd for Your people, providing for us and protecting us. Lord, I thank You that You are *my* shepherd. You've guided me throughout my life, but Lord, would You shepherd me, lead me, in this decision I have to make today? Do I make that job change or not?'

"Then I might go on to the next part of the verse, 'There is nothing I lack.' 'And, Good Shepherd, we have needs in our family right now. I don't know how I am going to pay all of our bills this month, but I know You have more resources than I can imagine. Please help me. And, Lord, shepherd my children today; meet all their needs. Please provide for my daughter. Meet her emotional needs. She has been wanting a heart friend who loves You. Help my son in school; he struggles with discipline. Train him to be a disciplined man. And Lord, I think about Nancy, our pastor's wife, who has cancer. Lord, she needs healing. Please provide healing for her. Give the doctors the wisdom and skill they need to treat her well.'

"As we pray our way through the passage, all kinds of needs come to mind, needs in our own lives and in the lives of others. Using a passage in this way both helps us to meditate on the Word more deeply and prompts us to pray in specific, biblically grounded ways."

The Word Shapes Prayerful Imagination

As we saw in chapter 7 of this book, the psalms often speak in word pictures and that means we have to use our imaginations. I asked Don if the imagination plays an important role in bringing together the spiritual truths of Scripture and the needs in our lives.

He responded, "Definitely. God gave us an imagination, and we are to use it for our good and God's glory. When we speak about the imagination, we're not talking about what some people call 'visualization,' by which we are imagining the world the way we want it—for example, 'Think world peace!' No, in using our imaginations we are thinking about Scripture and guided by Scripture to think and pray in certain directions."

I added, "So, instead of having to come up with how to pray for people out of thin air, we are guided in our prayers by Scripture itself."

Whitney said, "With this approach you think of things you would never think to pray about because the text prompts you, and you pray about the same old people and issues but in brand-new, fresh ways. For example, let's say today you are praying for your two children using Psalm 23. But tomorrow you're praying through Psalm 139:5–7: 'Where can I go to escape Your Spirit? Where can I flee from Your presence?' (v. 7). Prompted by that psalm, you might pray, 'Lord, may my children sense Your presence wherever they go today. Show them that You are actively involved in their lives!' The next day you pray through Psalm 1, and you pray that God would make your children people who meditate deeply on the Word of God. So each day you are praying for God to bless your children, but, because you are going through a different passage every day, you are praying for them in a wide variety of ways."

I commented, "The thing I love about this approach is that it is simple, and it really allows you to do two things in your prayer time. It gives you a basis for reflecting more deeply on God's Word . . ."

Whitney interjected, "That's meditation . . ."

I continued, "And then in thinking about who God is and what He has done, you pray, bringing the truth of Scripture to bear on needs in your life and the lives of those for whom you need to pray. The beauty is that this also forms us in the way we think about God and the way we think about life. So it seems to me that the Scriptures then become formative so that using them as the structure of our prayer guides us into how we should think and how we should pray. It teaches us to pray biblically!"

Whitney agreed wholeheartedly and pointed out that the psalms are especially conducive to use in this approach to prayer. "Remember, the psalms were originally inspired by God for the purpose of being sung to God. God gave them to us so we would sing and pray them back to God. That's why I think it's the best book in the Bible for praying through Scripture. God, in effect, said, 'I want you to praise Me and sing praises to Me, but you don't know how to do that. I'm invisible to you. You know nothing of Me unless I reveal Myself to you.' So He gives us the psalms so we know what to say as we worship and pray to Him. The psalms teach us how God wants to be approached, and they do so in authentic, human ways with which we can identify."

In chapter 7, David Howard spoke of the wide range of emotions in the psalms and thus the relevance of the psalms for all aspects of our lives. As both David and Don pointed out, this makes the psalms especially helpful in giving structure and guidance to our prayers. So this method uses the Scriptures in a way that lays a foundation for a robust prayer life.

Prayer Is Relationship

By analogy, think for a moment about a marriage relationship. If every time my wife and I went out on a date we sat down at the same place and said exactly the same things the same way, it would get old quickly. What Don had given us is a format, an approach to prayer that could help our prayer lives be more spontaneous and interactive. God leads us through His Word in how to pray, and we talk to Him as we think of specific needs in our lives and the lives of those around us or around the world. Such spontaneity can lead to delight and discovery, just as it does in our other relationships. I still keep a list of the various people, ministries, and needs for which I need to pray systematically each week, but now the Holy Spirit uses the Scriptures to lead me to pray for each in a wide variety of ways, most of which I would never have thought of on my own.

Whitney commented, "Prayer then becomes like a real conversation with a real person. It's not me showing up and saying, 'Lord, I've got my list again, so please be patient,' as if the Lord is there with His arms folded, tapping His fingers, 'OK, hurry up. Let's go through the list again; I've got a universe to run you know.' When we pray through a passage of Scripture, it's like a real conversation with a real person because the Bible is God speaking to us. We let God initiate the conversation through His Word. You can do this whether you have four minutes or four hours. Anyone can do it."

Staying Out of Religious Ruts?

I asked Don if this method could also become an empty religious ritual.

He answered, "Any method could if our hearts are not right or if we are not giving real attention to what we are doing. However, after twenty-five years it hasn't done so for me. Think about it. You have 150 psalms. I rarely get through an entire psalm, unless it's very brief. So I am always in fresh territory. The key is making sure I have enough emotional space to give focused attention to the Word."

I continued, "We have talked a good deal about the psalms. What other parts of Scripture are especially conducive for this approach to prayer?"

Whitney responded, "When I teach on this approach, I say the next best place to do this is the New Testament letters, although almost any part of Scripture can work. However, the New Testament letters work well since many people are familiar with the prayers of Paul in those letters, but I argue we should pray the whole letter. In nearly all the New Testament letters, virtually every verse is packed with truth. Almost every verse suggests something to pray about. I'm going to preach on Romans 8:31 in chapel in a few minutes. 'If God is for us, who is against us?' In praying that verse, you can delight yourself in the idea that God is for you. 'Lord, I praise You that You are for me!' He's shown that in the cross of Christ, for instance. The verse continues, 'Then who can be against us?' Whether it's the world or the flesh, the devil, your boss, a neighbor . . . who are they? You could pray, 'Lord, these enemies of mine are no match for You! And Lord, I want to pray for my persecuted brothers and sisters in . . .' You get the idea. How many hundreds of chapters do we have in the Bible? It's inexhaustible. That's why using Scripture to shape our prayers doesn't become routine."

I added, "So if you approach the Scripture with a heart that is open to the Lord, open to growth, longing for the Lord in relationship with Him, this gives you a tremendous reservoir of ideas and challenges and thoughts that then feed your talk with God."

Whitney continued, "I find it goes both ways. Because of the Holy Spirit, we do have this Godward orientation, so we are looking for something in God's Word that will respond to the deep calls of our heart. Scripture does that. But some days my heart is cold. I get up to pray, and I don't feel like it. I'm sleepy! Nevertheless, God said to Jeremiah, 'Is not my word like a hammer and a fire?' (see Jer. 23:29). I can plunge the fire of God's Word into my heart, and in a couple of minutes, I usually do feel like praying. As the Word talks about God being my Shepherd,

I begin to feel Him being my Shepherd. I begin to respond with all of my heart, soul, mind, and strength. When I come with a hungry heart, I find that the Word feeds that hunger. When I come with a cold heart, I find that the Word of God ignites my heart again."

Conclusion: A Final Word of Encouragement

It was about time for us to wrap up our conversation. Within the hour Don would be speaking to several hundred students, faculty, and staff in our chapel. His words had been encouraging and practical, yet I knew that most of us need lots of encouragement in these spiritual disciplines! So I ended our interview with the question, "Don, if you could speak to those people out there who are struggling to engage God in prayer and in the Word, what would be your word of encouragement to them?"

Whitney concluded, "I would give this word of encouragement: Being consistent in God's Word and prayer is doable. You may have had decades of sporadic time in God's Word and decades of boredom in prayer, and the hardest thing for me to do right now is to convince you that this is doable. But not only is it doable; it is enjoyable because God Himself is our real source of joy. Believe that. If you will try this method for a month to six weeks, you will find yourself hungering for more time with God."

"Don Whitney, thank you for being with us today. I think your insights will be helpful for people."

Don shook my hand, smiled, and said, "I enjoyed it, and I pray God will make it so."

We made our way to the chapel for a time of worship with the rest of the campus. As we walked down the hall, I found myself looking forward to a time when I could get alone and put the things we had discussed into practice.

Summary & Application

Summation

- Sometimes our struggle with spiritual disciplines like reading the Bible has to do with our methodology. Meditation is the key to delighting in Scripture and being changed by it.
- Meditation means to think deeply about the Scripture, and we can meditate on a passage by asking questions about the passage or thinking through the passage one word at a time.
- We also need to read constantly through Scripture's grand story, so that we understand the context of the passages we are reading.
- We can use meditation on Scripture as a foundation for an exciting prayer life. Use the words of a passage to voice specific requests to God for the various needs in your life and the needs in the lives of those for whom you wish to pray.
- Praying the Scriptures becomes relational as we speak to God and He speaks to us through His Word.

Conversation

1. What are the various ways you are involved currently in reading God's Word and prayer? Has there been a time in the past that you were consistent in these spiritual practices? If so, what helped you be consistent at that time?

2. How do you respond to the idea that the key to enjoying Scripture is to meditate on it? Why do many Christians feel pressure to rush through a reading for the day rather than meditating deeply on the Bible?

3. What would have to change in your life for you to make more room for a consistent, daily time for meditating on God's Word? What would be the benefits of those changes?

4. Read through Psalm 23, using the words of the psalm to praise and thank God for specific things in your life and to ask God for help with specific needs in your life or the lives of your family members.

Transformation

If you have not already done so, take a moment to explore the Bible reading plans in the back of this book. Consider reading through the Bible in the next year. As you read each day, take a few minutes to meditate more deeply on one or two verses that stick out to you, using those verses to lead you in prayer.

CHAPTER 14

Reading the Bible in Times of Sorrow and Suffering

A Conversation with Michael Card

Casting all your care on Him, because He cares about you.

—1 Peter 5:7

 "We live in a death-impregnated world." Not a happy thought but true. Dr. William Lane, who spoke those words, experienced that truth first-hand over a decade ago, dying in the painful grasp of multiple myeloma, an especially vicious form of cancer. Through Bill's life, but ultimately through his death, Michael Card and I became close friends.

While at Western Kentucky University Mike was studying wildlife management when God intercepted him through a bushy-haired religion professor with a booming voice. A Harvard-trained Ph.D., Bill's knowledge and interpretation of the New Testament grabbed Mike by the imagination and never let go. One day Bill, knowing that Mike had a gift for music, suggested that Card put a passage of Scripture to music and, as they say, the rest is history. Mike would go on to write some of the best-known Christian songs of the past thirty years, selling more than four million albums and writing nineteen number one hits. Mike's music combines excellence of musicality with deep, authentic reflection on the Scriptures. Unlike much of what floats from contemporary Christian airwaves, his songs might be tagged "Scripture infused" and "theologically robust." At heart Mike is a Bible teacher, and that passion comes through in his music. Beyond the music that orientation to Scripture has expressed itself in numerous books, articles, community Bible studies, radio programs, and speaking engagements around the world; this all started with Bill, who "walked with" Mike for twenty-five years.

Although we never lived in the same place, Bill Lane also mentored me for almost a decade. During the final phase of writing my dissertation on the book of Hebrews, I contacted Bill. Soon he would be publishing a massive two-volume commentary on Hebrews, and I wanted to interact with him on the book's structure. The winsome scholar opened his life to me, taking my ideas seriously, and he eventually presented my work to the world in the introduction to his highly acclaimed commentary. Until his death, Bill and I had a meal together at the annual national meeting of the Society of Biblical Literature and talked on the telephone from time to time. Like Mike, my life has been marked by Bill Lane.

It was not until Bill had died that Mike and I became friends. Our mutual relationship with Bill gave us a connection, a foundation for a special kind of community, and our friendship has become important to me, offering me prayer support, encouragement, stimulating conversation, a wider circle of friends, and camaraderie. Branching off from the path of death, run paths of life. Not only are sorrow and suffering woven into the fabric of our faith, these threads add beautiful hues and tones. To shouts of praise must be added lament. Lament takes us back to God in our suffering.

Over the past few years, my friend Mike Card has been studying the laments in Scripture, so I invited him to join me for a chat about reading the Bible in times of sorrow and suffering. We met late in the spring of 2009 at Mole End studio, nestled in the beautiful hills near Franklin, Tennessee. We settled back in a couple of comfortable chairs and started our talk.

What Is Lament?

"So, Mike, how would you define *lament*?"

Mike, dressed in his normal outfit of jeans and comfortable shirt, could pass for the wildlife management agent he almost became. He answered, "Lament is a form of prayer or even worship. We could define it as 'a difficult conversation we have with God,' a conversation that has to do with disappointment, suffering, anger, and even bitterness. We might normally think we wouldn't share such negative emotions with God, but the Bible is full of people like David, Asaph, Job, Habakkuk, and Jeremiah, who in essence cry out to God, 'When I needed You the most, that's when You were farthest from helping me. What's going on?' So lament is modeled for us in the Bible."

I added, "In modern church life we place a lot of emphasis on praise, as we should, but lament seems to add a voice to the dark side of our experiences, experiences that might push us away from God."

Mike responded, "It allows us to stay connected to God at a time when we might be tempted to become disconnected. On the cross Jesus laments, 'Why have You forsaken Me?' He felt abandoned. That's probably the most significant lament in the Bible. If Jesus could lament, why can't we?"

As I thought about Mike's description of what lament is, and especially about its relational nature, it reminded me of the honesty required in relationships. I mentioned this to Mike. "If you're going to have a healthy relationship with your wife, for instance, you have to be willing to be honest about all aspects of the relationship."

Card interjected, "Especially the hard aspects."

I added, "How you navigate the difficulties in a relationship is the key to long-term health in the relationship."

"And can't we understand that God wants that kind of relationship with us?" Mike continued. "Why do we think God wants us only on our good days? He's paid a price to live in relationship with us on our worst days; in the worst moments of your life God loves you so much He wants to be there."

Perspective in a Dark World

We had a well-known scholar, Calvin Seerveld, come and speak at Union a few months before my interview with Mike, and Mike came down to see him because Calvin is a friend of his and has taught Mike a lot about reading the Bible in fresh ways. I mentioned that "one of the things Seerveld said that struck me was that the laments help us to worship in moments of powerlessness. We see overwhelming evil in the world that we as human beings have no hope of eradicating. Calvin said the laments give voice to trust in God in the face of such overwhelming evil."

Mike responded, "The laments lead us to fresh perspective on God and the world. We remember that this is God's world, and God will hold evil accountable, maybe not on the timetable we would want, but that accountability will come. So we see evil and the power of evil in a different light. We sing to God about our sorrow over evil and cry out to God for justice.

"But we also see that God uses our suffering in ways that we would not have imagined. Job, for instance, has to have his perspective adjusted about who God is and who he (Job) is. He voices his rights, and he clings to his expectations about the treatment he should receive from God, as if Job is the center of the universe. Then God shows up, and God doesn't answer a single one of Job's questions, making clear that God Himself is the center of the universe; so He gives Job this tremendous dose of perspective."

To this I said, "Isn't one of the cool things about the laments what we might call 'the Job principle.' Job, through horrible suffering, after crying out honestly to God, didn't end up with answers to all his philosophical and theological questions; he ended up with a deeper relationship with God."

Mike responded, "God graciously shows up, not in spite of our honesty but in the midst of it. Job kept crying out for answers: 'God, why is all this happening to me! How could you let a righteous person suffer like this!' So he complains to God, and he cries out for God to answer. But God never does give him answers. But in the end He gives Job more of Himself. Job gets a closer walk with God. Sometimes I feel like God graciously puts up with the complaining part of our laments and says, 'When you're finished, we can reconnect.'"

I interjected, "So lament leads us through a process to God Himself."

Mike added, "Lament teaches us that we have to go through the process of dealing with our suffering before God. You don't just stuff your feelings down and put a good face on it, like a lot of us tend to do. You need to go through the process of pouring your heart out to God. And if you don't have the language for it, the Bible will give you the language; many of the psalms are laments. There are community laments and individual laments. There are laments for times when we have sinned (contrition laments) and laments for times when our suffering seems 'innocent.'"

An Unwelcomed Moment of Opportunity

As I mentioned at the beginning of this chapter, Mike lost his dearest mentor when Bill Lane died, but he has had several losses in the past few years. I said to him, "You and I have a friend, Denny, who went to be with the Lord not too long ago. You and Denny were close; he was your pastor for a number of years. How did the laments of the Scripture help you work through your grief and lead you in worship during that time after his death?"

"The day Denny died was an interesting day," Mike responded, "because my mother died that same day, and they were buried on the same day. It was right at the tail end of three or four years of dealing with laments and having lament services at some of my concerts.

"I think laments give you, what I call 'disturbing clarity.' After Denny's death and my mother's death, I spent a time weeping, and since then, I've picked up the phone to call Denny and realized he's not there to call anymore. I think there's an ongoing aspect to lamenting and mourning the death of someone. But this disturbing clarity business—I think you see things more clearly through the laments. You see this in David's life when Bathsheba's baby dies. David is on the floor face-down, fasting, and all the servants are afraid to tell him that the baby has died. But when he finds out, he washes his face, goes to the temple, and says that verse you hear at every infant funeral, 'I'll go to him, but he won't come to me.' Everyone is sort of amazed at the change. The baby died, and now David is responding in an unexpected way. I think he was writing Psalm 51 while he was lamenting the death of that little baby, and that psalm of lament shows astounding clarity."

I added, "Wouldn't we say that for all of us it is those most difficult experiences of life that really take us to greater depths and clarity in our relationship with God?"

Mike responded, "Yeah. Our times of suffering seem to be what God uses the most."

I continued, "That's one reason this topic we're talking about—how we read the Bible in times of sorrow and suffering—is so important. Everyone goes there, and from a biblical perspective suffering constitutes a moment of opportunity."

Mike continued with an illustration from the life of Jesus. "Think about this. In Jesus' life, the moment Jesus is most being used by God—what is He doing? He's lamenting on the cross. 'Why have You forsaken Me?' The question I ask people is, 'Could it be that the point where we are being most used by God is *not* when we're writing commentaries or producing records or doing the things we think of as being productive? Could it be that the moments in our lives when we experience the most intense suffering and the most intense struggles are when God is using us the most?'"

A Missing Element in Modern Worship

God turns our suffering inside out. How we spiritually process our sufferings plays an important role in our growth in following Christ. And yet, as I think about the laments of the Bible, which are there to help us come to God in the midst of our sufferings, they seem to play virtually no role in modern worship. I had mentioned this to David Howard in our conversation about the psalms, and I now mentioned this to Mike.

He responded, "They play hardly any role at all. We don't make a place in our church worship times for people who are suffering and are honest about their struggles with their suffering."

I continued, "I tell my students I don't remember coming to church recently and hearing someone begin a praise chorus or hymn that says (singing), 'Oh God, I hate my life today! Things really stink!'" Mike laughed, and I asked, "What do you think has contributed to the church's neglect of this significant aspect of Scripture?"

"We don't think biblically," Mike replied. "We allow ourselves to be shaped by this culture—this 'I'm OK, you're OK' culture. We may be struggling deeply, but we don't feel the freedom to be honest about it. The laments involve brutal honesty, and that kind of honesty is what we're encouraged to embrace. That is why, at churches or in concerts around the country, we've done lament services where we use a word picture of *temple* or *tabernacle*. We build a 'house of prayer' by reading or singing laments with the understanding that this is a safe place where a person can go in and have honest conversations with God and offer up all kinds of suffering in worship."

I didn't completely understand. "Explain what you mean by that. You said you build a house—"

Mike explained, "Figuratively. With songs and prayer in a worship service context. We start out laying the foundation by reading laments from the Scriptures; then we sing songs on the themes we have read, building up the walls of the house of prayer. I think prayer and worship create a sacred space for people, a place where they can really connect with and be honest with God. You have to lead people there. You have to say it's OK to cry. Tears are good."

I interjected, "And you're not trying to be emotionally manipulative?"

"No," Mike replied. "The thing is, you don't have to be. If you lay that basic biblical foundation, when you show Job or David or Jeremiah lamenting, and then you come together corporately, people naturally open their hearts to God, in their pain, their sorrow over their sin, or other personal expressions of sadness."

The Relevance of the Laments for Real Life

I added, "I can think of many ways a worship time that included laments would be relevant to people I know in my church; it would give them a voice for their struggles. In the psalms there are laments of contrition, expressing sadness over sin. There are laments of betrayal, which would be relevant for someone whose spouse had left. There are also laments that deal with sickness, for example, and we have people in our church struggling with cancer."

Mike reflected, "There's a whole category in the psalms called 'disease laments.' We don't know what it was, but apparently David had a life-threatening illness at one point. In certain psalms David describes what seems to be a disease he had that almost killed him. The interesting thing to me, George, is whenever he talks about this disease, what really bothers him the most isn't the disease, although it's horrible. His tongue sticks to the roof of his mouth, and his bones are on fire, and that sort of thing. What really causes him to suffer is a group of people like Job's friends who are standing around him and saying, 'You're just getting what you deserve!' How many people in our churches have had that kind of experience? My sister lost two babies, in two separate pregnancies, in thirteen months. Someone in her church actually came up and said, 'You must have done something wrong, or God wouldn't have done that to you.' That was in some ways a more intense part of her suffering than losing the babies."

I responded, "Poor theology leads to poor treatment of people. One way we could walk with people who are going through an illness would be to have worship times that minister to them.

From a James 5 perspective, we should at times gather around them, lay hands on them, and pray over them. We need to ask God for healing."

"And He does choose to heal sometimes," Mike added.

I continued, "But we also could include times of lament in our worship services."

Mike commented, "That could give people an opportunity to lift up their cancer to God as an act of worship. David said, 'The sacrifice pleasing to God is a broken spirit' (Ps. 51:17). Of course David was lamenting his sin at that point, but the principle is the same. In worship a person with an illness might say to God, 'See, Lord, all I've got to give at this point is my confusion over this cancer.' Maybe that thing that's hurting me the most could be the most precious thing I have to offer to the Lord."

I remembered a serious fall I had from a ladder in 2006. Broken foot. Internal injuries. Damage to my right lung. My wife asked the doctor if I could die. He said, "Sure." I was so worn out emotionally and physically from the situation that I really didn't have anything to give God except my condition. So I turned to God in the middle of the night when I would wake up in pain and say, "Lord, I don't have anything else I can do here. I can hardly pray. This is Your moment. This is something I give to You to use the way that You will." I mentioned this to Mike.

He reflected, "In a sense, isn't that what Jesus does on the cross? He offers up His suffering, the thing that hurts Him most, as an act of worship. God uses suffering to save the world. And once again the fact that God enters into our suffering and uses it is the best reason for worshipping Him that I can think of."

I added, "And through worship we regain perspective on our situations."

"That's the wonderful thing about the laments; we are not left to wallow in our suffering. They turn our hearts to God. What almost all of the laments do is begin with deep struggle and conclude with renewed perspective. So if our worship services included times of lament, they could lead us to new depths in our worship and a way forward in our suffering."

An Example from Lamentations

I wanted us to look to an example of that pattern—honest struggle before God, which leads us to renewed perspective—in a particular lament in Scripture. We chose Lamentations 3. As Mike and I work through this passage, I want to invite you as the reader to think about your own life and experiences. Maybe you can identify with this lament. I asked Mike to set the scene for us.

He explained, "This lament comes from Jeremiah, and Jeremiah has witnessed God use an invading army to destroy Jerusalem and the temple. God's judgment was devastating, and Jeremiah was right in the middle of it. He was the only prophet to be destroyed by what he prophesied. So he's called the 'weeping prophet.' He was a person for whom tears were pretty close to the surface."

Mike continued, "With chapter 3, Lamentations becomes personal. Up to this point, it's all been 'us' and 'we,' the people of Israel who have suffered. But now in chapter 3 Jeremiah shifts and says 'I.'

> I am the man who has seen affliction, by the
>   rod of his wrath.
> He has driven me away and made me walk in
>   darkness rather than light;
> indeed, he has turned his hand against me
>   again and again, all day long.
> He has made my skin and my flesh grow old and
>   has broken my bones. (Lam. 3:1–4 NIV)

"Wow," I commented. "Aren't there times when we feel physically and emotionally depleted like that? We feel emotionally like our bones have been broken. We feel crushed because of our experiences, and we feel like God's hand is against us."

Mike continued, "'He has besieged me and surrounded me with bitterness and hardship'" (v. 5 NIV). "See?" Card said. "He feels like God has become his enemy. God is laying siege against Jeremiah."

In the ancient world an invading army would lay siege to a city, circling and closing in the inhabitants so there was no escape. Jeremiah here uses that word picture.

I commented, "And what he's doing is expressing his emotions. He feels trapped!"

Mike replied, "Jewish tradition says Jeremiah wrote this in a cave overlooking Jerusalem, and he was watching the temple be destroyed. That's a hard thing—for a righteous Jew to see God's house destroyed. Then he writes . . .

> He has made me dwell in darkness like those
>   long dead.
> He has walled me in so I cannot escape; he has
>   weighed me down with chains.
> Even when I call out or cry for help, he shuts out
>   my prayer.
> He has barred my way with blocks of stone; he
>   has made my paths crooked.
> Like a bear lying in wait, like a lion in hiding,
> he dragged me from the path and mangled me
>   and left me without help.
> He drew his bow and made me the target for his
>   arrows. (Lam. 3:6–12 NIV)

"Think of the imagery in this passage!" I exclaimed. "He feels like God has walled him in and shut out his prayers. He feels like God is a wild animal that has dragged him off the path of life, mangled him, and left him torn apart! He feels like the bull's-eye in God's target practice! These words are excruciating and brutally honest!"

Mike responded, "It is amazingly graphic language. Some people would be surprised to find this is in the Bible. Remember, he is saying all this to God! 'God, *You* have treated me this way—your prophet! Remember me? Why is this happening to me?'"

Mike continued reading,

> He pierced my heart with arrows from his
>   quiver.
> I became the laughingstock of all my people;
>   they mock me in song all day long.
> He has filled me with bitter herbs and sated me
>   with gall.
> He has broken my teeth with gravel; he has
>   trampled me in the dust.
> I have been deprived of peace; I have forgotten
>   what prosperity is.
> So I say, "My splendor is gone and all that I had
>   hoped from the LORD."
> I remember my affliction and my wandering,
>   the bitterness and the gall.
> I well remember them, and my soul is downcast
>   within me. (Lam. 3:13–20 NIV)

Mike responded, "There's a great passage with which people can connect. How many of us have felt like our heart was punctured? How many of us have been laughed at and felt like we had been stomped in the dust? Jeremiah says that all he had hoped for from the Lord is gone. He is in despair."

I commented, "So he feels hopeless. He doesn't feel like he has a future. He really is struggling with depression. But he doesn't stay there, does he?"

A Turning in Lament

Mike replied, "No! It's important to see that right at the moment he mentions depression ('my soul is downcast within me'), that's when the lament turns a corner. Verse 21: 'Yet this I call to mind . . .' 'Yet.' There is the contrast between where Jeremiah has been emotionally in the first twenty verses of the chapter and a new perspective that is dawning on him. 'This I call to mind.' A lot of times in lament literature, the act of remembering has redemptive value; it is a way out. Look at what follows:

> Yet this I call to mind, and therefore I have
>   hope:
> Because of the LORD's great love we are not con-
>   sumed, for his compassions never fail. They
>   are new every morning; great is your faithful-
>   ness. (vv. 21–23 NIV)

"Now is this the same guy? The guy who wrote the first twenty verses of Lamentations 3? What's happened? He's gotten a new perspective because he has remembered something."

I interjected, "Because he has remembered God. He reconsiders God Himself and God's character—what is true about God."

Mike continued, "And now he is not just looking at his situation, his experiences. That is what the laments are designed to do. They bring us to God through the door of brutally honest prayer. We lay before God how bad things have gotten in life. But then the laments realign our perspective to a focus on God Himself. Here Jeremiah's perspective gets realigned, and it turns on the Hebrew word *ḥesed*, which refers to God's covenant love or 'great love' as it is translated here."

I asked, "Explain what you mean by that and how our understanding of God's love might affect the way we approach reading the Bible in our times of sorrow and suffering."

Mike thought for a moment and then gestured with his hands as he said, "The Hebrew word *ḥesed* is translated fourteen different ways in the King James Version, so it is a complex word. It occurs 250 times in the Old Testament. The NIV usually translates it as 'loving-kindness.' I've got an even longer translation: *ḥesed* is when the person from whom I have a right to expect nothing gives me everything. 'Because of the Lord's *great love* we are not consumed.' God is essentially understood to be a God of unexpected and elaborate mercy. If you grasp that truth, if you understand that He really loves you, it will adjust your perspective even in the midst of horrible circumstances."

I commented, "In a different way it addresses the other side of the suffering question Job deals with. The bad theology that

Job addresses says, 'Bad things happen to bad people.' The theology of God's grace addresses the bad theology that says, 'Good things only happen to good people.' This understanding of God's great love, His grace, says, 'Good things, by God's mercy, happen to bad people,' people who deserve judgment."

Mike continued, "To me, the older I get, grace gets more and more amazing because I have no right to expect anything from Him. God's character, the fact that He has revealed Himself as a God of *hesed*, gives us the freedom to come to Him in our suffering. His character gives us a basis for entering into lament in worship. This is not *just* grumbling."

I added, "Like the wanderers in the wilderness."

"Like the wanderers in the wilderness," he echoed. "It is a bringing of our complaints to God on the basis of His faithfulness!"

I interjected, "So lament is grounded in God's covenant love, His faithfulness."

Mike continued, "Yeah. It is coming to God and saying, 'When I needed You the most, that's when You seemed farthest away from helping me. Now I know You are a faithful God! What are we going to do about this?' And it involves coming around, through worship, to a place where we see the faithfulness of God more clearly."

Conclusion: Life Beyond the Wall of Suffering

As we wrapped up our conversation, I asked Mike what he would like to say to those who might hear or read our interview, who are suffering and need to discover the grace of the Bible's laments.

Mike responded, "I would point to that image that we just read in Lamentations 3, which is not an image that has ever really commended itself to me much—that image of being walled in. My prayer for those of you who feel walled in is this: that you would turn and look in a fresh way at this lament literature and that you would realize that Someone is waiting beyond the wall. Someone is ready to break down the wall or climb over the wall.

The fact that you are looking at a wall right now doesn't mean that this is a dead end. There is life beyond the wall because the God of *ḥesed* is on the other side of that wall. The laments are a way out or over, a way back to your connection with God. Ultimately that is what I hope. I hope those of you who have interacted with this material will say with Job, 'My ears have heard of You, but now my eyes see You.' That would be a good thing."

As I thanked Mike for his time, it dawned on me that Michael and I have these kinds of conversations all the time, putting our heads together about what is going on in Scripture. We both love talking about the Bible, talking about how it adjusts our lives, our perspectives. In part we learned that love from our friend Bill Lane. As we left the studio, we walked out into this "death-impregnated world" of which Bill spoke, a world of suffering in which laments are not only appropriate but welcomed by our God of *ḥesed*.

Summary & Application

Summation

- Lament may be defined as "a difficult conversation we have with God," a conversation having to do with our disappointment, suffering, anger, and even bitterness.
- The laments of the Bible lead us to fresh perspective on God and the world: our faithful God will judge evil, and He uses our suffering for good.
- We need to rediscover lament in modern worship; it is biblical and forms an important aspect of relationship with God.
- Laments of the Bible lead us back to God in our sorrow and suffering. Almost all of the laments come to a turning point in which the person lamenting begins to praise God.

Conversation

1. What is a difficult experience you have had in your life? How did that experience affect you, both positively and negatively?
2. How did you process that experience in your relationship with God?
3. What part of this chapter surprised you the most?
4. Why do you think the church has lost lament as an aspect of its worship? How might your church use lament in worship?
5. What is the difference between lament and grumbling against God?
6. In what ways is lament in the Bible grounded in God's faithfulness?

Transformation

Either alone or with a few close friends, read a lament from the book of Psalms (e.g., Ps. 38; 42; 43; 55; 69; or 73). Use the lament to pray to God, expressing your heartache over your suffering, the suffering of someone close to you, or the suffering caused by profound and pervasive evil in the world. Take time to grieve before the Lord. Then allow the psalm to lead you to praise for God's faithfulness in the midst of suffering.

CHAPTER 15

Reading the Bible with the Family

A Conversation with Pat Guthrie

These words that I am giving you today are to be in your heart.
Repeat them to your children.

—Deuteronomy 6:6–7

 W. E. Channing once wrote, "God be thanked for books! They are the voices of the distant and the dead, and make us heirs of the spiritual life of past ages." That is true of books in general, of course, as they are passed down to us from generations past, but to the Bible must be given pride of place among the high-impact books that fall into our hands from those who have gone before.

Our memorials table sits symbolically in the middle of our home's gathering room. The table has a glass top through which you can see the contents of a large drawer. In the drawer we place reminders, "memorials," of what God has done for us as a family. There rests Grandpa Ruschhaupt's German *Die Bibel* (The Bible). Martin Luther crafted the translation in the early sixteenth century while holed up at Wartburg Castle. As "the King James Version" for German-speaking people, the *Lutherbibel* has had a profound influence on German as a modern language; and our copy, published in 1915, is a cherished heirloom. One of the highlights of Pat's year when she was a little girl was spending a week at the home of her Grandma and Grandpa Ruschhaupt, who were farmers. In the evenings everyone gathered around for supper, enjoying good food and rest from the day's hard work, and they always had devotions before they went to bed. Pat remembers vividly sitting on the couch in that simple, white farmhouse, windows open to allow the breezes of the evening to cool the heat of a south Texas summer. Grandpa, devotional book and Bible in hand, read to the family in English, and Pat always asked Grandpa to read from the German Bible as well. These are some of my wife's earliest and happiest memories.

My Great-Grandaddy Carnahan, involved in both farming and the lumber industry in early twentieth-century Arkansas, was a prominent Baptist layman and played host to Baptist statesmen, like the great George W. Truett, as they passed through his area. I inherited Great-Grandad's King James Version of the Bible. Notes scribbled here and there in its brown and fragile pages, it now sits on a shelf in my study at home.

Our families mold us in a myriad of ways. These copies of the Bible, passed down from generation to generation, serve as tangible reminders of a vitally important part of our heritage and one that we want to pass on to our children; we want our children to take the Bible into their hands and hearts. My wife Pat and I have tried to be proactive in thinking through how we might shape Joshua and Anna's hearts in line with the Scriptures. Too often our efforts must be tagged "fallen and failed"; I especially have not been as consistent as I should have been. Yet we have kept at it, and I thought it might be helpful to let other families in on some of the things we have learned in our seventeen years of parenting.

So on a snowy day in February, when schools were closed because of the inclement weather and the kids were in the front yard, on the other side of the pond, building a snowman, Pat and I sat down for a talk about how families might integrate the Bible into their busy lives. As we drank hot tea by the fire and munched on Pat's chocolate chip scones (for which she is famous among our friends), I said, "Honey, thank you for talking to me today!"

She responded, "Well, I always love to talk to you, George."

Building Your Home on the
Foundation of Scripture

I started the conversation with, "Let's talk first in terms of goals. How would you describe what we wanted to accomplish as we taught our kids the Bible?"

To Love God

Pat answered, "First of all, the Lord really is the most important part of our lives. My heart's desire has always been to pass on a sincere love for God to our children. Biblically, loving God and loving His Word are inseparable. Love for God is expressed in part by obedience to God. We have tried to orient our kids to the Bible from the beginning so they would grow to love the Lord and learn what it means to walk closely with Him."

One of the dynamics we see in Scripture is the pairing of love for God with obedience to God. As Pat said, love is expressed through obedience. For instance, Jesus identified "loving God" as the most important commandment. That command is part of the *Shemah* (Deut. 6:4–7), one of the most foundational passages in Judaism:

> Listen, Israel: The LORD our God, the LORD
> is One. Love the LORD your God with all your
> heart, with all your soul, and with all your
> strength. These words that I am giving you
> today are to be in your heart. Repeat them to
> your children. Talk about them when you sit in
> your house and when you walk along the road,
> when you lie down and when you get up.

Notice how a deep devotion to the words of God follows on the heels of love for God in this passage. To live the words, therefore, is a relationship commitment to God. I interjected, "So interaction with the Bible is oriented to relationship with God."

"Very much relationship oriented," she replied. "Basically, we wanted them to know the Bible because we wanted them to know God."

A Biblical View of the World

As we talked, Joshua and Anna had come in from the cold outside taking a brief break from the winter wonderland, rummaging around in the kitchen for a snack as we talked. I picked up the conversation, pointing to a second reason for teaching our children to "desire the pure milk" of God's Word (see 1 Pet. 2:2). "We also want our children to embrace a biblical view of the world. We want them to see the world with 'biblical eyes,' in other words. At Union, the university where I teach, we talk a lot about helping students grasp a 'biblical worldview.' Such a view of the world has to do with interpreting reality with the Bible as the primary reference point."

Let me make clear that the Bible doesn't directly address every subject in the world. There are no iPods or movie ratings in the Bible, for instance. Yet the Bible *does* provide us with a wealth of wisdom on how life should be approached in the modern world and how we might respond to such issues as technology or entertainment. The Bible provides the framework from which reality can be interpreted or understood. For instance, we can assess the relative value of things, people, or activities by thinking deeply about what God values, and the Bible tells us what God values. C. S. Lewis famously said, "I believe in Christianity as I believe that the sun has risen: not only because I see it, but because by it I see everything else." For us the biblical view of the world makes sense and makes sense of everything else. It gives us a profound point of reference from which to see the world and everything in it.

Pat added, "Everything, all of reality, must be understood with respect to what God's Word says is true. Nothing falls outside the purview of His truth."

I continued, "As an example, one of our presuppositions as we approach life and our relationships with one another in the family is that all of us are sinners. (If you doubt that children are sinners, volunteer to work in a preschool class for a day!) When Anna was three years old and was defiant, stubbornly refusing to be obedient on an issue, we did not say, 'Oh, isn't that cute!'

We disciplined her and taught her to have a soft heart toward her parents."

Pat interjected that we were not just after restraining outward behavior. We were attempting to shape the kids' hearts. "I often used Play-Doh and a rock as an illustration for the children," Pat said. "I would show them the Play-Doh and say, 'This is soft; I can work with it. The rock is hard. It is not nice to work with like the Play-Doh. You need to have a soft heart toward Mommy and Daddy.'"

I thought about other ways this understanding of sin affected us. "When Joshua intentionally hurt his sister in some way, we treated it as sin. He had to go to Anna and say, 'Anna, I was wrong for pushing you out the window. (Pat laughed and added, "He never did that!") Will you forgive me?' At times she would respond, 'No!' initially but then, given time, would give forgiveness."

Pat and I assumed we were sinners too. Our kids need to see the truth of repentance and restoration modeled in us. When I lost my temper and spoke too harshly to the children, we treated it as sin. Many times I have gotten on my knees in front of my children and asked them to forgive me for something I have done wrong. I still have to ask their forgiveness at times.

Accordingly, each of us has learned to name our sin and take responsibility for it, ask for forgiveness from the person offended and from the Lord, and experience restoration in our relationships. That pattern comes from a biblical view of reality and lays an important foundation for our children, preparing them to understand the nature of the gospel of God's grace. People are not basically good and just make innocent mistakes. We are sinners, rebel against God's ways, and hurt those around us. With this understanding, children have a framework from which to understand their struggles with sin and God's exorbitant love and restoration. We wanted Joshua and Anna to read and understand the Bible because we wanted them to interpret reality the way the Bible does.

Principles for Living Life Well

A third reason for giving our children a solid orientation to the Bible has to do with teaching them to live well as they learn to live by God's principles. I asked Pat to give examples of what we mean by living according to God's principles.

Sabbath as an Example

She first mentioned the Sabbath principle. "I think of the Sabbath principle as being a lot of fun."

I added, "We draw the Sabbath principle from many passages, especially in the Old Testament but also in the Gospels. Through those passages we see that God has built rhythm into the universe ('[God] rested on the seventh day,' Gen. 2:2) and has given Sabbath as a gift to us as His people. The principle says we need to have times of rest from work, special celebration, focus on worship, and even ministry to others. The Sabbath is not a law for us; it is a gift and should be received as a gift. We primarily try to block off a time every week (perhaps Saturday morning or all day on Sunday) for serious rest, breaking the cycle of relentless deadlines, the push and shove of modern life. Not only is Sabbath tied to creation in the Bible; it also is related to the Exodus. If you think about it, slaves don't get a day off. Sabbath is an expression of freedom from work, offering emotional, physical, and spiritual renewal. Too many people in modern American culture are in effect slaves who need a break." I asked Pat, "What are some other manifestations of Sabbath in our family?"

Pat answered, "When the children were younger, one of the things we did was have a 'Sunday box.' In the Sunday box were toys, games, books, and puppets that could only be brought out on Sunday. The children really looked forward to coming home from church and getting out the Sunday box.

"We also have been doing what we call 'Sabbath tea' for about fifteen years. Basically Sabbath tea is a special weekly meal for the family. We decorate the table. When Anna was little, she loved to go out and bring in flowers (and she still does this at times!). We use candles and put on beautiful music. For Sabbath tea we have finger foods, like popcorn, scones, apples and caramel, pigs in a blanket, cheese tarts, cheese and crackers; and, of course, each person has his or her own little pot of tea."

I pointed out, "It is a time of celebration and fun, and we often talk about what we have been learning from the Bible, or theological issues, or some issue that has come up in a book or a sermon. Sometimes the discussions have been planned, but they often have been spontaneous. And the timing of the meal has varied through the years."

Pat added, "Depending on our schedule at church, we at times have had Sabbath tea on Sunday evenings, but since our small groups have often met on Sunday nights, Sabbath tea gets shifted to Saturday night at times."

The kids love Sabbath tea. I remember occasions when our schedule has been disrupted in some way, and we have said, "Do you want to go out to eat tonight?" And the kids have always responded, "We can't do that! It's Sabbath tea night!" The rhythm is well established in our family and does much to build a rhythm into the go and flow of our lives. It has not always been easy. We get overscheduled sometimes and do not take a block of time to rest as we should. But generally our commitment to the Sabbath principle has been a great gift, a source of renewal and rhythm in our busy lives.

Focused on the Needs of Others

Another example of how we have tried to incorporate biblical principles into the life and mind-set of our family has to do with caring for the poor. The Bible is clear that God cares about how we respond to the needs of the poor and most vulnerable in the world. In addition to giving to the ministries of our church (which is committed to caring for the poor in our immediate area), we have, for example, participated in Samaritan's Purse's Operation Christmas Child, which sends millions of gift-laden shoe boxes to needy children around the world each Christmas. Pat mentioned, "And we always took pictures of the kids with their boxes; so we saw our kids grow up in those pictures and grow in their joy over participating in that ministry. It was so much fun for them to fill their boxes with things they had picked out. I have also encouraged Joshua and Anna to write notes to put in their shoe boxes along with a picture of themselves. We have actually had two of the children write us back! That was exciting!"

Through the years we have sponsored several children through the ministry of World Vision. At times we have encouraged the kids to pick out a special gift from the World Vision Christmas catalog that they would purchase with their own money and give to a needy family overseas. Joshua and Anna have given chickens, goats, and medical supplies. The main point, however, is that through the Scriptures they have embraced the value that God places on caring for the poor.

About four years ago Joshua mentioned to me that he would love to give one of the really big items in the World Vision Christmas catalog, pointing especially to a water well, which cost $10,000. "But Dad, I will never be able to save up that much money," he lamented. I encouraged him to pray about rallying other teenagers to give to such a project. In spring 2008 this burden on Joshua's heart again came bubbling to the surface, and we decided to invite the family of Jeff Palmer, the president of Baptist Global Response, for a meal. Jeff and I had attended Union University together in the late 1970s, and he has been extensively involved in relief and development projects around the world. Jeff encouraged Joshua and provided him with specific examples of needs across the globe. Not long after that meal, Joshua read the book *Do Hard Things* by Alex and Brett Harris. It challenged him to put his ideas into action. He and I started to plan. We contacted the IRS, developed a Web site, and started dreaming about fund-raising. Joshua's nonprofit, Dollar for a Drink (www.dollarforadrink.org), was born. In March 2009 Dollar for a Drink's first well was built in Darfur, Sudan, and services about six thousand people, many of whom previously had to walk four to six hours one way to get water. Just last week Joshua handed over a check that will pay for three more wells in Sudan in the coming year.

By God's grace our children are aware of the poor in the world and feel compelled to address poverty with the use of their personal resources. Such an orientation does not happen by accident. I confess that I have often been a poor model for my children with regard to caring for the needs of those around me. Yet the Bible, which reflects God's heart for the poor, keeps drawing us to that value, and we continue to learn how to respond.

Practical Practices for Teaching Your Children the Bible

Next I wanted us to talk about practical ways families can expose their children to the Bible. You may be a parent who is thinking, *OK, give me some practical help here. What can I do to get my kids into the Bible?* Well, there are no guarantees and no perfect plans, but perhaps what follows will help.

Approaches to Bible Reading and Listening

First, *you need patterns of Bible reading and/or listening in your family.* Families we know approach family devotions in various ways. I mentioned to Pat, "I think of our friends the Salazars, who have a time of Bible reading and discussion every day at a set time." I sent Mike, the dad, an e-mail, asking for specifics. Mike, who teaches chemistry at our university, explained:

> We do fairly simple things. We start early, usually between 6:00 and 6:30 depending on the day. We open with prayer and review memory work. The smaller ones are memorizing the books of the Bible, and the older ones are memorizing Scripture. We review what has already been memorized and then move on to learning more books and another verse or two. All that usually takes fifteen minutes. After memory work we read together. I have the kids alternate and read aloud. We usually read several chapters, but that depends on the book. We stop and

discuss, and the kids are free to interrupt to ask
a question or make a point. All this usually takes
between thirty and forty-five minutes.

Some families, like the Salazars, have a devotional time in
the morning; others, after supper or at bedtime.

In addition to devotional reading of the Bible, our friends
the Van Nestes have begun singing the psalms at supper time.
Ray also has a wonderful blog on which he reviews children's
literature and Bible resources (http://www.childrenshourbooks.
blogspot.com/). Similarly, Sarah Clarkson has recently published
Read for the Heart: Whole Books for WholeHearted Families (Apologia
Press, 2009), a rich repository for teaching your children to love
books and for teaching them to think biblically as they read
books (her blog is http://www.storyformed.com/). By the way, if
you want your kids to read the Bible, you need to lay a foundation
by teaching them to love reading good books.

Other friends of ours use a devotional guide like *Our Daily
Bread* or *My Utmost for His Highest.* Still others use some form of
catechism, systematic teaching through the theology found in
the Bible. My friend Bruce Ware has a wonderful book titled,
*Big Truths for Young Hearts: Teaching and Learning the Greatness of
God.* This book is designed to help parents begin to train their
children in basic theology.

Pat said, "When our kids were younger, we had reading
times from their story Bibles each night as they went to bed."
Story Bibles like *The Big Picture Story Bible* (Crossway, 2004) by
David Helm and Gail Schoonmaker or *The Jesus Storybook Bible*
(ZonderKids, 2007) by Sally Lloyd-Jones can be wonderful for
bedtime (or anytime!) reading.

I added, "Through the years we have tended to emphasize
individual 'quiet times' in the Word, setting aside time for each
member of the family to read in their Bible."

"As Joshua and Anna got older," Pat said, "We gave them
reading plans or basic Bible studies to do, so we were training
them along the way. George, I appreciate your emphasis on reading through the Bible; I think you have led us well in that way.

The first time I ever read through the Bible all the way was in college, and up to that point, it was a foreign concept to me."

This year we all are reading through the Bible chronologically (using the "Chronological Reading Plan" in the back of this book), and each member of the family is using the *Reader's Guide to the Bible* that I wrote. The *Reader's Guide*, as the name suggests, guides a person in reading the Bible day by day. It works in conjunction with the one-year chronological plan. For instance, the guide on day 1 of week 1 reads like this:

Day 1—Genesis 1–2

Notice how day 1 of creation relates to day 4, day 2 to day 5, and day 3 to day 6. Days 1, 2, and 3 tell of God's creation of "settings" to be inhabited, and days 4, 5, and 6 the "characters" that inhabit those settings. God builds both beauty and order into his creation. According to Gen. 2:2–3 God "rested" on the seventh day, blessed that day, and declared it holy. In declaring one day of the week special, he built an order and rhythm into the weekly routine of people that goes all the way back to the creation. Describe the order and "rhythm of rest" in your weekly patterns.

As we read through the Bible as a family, we talk about what we are reading. It has been natural for us to have open discussions about people, places, events, themes, and theological issues that pop up in the Bible. My children constantly ask questions, and virtually every week (and sometimes every day) Pat and I discuss various passages we are reading.

Pat said, "It is comfortable and natural for us to talk about the Bible when we 'sit in our house, or walk along the way, when we lie down, and when we rise up' to paraphrase Deuteronomy 6. That is what we do as a family."

As a dad and husband, this keeps me on my toes. I do not have all the answers, but I know good tools that can help me. If you are a parent, you need to have on hand some of the tools we have discussed in this book, beginning with a good study Bible and a Bible dictionary.

One of my favorite things we did when the children were small involved another bedtime practice. Once the lights were out and they were drifting off to sleep, the kids always listened either to "Jesus" music or Bible stories on tape (this was in the days of cassette tapes!).

I asked Pat to explain.

She said, "During the day we listened to all kinds of fun music, and they would watch shows like Barney or the Canadian show, *Mr. Dress-up*, which a friend from Canada videotaped for us. But when the kids were going to sleep, we wanted them to be thinking about the Lord and about Scripture. They might listen to music, like Michael Card's *Sleep Sound in Jesus*, but we also had wonderful dramatizations of Scripture on tape. One of these was called 'Bible Comes Alive' from *Your Story Hour* (http://www.yourstoryhour.org), and the other was from *The World's Greatest Stories* (http://www.worldsgreateststories.com/). Joshua and Anna learned a lot of Bible stories in this way, and they loved listening at night as they went to sleep."

I added, "I remember taking the children to a VeggieTales movie when Anna was about five or six. I think the movie was telling the story of the battle of Jericho in a VeggieTales sort of way, and the defenders were throwing slushies off the wall. At one point in the movie, Anna turned to me and whispered, 'Dad! That's not in the Bible!' She knew the real story very well." Pat laughed at the memory.

Then my wife said, "As Joshua and Anna have gotten older, they have continued to enjoy listening to biblically saturated music."

I commented, "For instance, both of the kids love the music of artists like my friend Michael Card. Mike's music reflects deeply on the Bible, its truths, and its stories. They still love Mike's music because, since it is grounded in Scripture, it has depth."

One of Mike's albums is on the book of Revelation. Once, when Joshua was about eight years old, he was walking around the house singing, "Fallen, fallen, fallen is Babylon; fallen is the city of doom!" Much of Scripture is etched on our children's brains through the medium of music.

Helping Them Get the Big-Picture Story

Second, not only do you need to have your family read and listen to the Bible, *you need ways to help your children enter the big-picture story of Scripture.* Whereas listening to Bible stories and music helps them learn the parts of Scripture, we also need to give the kids (and ourselves!) the big picture of Scripture.

Pat mentioned a couple of practices, in addition to reading through the Bible systematically, that have helped us in this regard.

"One of my favorite things has been doing an Easter tree during the weeks leading up to the celebration of Easter. I made a tree out of a simple branch, and we put it in a big coffee can with rocks in it. On the tree we hang ornaments, one at a time, which walk us through the whole story of the Bible, all the way from creation to the second coming of Christ. This is a great opportunity to walk the kids through the story of the Bible every year."

I asked her to explain how it works.

"Well," Pat continued, "each day we gather around the Easter tree and hear a part of the story. On the first day we read a passage about creation, and then we have a little ornament of the world that we hang on the tree. When the children were younger, they loved to get to hang the ornament each day and took turns doing so."

I interjected, "Then as the weeks progressed, we often asked them to talk back through the story of the Bible, using the ornaments."

I then mentioned that we also would do something similar during the Advent season, leading up to Christmas, but this time focused on the birth of Christ. We would read passages of Scripture each day and light one of the Advent candles.

Pat noted, "I have very fond memories of that. My parents often have been with us just before Christmas, and I remember us gathering around, reading Scripture, and lighting the candle. It is special because it reminds me of the devotional readings we used to do when I was down at Grandma and Grandpa Ruschhaupt's when I was growing up."

Listening to Scripture Taught

Third, *you need to train your children to listen to the Bible being taught.* God has given teachers and preachers of the Bible to the church as a gift. We cannot live what we don't understand, and we cannot understand what we don't hear. A basic skill involves teaching your children to participate in the community of faith as good listeners. This can be fostered even while the kids are young. It starts by patterns in the home. It can be extended in Bible classes at church, but it also can involve community worship services in which the Bible is being preached and taught.

Pat explained, "It was important to me, and it still is, that we sit together as a family at church. You and I would take our sermon notes. Each of the kids was given a little blank journal. Before they could even write, we had them draw pictures about what the pastor was speaking on. Then we would talk about it later. This set the pattern of paying attention to what was being said. As they got older, it was natural for them to take notes, and today Joshua and Anna like talking about the sermon at church. The patterns started when they were young."

I added, "At times we come home from church and talk about that day's sermon over lunch. Our kids enjoy such conversations. Joshua and Anna also regularly listen to great Bible teaching on MP3s, loading their iPods with wonderful messages that challenge them to grow spiritually in a wide variety of areas. It has been a joy to watch our kids blossom into the young adults they are, but their thirst for good teaching and preaching stems from those early years of learning to listen in church."

Conclusion

As we wrapped up our discussion, I thought of how much I appreciate my wife's passion for discipling our children. She loves the Lord, loves His Word, and lives the Word out authentically. For those of us who are Christian parents, our kids are much more likely to catch a vision for a life integrated around the Scriptures if they see such a life incarnated in us. God has called us, as flawed and fallen as we are, as disciplers of our children. For those of us who are parents, this role cannot be delegated to the pros at church. Their role is to supplement the life-on-life training we do at home. If our children are to learn to live deeply, lives rooted in the Scriptures, it needs to begin with us.

Pat and I have a vision for our children. We hope and pray that Joshua and Anna will have a powerful impact on the world, spreading the fame of Christ among the nations, and that their children—and their children's children—will also advance God's cause in their time, as they know and live God's powerful, relevant, life-orienting Word. Not surprisingly, Psalm 78 is one of our favorite passages:

> He established a testimony in Jacob
> and set up a law in Israel,
> which He commanded our fathers
> to teach to their children
> so that a future generation—
> children yet to be born—might know.
> They were to rise and tell their children
> so that they might put their confidence in God
> and not forget God's works,
> but keep His commands. (Ps. 78:5–7)

They were to "teach," "rise," and "tell." May we as parents do these things as we read the Bible with our families in the days to come.

The kids had come back in from the cold, and hot chocolate was waiting on them. We had finished our tea and scones and needed to get on to other, more mundane tasks of the day. As we closed, I said, "Pat, thanks for talking to me on this snowy day in West Tennessee. I really love talking to you. I have for twenty-two years."

She ended with, "Thanks, Lovie."

Summary & Application

Summation

- Reading the Bible teaches our children to love God, to think biblically, and to live well in the world.
- We need to establish patterns of Bible reading and listening in our families. Examples might include:
  - Having family devotions in the morning or evening
  - Singing biblically rich songs or psalms at the supper table
  - Using a devotional guide or some form of catechism
  - Reading to our children at bedtime or having them listen to Bible stories or songs
  - When the children are older, reading through a Bible reading plan together and discussing insights together at a mealtime
- We need to help our children (and ourselves) learn the "big picture" of the Bible's grand story. For example, in addition to the suggestions above:
  - Developing an Easter tree
  - Celebrating the story of Christ's birth at Advent
- From an early age, we need to train our children to listen to Scripture taught.
- We need to cultivate in our children a great love for God's Word!

Conversation

1. When you were growing up, did your family have a time when the Bible was read or discussed? If so, describe that experience.
2. What are the current patterns of Bible intake and interaction in your family? If you are single, with what "family" do you experience discussions on the Bible?
3. If you are a parent, what challenges do you face in implementing ideas in this chapter? What one thing would most help you overcome or ease those challenges?
4. Which part of this chapter was most challenging to you?
5. Which ideas in this chapter sound like they could be effective with your family? What would be the keys to success in implementing those ideas?
6. How might friends or your group pray for you concerning the incorporation of the Bible into your family's patterns of life?

Transformation

Read Deuteronomy 6:4–7 and Psalm 78:5–7 in three or four different translations, meditate on them, and answer the following questions: How would you describe the purpose or role of God's Word in each of these passages? How would you describe the role of the parent in each passage? What vision for the children is communicated by each passage? How might you live out these passages effectively?

CHAPTER 16

Reading the Bible with the Church

A Conversation with Buddy Gray and David Platt

Until I come, give your attention to public reading,
exhortation, and teaching.

—1 Timothy 4:13

In 2003 the human genome project mapped the approximately twenty thousand to twenty-five thousand genes in human DNA for the first time. From a biological standpoint, genes determine the particular characteristics of any organism. God is an amazing engineer to have made us so! Our genes determine how we will develop or, in some cases, deteriorate as our life progresses. The color of our eyes, our height, even our propensity to certain diseases are examples of how we have been woven in the cellular details of our physicality.

By analogy, churches too have a "genetic makeup"—beliefs and principles and commitments that shape, direct, and determine their spiritual existence, their community dynamics, and ultimately their impact on the world. It might seem a no-brainer that a church would have Scripture in the marrow of its bones, but unfortunately this is not always the case. In North America we are experiencing a "genetic" illness in the church, manifesting in a troubling, rapidly expanding biblical illiteracy. A recent survey by the Barna Group showed that only 4 percent of adults and just 9 percent of born-again Christians have a view of the world that is meaningfully informed by the Bible. As I pointed out in the introduction, another study done by LifeWay Research noted that only 16 percent of church people read the Bible every day, another 32 percent read the Bible at least once a week, and only 37 percent say that studying or reading the Bible has made a significant change in their lives. Clearly in the North American church there seems to be a disconnect between our professed commitment to Scripture as authoritative for believers and the actual experience of many Christians.

To explore how we might strengthen our interaction with the Bible in the context of local communities of faith, I drove five hours south of my home to Birmingham, Alabama, to interview pastors David Platt and Buddy Gray. David and Buddy are leading their respective churches to encounter God's Word in fresh and powerful ways. A Ph.D. in preaching, who had been dean of the chapel at New Orleans Seminary, David came to The Church at Brook Hills at the ripe old age of twenty-seven. With a maturity and spiritual depth that belies his years, David has led Brook Hills in an adventure grounded in Scripture and aggressively reaching far beyond the city limits of Birmingham. Buddy, on the other hand, has served Hunter Street Baptist Church for more than two decades, faithfully building a community deeply rooted in the Word, creatively crafting one of the strongest discipleship ministries in the South.

We met for our conversation in Hunter Street's expansive auditorium. After catching up a bit, reviewing what had been going on in our families and ministries, I started our conversation by asking these men what we are up against in the church at present. Mentioning the statistics given above, I asked, "David and Buddy, what about our culture fights against believers' hearing Scripture and responding to it in a way that is authentic and life changing?"

The Church as Part of God's Story

God-Centered Reading of the Bible

Buddy commented, "On one level many people are not reading and studying the Bible enough; that much seems clear. But I think what we are dealing with is more than just neglect of the Bible. Often when people do interact with the Scriptures, through reading or sermons or Bible studies, they tend to live at the level of information, as if information is what life is all about. With all the technology and information available in our world today, people think, *If I have access to the right information, that's enough.* So even when they think about the Bible, they think of it as a resource for finding information, for helping them live life more effectively. When they see the Bible as a self-help book, they 'google' it, randomly looking for answers to their particular issues. So they go to a passage, find the information they feel they need, and then move on. That approach can foster an 'it's all about me' attitude. The Bible becomes a tool that serves me."

David agreed and added, "We have programmed people to look at the Bible as a resource manual for life on Earth, as the book that has all the answers for all the questions we're asking. The reality is, I don't think that's why we have the Scriptures. They are not intended to be a resource manual for life on Earth. They don't answer all the questions we have, but they do address our primary needs in life—our need for forgiveness, for relationship with God, for right relationships with others, and the need to be conformed to Christ's image. Because we are 'self-help' oriented, too often we as Christians have become more content to go to the Christian bookstore and get good books there, neglecting our reading of the Bible. We think those books apply to us better than the Bible does, but the reality is, no book in the Christian bookstore can do what the Bible is divinely inspired to do: to transform us at the deepest levels in the way we think and live, to mold us into the image of Christ and show us our place in the grand story of Scripture."

I interjected, "It strikes me that we can almost train people to think of the Bible as a self-help tool with our preaching if we are not careful. A constant dose of topical sermons that are highly self-help oriented, detached from specific contexts in Scripture, can teach a pick-and-choose posture toward the Bible."

David agreed. "It certainly can. Of course the Bible is the most relevant book on the planet, but its message is a God-centered message, not a self-centered message."

Buddy continued, "As David said, what we need to help people see is that the Bible isn't primarily about them; it is all about God! The Bible is about knowing and loving God as He wants to be known and loved, coming into His presence, having your mind renewed to think about life the way He does. Once you begin to understand that the Bible is about God and not primarily about you, it takes on a whole different priority in your life—and a whole new relevance. If we are really God centered, it can make all the difference in how a church interacts with Scripture."

Information Overload and Bible Reading

Platt then pointed to a related problem in reading the Bible with the church. "I think another issue is that we, in our normal processes in life as individuals, are inundated with information, which leads to information overload and image overload. The people we lead in church are constantly immersed in all kinds of media, ideas, philosophies of life, and entertainment options, all of which pull at their minds and their desires."

Smiling, I interjected, "I just got an iPhone, and I am over-whelmed by the app options!"

David laughed and said, "So you joined the club?"

I answered, "Yep, and the technology is both amazingly help-ful and, at times, terribly distracting. I can check the weather, text someone, get a call on the phone, surf the Web, look up a Bible verse, check my e-mail, check movie times, make a bid on eBay, check my bank account, listen to music, check reviews on a restaurant, and get directions to that restaurant, all on the same device and in a matter of a few minutes! I am living what you are talking about. Too much information!"

Platt continued. "I know how you feel. We are maxed out in terms of our time, our ability to focus, and our desires. In a sense, to use a word picture, I think our spiritual stomachs are full from all kinds of stuff offered by this world, and you can't fill something that is already full. Like the space in our physical stomachs after a huge meal, we have no room left in the spiritual and emotional spaces of our lives. Our thoughts, our desires, and our energies are so used up, there's little space left for the Word of God."

I asked David, "What can we as leaders of the church do to combat the problem?"

He answered, "In order to counter the temptation, I think there's got to be a way for the church to show the supreme satisfaction that is found in the Word, a satisfaction that pulls our taste buds away from the things of this world toward the things of God. Whether we are dealing with teenagers who would rather spend hours on video games or adults who would rather spend hours in front of the TV, on the Internet, or shopping, the question is, How do we draw them to the Word in a way that changes their hearts, their desires? It's got to start little by little, showing that the Word is so much more satisfying than these things with which the world bombards us. Until we show the deep satisfaction that is found in God's Word, I think we're going to continue to see those statistics on biblical illiteracy getting worse and worse.

"And it has to begin with us as leaders. We as leaders need to get gut-level honest with ourselves and ask whether we ourselves find satisfaction in the Word; are immersed in the Word; are reading, studying, and memorizing the Word; are being transformed by the Word. If not, that's where we need to begin. We need to examine our own hearts and discover that God's Word can satisfy our deepest desires in life."

In thinking about David's comments, I remembered C. S. Lewis's words from his 1949 book *The Weight of Glory*: "It would seem that Our Lord finds our desires, not too strong, but too weak. We are half-hearted creatures, fooling about with drink and sex and ambition when infinite joy is offered us. . . . We are far too easily pleased."

God's Word is *desirable* because God and God's ways are desirable. Foundationally, we must deal with the appetites of our hearts and make room for the satisfying Word.

Seeing Ourselves in the Story

I interjected, "One result of a 'hyperlink' culture is that people have a hard time tracking with longer, sustained stories in literature generally and the Bible particularly. Biblical illiteracy is on the rise in part because people don't get the big picture of the Bible, how it all fits together and how they fit in the story. It seems to me that it's going to be important in some way for us to help people grasp that the Bible is about a developing story and that they have a place in that story."

Buddy responded, "When that begins to click in someone's mind, they begin to think about the Bible differently. They see the beauty of the flow of the story—creation, fall, redemption, restoration. They begin to see where the pieces fit. You are absolutely right. They can't understand their place in the story until the story starts sinking in, but when that happens, folks get really excited about the Bible. We as a church have read through the Bible in a year together, and that generates a lot of excitement. Especially as a pastor, when I know that everybody is reading through the Bible together, and I can build sermons around the reading for the week, that's exciting. There's a lot to be said for accountability and encouragement when everybody is on a Bible reading program together."

David added, "For the next year we as a church are implementing what we are calling 'the Radical Experiment.' We as individuals and as a community are going to pray for the entire world, read through the entire Word, commit to being involved in community groups, commit to capping our standard of living and using our financial resources for the advancement of God's causes in the world, and commit to giving one week of our time in gospel ministry outside of Birmingham for the sake of God's glory in the world. Our interaction with God's Word is at the heart of the Radical Experiment. I am preaching through the story of Scripture as the congregation is reading through the story of Scripture. We also have family devotional guides and small-group guides to go with the readings for the week, and there are Scripture memory verses for each week. We are excited about how this is going to shape our church."

Last year David came to Union for a series of messages. He and I had a couple of meals together and found that what God had put on his heart for Brook Hills dovetailed with the *Read the Bible for Life* Initiative with which I am involved at present. The book in your hands is a part of that initiative, and you can read more about it in the material at the back of this book. To make a long story short, Brook Hills is field-testing the Chronological Reading Plan and the *Reader's Guide to the Bible* I have developed, using these tools to guide the church through the reading of Scripture. The tools are designed to help a person track with the story of the Bible and apply biblical truth to life.

David continued, "We believe that as people really begin to build the framework of the story of Scripture, applying it to their lives week by week, they are going to see themselves more and more as a part of that story and that will change the way they think about and live their lives."

Helping the Church Read the Story

At this point Buddy continued the conversation. "If I could add to what David has just said, I want our folks to be so immersed in the Bible that they have a biblical mind-set—minds that are being transformed, shaped by the Scriptures. Romans 12:2 says, 'Do not be conformed to this age, but be transformed by the renewing of your mind, so that you may discern what is the good, pleasing, and perfect will of God.' Our natural tendency is to compartmentalize life into 'spiritual' and 'real' life, or into 'my life at church' and 'my life everywhere else.' As folks begin to be shaped by a biblical mind-set, they quit compartmentalizing life into different spheres because the Bible doesn't compartmentalize life in that way. God is the God of all of life. Family issues, business, school, friendships, time, resources, how we do church—all of life comes under the purview of Scripture. People begin realizing that God is interested in and speaks to all those areas of life."

A Theologically Trained Church

At this point I mentioned to Buddy, "I know that you are training people of all ages in theology, how to think about God, and us as human beings, and life in the world. Tell us about that."

Tapping the desk lightly, Gray smiled and picked up the conversation. "This is so exciting to me. About seven years ago I felt like I wanted to study more theology. I approached nine guys in the church, and every one of them said yes to being involved in a theology reading program. They didn't really know what they were saying yes to. We used Wayne Grudem's *Systematic Theology*, and if you've ever seen it, it weighs a ton. It's about fifteen hundred pages. We took a chapter a week, and everybody read, and we'd come together and discuss what we had read. That book, read that way, takes a year and a half to go through. About five or six months into it you could tell that these men were changed because their thinking about reality changed. They were changed because they'd begun to see the greatness of God. The most important thing about a person is his or her concept of God. Everything you are flows from who you think God is, whether you're an atheist or a true believer. By using Grudem, we were able to begin talking about the greatness of God. Lights started coming on in their hearts. It wasn't, 'Hey! I'm studying theology!' It was, 'I'm getting to know God!' Of course, the book itself is filled with Scripture."

I interjected, "I was going to say, one of the things about Grudem's book is that it is constantly referring to Scripture."

Buddy continued, "Over and over and over. And it made our guys want to go to Scripture and dig deeper. As the year and a half came to a close, I said, 'Guys, I want you to read this book

with other people.' They said, 'Absolutely.' Since they were getting to know God, they wanted to talk about God. They wanted
others to know what they were learning. They each got nine guys
together, and they read; and to make a long story short, we've
had about eight hundred people read through this big systematic
theology book. Some of the stories have been wonderful. A lady
stood up one day and said, '*Systematic Theology* changed my life!'
Everybody laughed. After her husband started to read about God
and felt comfortable with God and God's Word, he began to pray
with her. Now he's teaching their children about the greatness of
God. He's leading them in devotions every night. It has been the
most wonderful, encouraging thing.

"I've read *Systematic Theology* with tenth-grade boys, college
students, an eighty-two-year-old man, and everybody in between."

I asked, "Tenth-grade boys? *Systematic Theology*?"

Buddy laughed and said, "Absolutely. If someone had sat
me down when I was fifteen and walked me through *Systematic
Theology*, I'd be a far different person than I am now. These guys
get together and make bodily noises, and the next thing they're
talking about the nature of God and why it matters. I think, 'How
much fun is this?' I love it."

I have a seventeen-year-old son; he is such a great guy. If
I will spend an hour and a half to two hours with him in my
study, talking about issues in theology, he just loves it. As Buddy
had pointed out, theology can be exciting because God and what
God is up to in the world are exciting. We shouldn't assume that
people aren't interested in theology. As Dorothy Sayers once
said, "The dogma (theology) is the drama." When we understand
more about God and His purpose for us in the world, all the
world becomes a grand and exciting stage.

Buddy continued, "We've also added a track on biblical theology, basically how to read the Bible as one story. We have used a
little book called *The Drama of Scripture*. It lets people know the
big story. We let people read it for about four weeks or so, and
then we use Mark Dever's book, *Promises Made, Promises Kept*,
based on a sermon series he preached. The book shows how each

book of the Bible speaks about Christ. Dever shows how the message of each book contributes to the whole picture painted by Scripture. Once again I have people coming up to me and saying, 'I've been in church all my life, but for the first time everything's coming together. I begin to see what it's all about.'"

Secret Church

From time to time I have had students travel from our university down to The Church at Brook Hills to attend Secret Church, which also is designed to help people learn the big picture of Scripture. I asked David to explain what Secret Church is and what he wants it to accomplish.

Platt responded, "It's patterned after some experiences that God, by His grace, has given me among persecuted brothers and sisters around the world. When they come together, sometimes at the risk of imprisonment or even their lives, they want to make the most of their time studying the Word. They ask me to teach them the Bible for eight to twelve hours a day. When I came to Brook Hills, we said, 'Why can't we do that?' We don't go for eight to twelve hours straight, but we do normally go for six or seven hours straight. Periodically Secret Church lasts from 6:00 p.m. to midnight, and we gather together for intensive study in the Word. We went through an overview of the books in the Old Testament, as well as an overview of Old Testament theology in one night. We've done New Testament and how to study the Bible on other nights. Secret Church has covered theological topics like the doctrine of God, the Holy Spirit, the atonement, and angels and demons.

"The first time we did Secret Church, we had about a thousand people show up. We thought that was pretty neat. But it's gotten to the point where we pretty much have to take reservations now because our auditorium will be totally full with about twenty-five hundred people studying the Bible for six hours. There's a real hunger for depth and authenticity that can only be found in a deeper experience of God's Word. It's a great sight, to look out over a full auditorium of twenty-five hundred people at 12:30 in the morning, and they're all there with their Bibles open, studying the Word. It's one of the ways I've tried to address some of the things we're talking about. The goal is not just so they would know the Word but so they would be equipped to go into the world and teach the Word. That's why I say at the beginning of every night that we gather, 'The purpose is not just to have a Bible study. The purpose is so that you might know God more deeply and so that you might walk away from this place equipped to tell the nations how great God is.' That's the goal."

Continuing the Story: The Word in Worship

As we moved to the final phase of our conversation, I asked David and Buddy how the commitments of their respective churches to Scripture come together as their communities gather for worship.

David, resting his hands in front of him on the desk, answered by pointing to the book of Nehemiah. "The picture that comes to mind is Nehemiah 8:1–12. It is an incredible image of the centrality of the Word confronting the people of God and leading them to worship."

I interjected, "That is a great passage. Let's put it in context. Nehemiah 8 speaks of a time after the Babylonian exile, some 450 years before the birth of Christ. The Persians have allowed the Jewish people to go back home to Palestine; the wall around Jerusalem has just been rebuilt. The Word of God is brought out to the community. The passage really speaks of a reestablishment of the Jewish community on the basis of the rediscovery of God's Word."

David continued. "That's right. When I read Nehemiah 8, I am struck by their respect and reverence for God's Word, their hunger for the Word. I want that to be alive in the community of faith that I lead! The people in Ezra's day were saying, 'Bring out the book! We want to hear the Book!' Can you imagine if that attitude permeated our churches? As soon as Ezra started reading the Word, the people stood up in awe. I want the people in the church I lead to have that kind of reverence for God's Word because it demonstrates a reverence for God."

David added, "Notice that the Word of God and the worship of God are woven together throughout that passage. It is a false dichotomy to speak of the ministry of the Word and worship as two different things in a service."

I interjected, "The Word should infuse our worship, and worship should fill our hearts as we spend time in the Word."

David continued, "Absolutely. In Nehemiah 8 the Word penetrated the community of faith at a deep level, and they responded to the Word, grieving, confessing their sins, and then celebrating God's grace in worship. The preaching of the Word is exaltation of God in worship. Back in Nehemiah 8, nobody pulled out a guitar at all. All they'd done was open up the Word, and worship happened."

David embodies this picture of the penetrating Word presented in Nehemiah 8. A couple of years ago he spoke in our chapel at Union. For his message he "preached" the first eight chapters of Romans *from memory*. About five minutes into the message, everyone in the auditorium spontaneously stood to their feet and remained standing for the next twenty-five minutes. We were hearing the Word and worshipping God. It was a powerful, Nehemiah 8 moment.

Integrating the Word in Worship

Buddy then practically pointed to the ways his church incorporates the Word in worship services. "Our call to worship focuses on the reading of a passage of Scripture. When I lead in the pastoral prayer time, I'm careful to weave Scripture into my prayer. We pray Scripture. When we sing, we're careful that everything is biblically sound and grounded. We often sing songs that are Scripture songs, based entirely on the words of Scripture. We tell people that the song is from Psalms or Colossians, for instance, so they understand that what they are singing is based on the Word of God. When I preach, I have everyone stand to honor the reading of God's Word. When I finish, I say, 'This is the Word of the Lord,' and everyone responds, 'Thanks be to God.' I don't want that to be a meaningless ritual, but in a world that says there's no absolute truth, that practice is a way of honoring God as we read His Word."

Platt continued, "I was convicted a few months ago that we were not practicing an intentional, thoughtful reading of the Word in our worship times together. As part of our preaching, I think it's important to practice reading the text that we're preaching from, reading it as it was intended to be heard."

I added, "To give inflection in places—"

David continued, "Yes. And that involves preparation and a bit of work, to make sure we're reading it with the passion, or the anguish, or the solemnity and seriousness that is appropriate to a given passage. Reading the Scripture should not just be a throwaway moment in a worship time.

"We also have a variety of people, of various ages and roles in the church, involved in reading the Word in our worship services. I encourage them to think through and practice reading and let that Word sink into their hearts. Also, I want people to see leaders quoting the Word; or we'll have an elder or pastor start our worship service with reading the Word, and that will be the call to worship; or we will do a responsive reading. Those times are rich. We also involve children and students in reading the Word or quoting the Word. It's humbling and encouraging to see a six-year-old quote a chapter of Scripture in front of the community of faith."

Conclusion: Worship Through the Word Changes Us

This integration of Word and worship in a community of faith begins to build a rhythm into that community of faith. We hear the Word, sing the Word, pray the words of the Word, meditate on the Word, and seek to live the Word, allowing it to shape us as individuals, as families, and as churches in the way we think and the way we live. Our Word-oriented lives then become expressions of worship to God. Earlier Buddy mentioned Romans

12:2. The first verse of that chapter reads, "Therefore, brothers, by the mercies of God, I urge you to present your bodies as a living sacrifice, holy and pleasing to God; this is your spiritual worship." To present ourselves to God in response to His Word is worship. If we are reading the Bible with the church in the ways Buddy and David had described, the result will be application of the Word in the nitty-gritty details of day-to-day life in a way that is worshipful. As we said at the beginning of our conversation, the Bible is not designed to be a self-help manual for the self-centered. When Scripture begins to change us, drawing us into a God-centered life, showing us our place in God's story in the world, things begin to happen.

David gave an example of how a response to the Word can shape a community in exciting ways. "Last year I was teaching through James. We came to James 1:27: 'Pure and undefiled religion before our God and Father is this: to look after orphans and widows in their distress and to keep oneself unstained by the world.' I asked the leaders of our church, 'Does anyone know how many orphans we have here in our county?' No one did, so I called the Department of Human Resources (DHR) and asked them how many more foster homes they would need to take care of the kids who didn't have a home in our county. They thought I was kidding and laughed at me; they would need another 150 or so families to care for the other orphans. I asked if they could come and do a seminar at our church on how to be a foster family. We had 162 families show up. The people from DHR were weeping and began asking why we were doing this. It was a great opportunity to glorify God in response to His Word. Our folks, through responding to James 1:27 and caring for orphans, are expressing their love for God daily in a tangible way."

When we talk about the centrality of the Word in worship, we are not talking about the worship of the Word itself. As David had just shared, we are talking about being transformed by the Word as we walk with God in obedience. I asked Buddy what he would say to those who accuse us of placing too much emphasis on the Bible, as if we were worshipping it rather than God.

Buddy responded, "When we talk about loving the Bible, I know that we're sometimes accused of just loving a book. I'm always trying to figure out ways to explain to people that that's not the case because we as the church worship the God of the Book. John Piper has said, 'I love the Bible the way I love my eyes—not because my eyes are lovely, but because without them I can't see what's lovely.' What a wonderful way to put it. I love the Bible because it talks about the God I love. The Word should be a focus for what we do in the church because it draws us as the people of God to God Himself. This is the way He has chosen to reveal Himself to us as His people. As the community of faith, we walk with Him in relationship, which is a central theme of the Bible's story. But the way we continue to know Him and grow to know Him better as His people is to a great extent through the Bible. He speaks to us, His people, through its pages. He changes us and shows us how to live for Him and glorify Him in the world. So God's Word should be received as a great gift, and we as the church should read the Bible with receptive, thankful hearts."

As we wrapped up our conversation at the church and headed for lunch together, I thought about how much I enjoy and appreciate these guys. They are smart, energetic, and winsome as they lead their churches into an ever-deeper encounter with God's Word. They remind me of the leaders described in 1 Chronicles 12:32, "Who understood the times and knew what Israel should do." My prayer is that their tribe might increase and be used by God to reverse the trends of biblical illiteracy in the church in our day.

Summary & Application

Summation

- The Bible is not primarily about self-help information but rather transformation as we learn to live a God-centered life.

- Information overload fights against our intake of the Bible.
- We need to cultivate a supreme satisfaction with God's Word. God's Word is more satisfying than all that the world has to offer because God and God's ways are more desirable.
- A key to growth in reading the Bible is to grasp the Bible's grand story, to understand how all the parts of the Bible fit together.
- All of life should be integrated around a biblical view of the world.
- We will grow in reading the Bible as we grow in our understanding of theology—right teaching about God.
- When the church gathers, the Word should infuse our worship, and worship should fill our hearts as we spend time in the Word.

Conversation

1. How would you describe the DNA of your church? How would you describe the role Scripture plays in your church?

2. Why do you think church people don't read the Bible on a daily basis? What is your greatest challenge to spending time in God's Word?

3. What are the distractions in life that siphon your energies, desires, and attentions away from time in God's Word?

4. To what degree do you see the Bible as one big story? Where are the gaps in the story for you? What are the parts of the story with which you are most familiar?

5. How do you respond to the word *theology*? Why do David Platt and Buddy Gray emphasize the need for the study of theology in the chapter?

6. How might you be more engaged in reading the Bible with your church?

Transformation

Read Nehemiah 8:1–12 carefully. Identify the various parts of the passage that depict listening, understanding, and responding. Write down the experiences you have in your church that involve each of these three aspects of the intake of God's Word. What do you learn from this passage that might help you engage the Word more effectively in these experiences in your church?

APPENDIX

God's Story

Act 1: God's Plan for All People

Scene 1: Creation: The God of All of Life
Scene 2: Fall: Rejecting God's Vision for Life
Scene 3: Flood: God Judges and Makes a Covenant to Preserve
Life

Act 2: God's Covenant People

Scene 1: The People: God Calls a Covenant People
Scene 2: Deliverance: God Rescues His People
Scene 3: Covenant & Law: God Embraces and Instructs His
People
Scene 4: The Land: God's Place for His People
Scene 5: Kings and Prophets: God Shapes a Kingdom People
Scene 6: Kings and Prophets II: God Divides the Kingdom
People
Scene 7: Kings and Prophets III: The Southern Kingdom as
God's People
Scene 8: Exile: God Disciplines His People
Scene 9: Return: God Delivers His People Again

Act 3: God's New Covenant People

Scene 1:   Christ's Coming: God's True King Arrives
Scene 2:   Christ's Ministry: God's True King Manifests His
           Kingdom
Scene 3:   Christ's Deliverance of His People: God's Work
           through the Death, Resurrection, and Enthronement
           of His King
Scene 4:   Christ's Church: God's People Advance the Kingdom
Scene 5:   Christ's Second Coming and Reign: God's Future for
           the Kingdom

THE READ THE BIBLE FOR LIFE ONE-YEAR CHRONOLOGICAL READING PLAN

In the plan that follows, the material of the Bible has been organized to flow in chronological order. Since exact dating of some materials or events is not possible, the chronology simply represents an attempt to give you the reader the general flow and development of the Bible's grand story. Some passages are placed according to topic (e.g., John 1:1–3 in Week 1, Day 2; and many of the psalms). There are six readings for each week to give you space for catching up when needed.

Week I

ACT I: GOD'S PLAN FOR ALL PEOPLE

Creation: The God of All of Life

Day One
- [ ] Genesis 1–2

Day Two
- [ ] John 1:1–3
- [ ] Psalm 8; 104

Fall: Rejecting God's Vision for Life

Day Three
- [ ] Genesis 3–5

Flood: God Judges and Makes a Covenant to Preserve Life

Day Four Genesis 6–7

Day Five
- [ ] Genesis 8–9
- [ ] Psalm 12

Day Six
- [ ] Genesis 10–11

Week 2

ACT 2: GOD'S COVENANT
PEOPLE

The People: God Calls a Covenant People

Day One
❑ Genesis 12–13

Day Two
❑ Genesis 14–16

Day Three
❑ Genesis 17–19

Day Four
❑ Genesis 20–23

Day Five
❑ Genesis 24–26

Day Six
❑ Genesis 27–29

Week 3

Day One
❑ Genesis 30–33

Day Two
❑ Genesis 34–37

Day Three
❑ Genesis 38–40

Day Four
❑ Genesis 41–43

Day Five
❑ Genesis 44–46

Day Six
❑ Genesis 47–50

Week 4

Day One
❑ Job 1–5

Day Two
❑ Job 6–9

Day Three
❑ Job 10–13

Day Four
❑ Job 14–17

Day Five
❑ Job 18–21

Day Six
❑ Job 22–24

Week 5

Day One
❑ Job 25–28

Day Two
❑ Job 29–32

Day Three
❑ Job 33–36

Day Four
❑ Job 37:1–40:5
❑ Psalm 19

Day Five
❑ Job 40:6–42:17
❑ Psalm 29

Deliverance: God Rescues His People

Day Six
❑ Exodus 1–4

Week 6

Day One
❑ Exodus 5–9

Day Two
❑ Exodus 10–13

Day Three
❑ Exodus 14–18

Covenant and Law: God Embraces and Instructs His People

Day Four
❑ Exodus 19–21

Day Five
❑ Exodus 22–24

Day Six
❑ Exodus 25–28

Week 7

Day One
❑ Exodus 29–32

Day Two
❑ Exodus 33–36

Day Three
❑ Exodus 37–40

Day Four
❑ Leviticus 1–4

Day Five
❑ Leviticus 5–7

Day Six
❑ Leviticus 8–10

Week 8

Day One
❑ Leviticus 11–14

Day Two
❑ Leviticus 15–18

Day Three
❑ Leviticus 19–22

Day Four
❑ Leviticus 23–25

Day Five
❑ Leviticus 26–27
❑ Numbers 1–2

Day Six
❑ Numbers 3–5

Week 9

Day One
❑ Numbers 6–9

Day Two
❑ Numbers 10–13
❑ Psalm 90

Day Three
❑ Numbers 14–16
❑ Psalm 95
❑ Psalm 90

Day Four
❑ Numbers 17–20

Day Five
❑ Numbers 21–24

Day Six
❑ Numbers 25–28

Week 10

Day One
- [ ] Numbers 29–32

Day Two
- [ ] Numbers 33–36

Day Three
- [ ] Deuteronomy 1–3

Day Four
- [ ] Deuteronomy 4–7

Day Five
- [ ] Deuteronomy 8–11

Day Six
- [ ] Deuteronomy 12–15

Week 11

Day One
- [ ] Deuteronomy 16–19

Day Two
- [ ] Deuteronomy 20–23

Day Three
- [ ] Deuteronomy 24–-27

Day Four
- [ ] Deuteronomy 28–30

Day Five
- [ ] Deuteronomy 31–34

The Land: God's Place for His People

Day Six
- [ ] Joshua 1–2
- [ ] Psalm 105

Week 12

Day One
- [ ] Joshua 3–6

Day Two
- [ ] Joshua 7–10

Day Three
- [ ] Joshua 11–14

Day Four
- [ ] Joshua 15–18

Day Five
- [ ] Joshua 19–22

Day Six
- [ ] Joshua 23–24
- [ ] Judges 1

Week 13

Day One
- [ ] Judges 2–5

Day Two
- [ ] Judges 6–9

Day Three
- [ ] Judges 10–13

Day Four
- [ ] Judges 14–18

Day Five
- [ ] Judges 19–21

Day Six
- [ ] Ruth 1–4

Week 14

Kings and Prophets: God Shapes a Kingdom People

Day One
❑ 1 Samuel 1–3

Day Two
❑ 1 Samuel 4–8

Day Three
❑ 1 Samuel 9–12

Day Four
❑ 1 Samuel 13–16

Day Five
❑ 1 Samuel 17–20
❑ Psalm 59

Day Six
❑ 1 Samuel 21–24
❑ Psalm 91

Week 15

Day One
❑ Psalms 7; 27; 31; 34; 52

Day Two
❑ Psalms 56; 120; 140–142

Day Three
❑ 1 Samuel 25–27
❑ Psalms 17, 73

Day Four
❑ Psalms 35; 54; 63; 18

Day Five
❑ 1 Samuel 28–31;
1 Chron. 10

Day Six
❑ Psalms 121; 123–125;
128–130

Week 16

Day One
❑ 2 Samuel 1–4

Day Two
❑ Psalms 6; 9; 10; 14; 16; 21

Day Three
❑ 1 Chronicles 1–2
❑ Psalms 43–44

Day Four
❑ Psalms 49; 84; 85; 87

Day Five
❑ 1 Chronicles 3–5

Day Six
❑ 1 Chronicles 6
❑ Psalms 36; 39; 77–78

Week 17

Day One
❑ Psalms 81; 88; 92; 93

Day Two
❑ 1 Chronicles 7–9

Day Three
❑ 2 Samuel 5:1–10
❑ 1 Chronicles 11–12;
Psalm 133

Day Four
❑ 2 Samuel 5:11–6:23
❑ 1 Chronicles 13–16

Day Five

❏ Psalms 15; 23; 24–25; 47

Day Six

❏ Psalms 89; 96; 100; 101; 107

Week 18

Day One

❏ 2 Samuel 7
❏ 1 Chronicles 17
❏ Psalms 1–2; 33; 127; 132

Day Two

❏ 2 Samuel 8–9
❏ 1 Chronicles 18

Day Three

❏ 2 Samuel 10
❏ 1 Chronicles 19
❏ Psalms 20; 53; 60; 75

Day Four

❏ Psalms 65–67; 69; 70

Day Five

❏ 2 Samuel 11–12
❏ 1 Chronicles 20; Psalm 51

Day Six

❏ Psalms 32; 86; 102; 103; 122

Week 19

Day One

❏ 2 Samuel 13–15

Day Two

❏ Psalms 3; 4; 13; 28; 55

Day Three

❏ 2 Samuel 16–18

Day Four

❏ Psalms 26; 40–41; 58; 61; 62; 64

Day Five

❏ 2 Samuel 19–21
❏ Psalms 5; 38; 42

Day Six

❏ 2 Samuel 22–23
❏ Psalm 57

Week 20

Day One

❏ Psalms 97–99

Day Two

❏ 2 Samuel 24
❏ 1 Chronicles 21–22
❏ Psalm 30

Day Three

❏ Psalms 108; 109

Day Four

❏ 1 Chronicles 23–26

Day Five

❏ Psalms 131; 138; 139; 143–145

Day Six

❏ 1 Chronicles 27–29
❏ Psalm 68

Week 21

Day One

❏ Psalms 111–118

Day Two

❏ 1 Kings 1–2

❑ Psalms 37; 71; 94

Day Three
❑ Psalm 119:1–88

Day Four
❑ 1 Kings 3–4
❑ 2 Chronicles 1
❑ Psalm 72

Day Five
❑ Psalm 119:89–176

Day Six
❑ Song of Solomon 1:1–5:1

Week 22

Day One
❑ Song of Solomon 5:2–8:14
❑ Psalm 45

Day Two
❑ Proverbs 1–4

Day Three
❑ Proverbs 5–8

Day Four
❑ Proverbs 9–12

Day Five
❑ Proverbs 13–16

Day Six
❑ Proverbs 17–20

Week 23

Day One
❑ Proverbs 21–24

Day Two
❑ 1 Kings 5–6
❑ 2 Chronicles 2–3

Day Three
❑ 1 Kings 7–8
❑ Psalm 11

Day Four
❑ 2 Chronicles 4–7
❑ Psalms 134; 136

Day Five
❑ Psalms 146–150

Day Six
❑ 1 Kings 9
❑ 2 Chronicles 8
❑ Proverbs 25–26

Week 24

Day One
❑ Proverbs 27–29

Day Two
❑ Ecclesiastes 1–6

Day Three
❑ Ecclesiastes 7–12

Day Four
❑ 1 Kings 10–11
❑ 2 Chronicles 9
❑ Proverbs 30–31

Kings and Prophets II: God Divides the Kingdom People

Day Five
❑ 1 Kings 12
❑ 2 Chronicles 10

Day Six
❑ 1 Kings 13–14
❑ 2 Chronicles 11–12

Week 25

Day One
- [ ] 1 Kings 15:1–24
- [ ] 2 Chronicles 13–16

Day Two
- [ ] 1 Kings 15:25–16:34
- [ ] 2 Chronicles 17

Day Three
- [ ] 1 Kings 17–19

Day Four
- [ ] 1 Kings 20–21

Day Five
- [ ] 1 Kings 22
- [ ] 2 Chronicles 18-20

Day Six
- [ ] 2 Kings 1–4

Week 26

Day One
- [ ] 2 Kings 5:1–8:15

Day Two
- [ ] 2 Kings 8:16–29; 2 Chronicles 21:1–22:9

Day Three
- [ ] 2 Kings 9–11; 2 Chronicles 22:10–23:21

Day Four
- [ ] 2 Kings 12–13
- [ ] 2 Chronicles 24

Day Five
- [ ] 2 Kings 14–15
- [ ] 2 Chronicles 25–27

Day Six
- [ ] Jonah 1–4

Week 27

Day One
- [ ] Amos 1–5

Day Two
- [ ] Amos 6–9

Day Three
- [ ] Hosea 1–5

Day Four
- [ ] Hosea 6–9

Day Five
- [ ] Hosea 10–14

Day Six
- [ ] Isaiah 1–4

Week 28

Day One
- [ ] Isaiah 5–8

Day Two
- [ ] Isaiah 9–12

Day Three
- [ ] Micah 1–4

Day Four
- [ ] Micah 5–7

Kings and Prophets III: The Southern Kingdom as God's People

Day Five
- [ ] 2 Kings 16–17
- [ ] 2 Chronicles 28

Day Six
❏ Isaiah 13–17

Week 29

Day One
❏ Isaiah 18–22

Day Two
❏ Isaiah 23–26

Day Three
❏ 2 Kings 18:1–8
❏ 2 Chronicles 29–31
❏ Psalm 48

Day Four
❏ Isaiah 27–30

Day Five
❏ Isaiah 31–35

Day Six
❏ Isaiah 36–37
❏ 2 Kings 18:9–19:37
❏ 2 Chronicles 32:1–23
❏ Psalm 76

Week 30

Day One
❏ Isaiah 38–39
❏ 2 Kings 20:1–21
❏ 2 Chronicles 32:24–33

Day Two
❏ Isaiah 40–42
❏ Psalm 46

Day Three
❏ Isaiah 43–45
❏ Psalm 80

Day Four
❏ Isaiah 46–49
❏ Psalm 135

Day Five
❏ Isaiah 50–53

Day Six
❏ Isaiah 54–58

Week 31

Day One
❏ Isaiah 59–63

Day Two
❏ Isaiah 64–66

Day Three
❏ 2 Kings 21
❏ 2 Chronicles 33

Day Four
❏ Nahum 1–3

Day Five
❏ Zephaniah 1–3

Day Six
❏ 2 Kings 22–23
❏ 2 Chronicles 34–35

Week 32

Day One
❏ Habakkuk 1–3

Day Two
❏ Joel 1–3

Day Three
❏ Jeremiah 1–4

Day Four
❏ Jeremiah 5–8

Day Five
❑ Jeremiah 9–12

Day Six
❑ Jeremiah 13–16

Week 33

Day One
❑ Jeremiah 17–20

Day Two
❑ Jeremiah 21–24

Day Three
❑ Jeremiah 25–28

Day Four
❑ Jeremiah 29–32

Day Five
❑ Jeremiah 33–37

Day Six
❑ Jeremiah 38–40
❑ Psalms 74; 79

Week 34

Exile: God Disciplines His People

Day One
❑ 2 Kings 24–25
❑ 2 Chronicles 36:1–21
❑ Jeremiah 52

Day Two
❑ Jeremiah 41–44

Day Three
❑ Obadiah
❑ Psalms 82; 83

Day Four
❑ Jeremiah 45–48

Day Five
❑ Jeremiah 49–50

Day Six
❑ Jeremiah 51; Psalm 137

Week 35

Day One
❑ Lamentations 1:1–3:36

Day Two
❑ Lamentations 3:37–5:22

Day Three
❑ Ezekiel 1–4

Day Four
❑ Ezekiel 5–8

Day Five
❑ Ezekiel 9–12

Day Six
❑ Ezekiel 13–16

Week 36

Day One
❑ Ezekiel 17–20

Day Two
❑ Ezekiel 21–24

Day Three
❑ Ezekiel 25–28

Day Four
❑ Ezekiel 29–32

Day Five
❑ Ezekiel 33–36

Day Six
❏ Ezekiel 37–40

Week 37

Day One
❏ Ezekiel 41–44

Day Two
❏ Ezekiel 45–48

Day Three
❏ Daniel 1–3

Day Four
❏ Daniel 4–6

Day Five
❏ Daniel 7–9

Day Six
❏ Daniel 10–12

Week 38

*Return: God Delivers His
People Again*

Day One
❏ 2 Chronicles 36:22–23
❏ Ezra 1–3

Day Two
❏ Ezra 4–6

Day Three
❏ Haggai 1–2

Day Four
❏ Zechariah 1–7

Day Five
❏ Zechariah 8–14

Day Six
❏ Esther 1–5

Week 39

Day One
❏ Esther 6–10

Day Two
❏ Malachi 1–4
❏ Psalm 50

Day Three
❏ Ezra 7–10

Day Four
❏ Nehemiah 1–4

Day Five
❏ Nehemiah 5–7

Day Six
❏ Nehemiah 8–10

Week 40

Day One
❏ Nehemiah 11–13
❏ Psalm 126

ACT 3: GOD'S NEW
COVENANT PEOPLE

*Christ's Coming: God's True
King Arrives*

Day Two
❏ Psalm 106
❏ John 1:4–14

Day Three
❏ Matthew 1
❏ Luke 1:1–2:38

Day Four
- Matthew 2
- Luke 2:39–52

Day Five
- Matthew 3
- Mark 1:1–11
- Luke 3
- John 1:15–34

Christ's Ministry: God's True King Manifests His Kingdom

Day Six
- Matthew 4:1–22
- Matthew 13:54–58
- Mark 1:12–20
- Mark 6:1–6
- Luke 4:1–30; 5:1–11
- John 1:35–2:12

Week 41

Day One
- Matthew 4:23–25; 8:14–17
- Mark 1:21–39
- Luke 4:31–44

Day Two
- John 3–5

Day Three
- Matthew 8:1–4; 9:1–17; 12:1–21
- Mark 1:40–3:21
- Luke 5:12–6:19

Day Four
- Matthew 5–7
- Luke 6:20–49; 11:1–13

Day Five
- Matthew 8:5-13; 11:1–30
- Luke 7

Day Six
- Matthew 12:22–50
- Mark 3:22–35
- Luke 8:19–21; 11:14–54

Week 42

Day One
- Matthew 13:1–53
- Mark 4:1–34
- Luke 8:1–18

Day Two
- Matthew 8:18–34; 9:18–38
- Mark 4:35–5:43
- Luke 8:22–56; 9:57–62

Day Three
- Matthew 10; 14
- Mark 6:7–56
- Luke 9:1–17
- John 6

Day Four
- Matthew 15
- Mark 7:1–8:10

Day Five
- Matthew 16
- Mark 8:11–9:1
- Luke 9:18–27

Day Six
- Matthew 17–18
- Mark 9:2–50
- Luke 9:28–56

Week 43

Day One

❑ John 7–9

Day Two

❑ Luke 10
❑ John 10:1–11:54

Day Three

❑ Luke 12:1–13:30

Day Four

❑ Luke 14–15

Day Five

❑ Matthew 19
❑ Mark 10:1–31
❑ Luke 16:1–18:30

Day Six

❑ Matthew 20
❑ Mark 10:32–52
❑ Luke 18:31–19:27

Week 44

Christ's Deliverance of His People: God's Work through the Death, Resurrection, and Enthronement of His King

Day One

❑ Matthew 21:1–22; 26:6–13
❑ Mark 11:1–26; 14:3–9
❑ Luke 19:28–48
❑ John 2:13–25; 11:55–12:36

Day Two

❑ Matthew 21:23–22:14
❑ Mark 11:27–12:12
❑ Luke 20:1–19

❑ John 12:37–50

Day Three

❑ Matthew 22:15–23:39
❑ Mark 12:13–44
❑ Luke 20:20–21:4; 13:31–35

Day Four

❑ Matthew 24–25
❑ Mark 13
❑ Luke 21:5–38

Day Five

❑ Matthew 26:1–5, 14–35
❑ Mark 14:1–2, 10–31
❑ Luke 22:1–38
❑ John 13

Day Six

❑ John 14–17

Week 45

Day One

❑ Matthew 26:36–75
❑ Mark 14:32–72
❑ Luke 22:39–71
❑ John 18:1–27

Day Two

❑ Matthew 27:1–31
❑ Mark 15:1–20
❑ Luke 23:1–25
❑ John 18:28–19:16

Day Three

❑ Matthew 27:32–66
❑ Mark 15:21–47
❑ Luke 23:26–56
❑ John 19:17–42
❑ Psalm 22

Day Four
- ❏ Matthew 28
- ❏ Mark 16
- ❏ Luke 24
- ❏ John 20–21

Christ's Church: God's People Advance the Kingdom

Day Five
- ❏ Acts 1–4
- ❏ Psalm 110

Day Six
- ❏ Acts 5–8

Week 46

Day One
- ❏ Acts 9–11

Day Two
- ❏ Acts 12–14

Day Three
- ❏ James 1–5

Day Four
- ❏ Galatians 1–3

Day Five
- ❏ Galatians 4–6

Day Six
- ❏ Acts 15–16

Week 47

Day One
- ❏ Acts 17:1–18:18

Day Two
- ❏ 1 Thessalonians 1–5

Day Three
- ❏ 2 Thessalonians 1–3

Day Four
- ❏ Acts 18:19–19:41

Day Five
- ❏ 1 Corinthians 1–4

Day Six
- ❏ 1 Corinthians 5–8

Week 48

Day One
- ❏ 1 Corinthians 9–11

Day Two
- ❏ 1 Corinthians 12–14

Day Three
- ❏ 1 Corinthians 15–16

Day Four
- ❏ 2 Corinthians 1–4

Day Five
- ❏ 2 Corinthians 5–9

Day Six
- ❏ 2 Corinthians 10–13

Week 49

Day One
- ❏ Acts 20: 1–3
- ❏ Romans 1–4

Day Two
- ❏ Romans 5–8

Day Three
- ❏ Romans 9–12

Day Four
- [ ] Romans 13–16

Day Five
- [ ] Acts 20:4–23:35

Day Six
- [ ] Acts 24–26

Week 50

Day One
- [ ] Acts 27–28

Day Two
- [ ] Philippians 1–4

Day Three
- [ ] Philemon
- [ ] Colossians 1–4

Day Four
- [ ] Ephesians 1–4

Day Five
- [ ] Ephesians 5–6; Titus 1–3

Day Six
- [ ] 1 Timothy 1–6

Week 51

Day One
- [ ] 1 Peter 1–5

Day Two
- [ ] Hebrews 1–4

Day Three
- [ ] Hebrews 5–8

Day Four
- [ ] Hebrews 9–13

Day Five
- [ ] 2 Timothy 1–4

Day Six
- [ ] 2 Peter 1–3
- [ ] Jude

Week 52

Day One
- [ ] 1 John 1–5
- [ ] 2 John
- [ ] 3 John

Day Two
- [ ] Revelation 1–5

Day Three
- [ ] Revelation 6–10

Day Four
- [ ] Revelation 11–13

Day Five
- [ ] Revelation 14–18

Christ's Second Coming and Reign: God's Future for the Kingdom

Day Six
- [ ] Revelation 19–22

THE READ THE BIBLE FOR LIFE
4 + I PLAN

The 4 + 1 Plan offers a refreshing way to read through the Bible in a year. You will read at four different places in Scripture plus the Psalms. Over the course of the year you will read through Psalms twice. The plan is "semi-chronological" at points. Specifically, the prophets of the Old Testament and the letters of the New Testament have been placed in a rough chronological order. There are six readings per week, which will give you a day to catch up if you need it and a "Sabbath rest" if you don't.

READ THE BIBLE FOR LIFE

4+1 PLAN

Day				
WEEK 1				
☐ 1	Genesis 1	I Chronicles 1	John 1:1–18	Psalm 1
☐ 2	Genesis 2	I Chronicles 2	John 1:19–34	Psalm 2
☐ 3	Genesis 3–4:16	I Chronicles 3	John 1:35–51	Psalm 3
☐ 4	Genesis 4:17–5:32	I Chronicles 4	John 2	Psalm 4
☐ 5	Genesis 6–7	I Chronicles 5	John 3:1–21	Psalm 5
☐ 6	Genesis 8:1–9:17	I Chronicles 6	John 3:22–36	Psalm 6
WEEK 2				
☐ 7	Genesis 9:18–10:32	I Chronicles 7	John 4:1–24	Psalm 7
☐ 8	Genesis 11	I Chronicles 8	John 4:25–45	Psalm 8
☐ 9	Genesis 12–13	I Chronicles 9	John 4:46–54	Psalm 9

☐	10	Genesis 14–15	I Chronicles 10–11	John 5:1–18	James 5:1–6	Psalm 10
☐	11	Genesis 16–17:14	I Chronicles 12	John 5:19–29	James 5:7–12	Psalm 11
☐	12	Genesis 17:15–18:21	I Chronicles 13–14	John 5:30–47	James 5:13–20	Psalm 12
WEEK 3						
☐	13	Genesis 18:22–19:38	I Chronicles 15	John 6:1–21	Galatians 1:1–10	Psalm 13
☐	14	Genesis 20–21	I Chronicles 16	John 6:22–40	Galatians 1:11–24	Psalm 14
☐	15	Genesis 22–23	I Chronicles 17–18	John 6:41–59	Galatians 2:1–10	Psalm 15
☐	16	Genesis 24	I Chronicles 19–20	John 6:60–71	Galatians 2:11–21	Psalm 16
☐	17	Genesis 25	I Chronicles 21–22	John 7:1–14	Galatians 3:1–14	Psalm 17
☐	18	Genesis 26	I Chronicles 23	John 7:14–24	Galatians 3:15–29	Psalm 18
WEEK 4						
☐	19	Genesis 27	I Chronicles 24–25	John 7:25–36	Galatians 4:1–7	Psalm 19
☐	20	Genesis 28–29:30	I Chronicles 26	John 7:37–52	Galatians 4:8–20	Psalm 20
☐	21	Genesis 29:31–30:43	I Chronicles 27–28	John 7:53–8:11	Galatians 4:21–31	Psalm 21
☐	22	Genesis 31	I Chronicles 29	John 8:12–30	Galatians 5:1–15	Psalm 22

☐	23	Genesis 32–33	2 Chronicles 1–2	John 8:31–47	Galatians 5:16–26	Psalm 23
☐	24	Genesis 34–35	2 Chronicles 3:1–5:1	John 8:48–59	Galatians 6:1–10	Psalm 24
WEEK 5						
☐	25	Genesis 36	2 Chronicles 5:2–14	John 9:1–23	Galatians 6:11–18	Psalm 25
☐	26	Genesis 37	2 Chronicles 6	John 9:24–41	1 Thessalonians 1	Psalm 26
☐	27	Genesis 38	2 Chronicles 7–8	John 10:1–21	1 Thessalonians 2:1–8	Psalm 27
☐	28	Genesis 39–40	2 Chronicles 9	John 10:22–42	1 Thessalonians 2:9–16	Psalm 28
☐	29	Genesis 41	2 Chronicles 10–11	John 11:1–16	1 Thessalonians 2:17–3:5	Psalm 29
☐	30	Genesis 42	2 Chronicles 12–13	John 11:17–37	1 Thessalonians 3:6–13	Psalm 30
WEEK 6						
☐	31	Genesis 43	2 Chronicles 14–15	John 11:38–57	1 Thessalonians 4:1–12	Psalm 31
☐	32	Genesis 44	2 Chronicles 16–17	John 12:1–19	1 Thessalonians 4:13–18	Psalm 32
☐	33	Genesis 45	2 Chronicles 18–19	John 12:20–36	1 Thessalonians 5:1–11	Psalm 33
☐	34	Genesis 46	2 Chronicles 20	John 12:37–50	1 Thessalonians 5:12–28	Psalm 34

	#					
☐	35	Genesis 47	2 Chronicles 21–22	John 13:1–20	2 Thessalonians 1:1–4	Psalm 35
☐	36	Genesis 48	2 Chronicles 23	John 13:21–38	2 Thessalonians 1:5–12	Psalm 36
WEEK 7						
☐	37	Genesis 49:1–27	2 Chronicles 24	John 14:1–14	2 Thessalonians 2:1–12	Psalm 37
☐	38	Genesis 49:28–50:26	2 Chronicles 25	John 14:15–31	2 Thessalonians 2:13–17	Psalm 38
☐	39	Exodus 1–2	2 Chronicles 26–27	John 15:1–17	2 Thessalonians 3:1–5	Psalm 39
☐	40	Exodus 3–4	2 Chronicles 28	John 15:18–27	2 Thessalonians 3:6–18	Psalm 40
☐	41	Exodus 5–6	2 Chronicles 29	John 16:1–15	1 Corinthians 1:1–9	Psalm 41
☐	42	Exodus 7–8	2 Chronicles 30	John 16:16–33	1 Corinthians 1:10–17	Psalm 42
WEEK 8						
☐	43	Exodus 9	2 Chronicles 31	John 17:1–19	1 Corinthians 1:18–31	Psalm 43
☐	44	Exodus 10–11	2 Chronicles 32	John 17:20–26	1 Corinthians 2:1–5	Psalm 44
☐	45	Exodus 12	2 Chronicles 33	John 18:1–18	1 Corinthians 2:6–16	Psalm 45
☐	46	Exodus 13–14	2 Chronicles 34	John 18:19–40	1 Corinthians 3:1–9	Psalm 46
☐	47	Exodus 15	2 Chronicles 35	John 19:1–16a	1 Corinthians 3:10–23	Psalm 47

	Day	Exodus	2 Chronicles / Job	John / Mark	1 Corinthians	Psalm
☐	48	Exodus 16–17:7	2 Chronicles 36	John 19:16b–27	1 Corinthians 4:1–13	Psalm 48
WEEK 9						
☐	49	Exodus 17:8–18:27	Job 1	John 19:28–37	1 Corinthians 4:14–21	Psalm 49
☐	50	Exodus 19	Job 2	John 19:38–20:10	1 Corinthians 5:1–13	Psalm 50
☐	51	Exodus 20	Job 3	John 20:11–23	1 Corinthians 6:1–11	Psalm 51
☐	52	Exodus 21:1–32	Job 4-5	John 20:24–31	1 Corinthians 6:12–20	Psalm 52
☐	53	Exodus 21:33–22:15	Job 6-7	John 21:1–14	1 Corinthians 7:1–9	Psalm 53
☐	54	Exodus 22:16–23:19	Job 8-9	John 21:15–25	1 Corinthians 7:10–16	Psalm 54
WEEK 10						
☐	55	Exodus 23.20–24.28	Job 10	Mark 1:1–20	1 Corinthians 7:17–24	Psalm 55
☐	56	Exodus 25	Job 11–12	Mark 1:21–39	1 Corinthians 7:25–31	Psalm 56
☐	57	Exodus 26	Job 13–14	Mark 1:40–2:12	1 Corinthians 7:32–40	Psalm 57
☐	58	Exodus 27	Job 15–16	Mark 2:13–28	1 Corinthians 8:1–13	Psalm 58
☐	59	Exodus 28	Job 17	Mark 3:1–12	1 Corinthians 9:1–14	Psalm 59
☐	60	Exodus 29	Job 18–19	Mark 3:13–30	1 Corinthians 9:15–27	Psalm 60

WEEK 11

☐	61	Exodus 30	Job 20–21	Mark 3:31—4:9	I Corinthians 10:1–13	Psalm 61
☐	62	Exodus 31–32	Job 22–24	Mark 4:10–25	I Corinthians 10:14–22	Psalm 62
☐	63	Exodus 33	Job 25–27	Mark 4:26–41	I Corinthians 10:23—11:1	Psalm 63
☐	64	Exodus 34	Job 28	Mark 5:1–20	I Corinthians 11:2–16	Psalm 64
☐	65	Exodus 35:1–29	Job 29–30	Mark 5:21–43	I Corinthians 11:17–34	Psalm 65
☐	66	Exodus 35:30—36:38	Job 31	Mark 6:1–13	I Corinthians 12:1–11	Psalm 66

WEEK 12

☐	67	Exodus 37–38	Job 32	Mark 6:14–29	I Corinthians 12:12–20	Psalm 67
☐	68	Exodus 39	Job 33	Mark 6:30–44	I Corinthians 12:21–31	Psalm 68
☐	69	Exodus 40	Job 34	Mark 6:45–56	I Corinthians 13	Psalm 69
☐	70	Leviticus 1–2	Job 35	Mark 7:1–13	I Corinthians 14:1–12	Psalm 70
☐	71	Leviticus 3:1—4:21	Job 36	Mark 7:14–30	I Corinthians 14:13–25	Psalm 71
☐	72	Leviticus 4:22—5:13	Job 37	Mark 7:31—8:10	I Corinthians 14:26–40	Psalm 72

WEEK 13

☐					
73	Leviticus 5:14–6:30	Job 38:1–40:5	Mark 8:11–26	1 Corinthians 15:1–11	Psalm 73
74	Leviticus 7	Job 40:6–41:34	Mark 8:27–9:1	1 Corinthians 15:12–19	Psalm 74
75	Leviticus 8	Job 42	Mark 9:2–13	1 Corinthians 15:20–34	Psalm 75
76	Leviticus 9–10	Proverbs 1	Mark 9:14–32	1 Corinthians 15:35–49	Psalm 76
77	Leviticus 11	Proverbs 2–3	Mark 9:33–50	1 Corinthians 15:50–58	Psalm 77
78	Leviticus 12	Proverbs 4–5	Mark 10:1–16	1 Corinthians 16:1–11	Psalm 78
WEEK 14					
79	Leviticus 13	Proverbs 6–7	Mark 10:17–34	1 Corinthians 16.12–24	Psalm 79
80	Leviticus 14:1–32	Proverbs 8	Mark 10:35–45	2 Corinthians 1:1–11	Psalm 80
81	Leviticus 14:33–57	Proverbs 9–10	Mark 10:46–52	2 Corinthians 1:12–22	Psalm 81
82	Leviticus 15	Proverbs 11	Mark 11:1–14	2 Corinthians 1:23–2:4	Psalm 82
83	Leviticus 16	Proverbs 12	Mark 11:15–33	2 Corinthians 2:5–17	Psalm 83
84	Leviticus 17	Proverbs 13	Mark 12:1–17	2 Corinthians 3:1–11	Psalm 84
WEEK 15					
85	Leviticus 18	Proverbs 14	Mark 12:18–34	2 Corinthians 3:12–18	Psalm 85

☐	86	Leviticus 19	Proverbs 15	Mark 12:35–44	2 Corinthians 4:1–6	Psalm 86
☐	87	Leviticus 20	Proverbs 16–17	Mark 13:1–13	2 Corinthians 4:7–18	Psalm 87
☐	88	Leviticus 21–22	Proverbs 18–19	Mark 13:14–31	2 Corinthians 5:1–10	Psalm 88
☐	89	Leviticus 23	Proverbs 20	Mark 13:32–14:11	2 Corinthians 5:11–21	Psalm 89
☐	90	Leviticus 24:1–25:22	Proverbs 21	Mark 14:12–31	2 Corinthians 6:1–13	Psalm 90
WEEK 16						
☐	91	Leviticus 25:23–55	Proverbs 22–23	Mark 14:32–42	2 Corinthians 6:14–7:1	Psalm 91
☐	92	Leviticus 26	Proverbs 24	Mark 14:43–52	2 Corinthians 7:2–16	Psalm 92
☐	93	Leviticus 27	Proverbs 25–26	Mark 14:53–65	2 Corinthians 8:1–15	Psalm 93
☐	94	Numbers 1	Proverbs 27–28	Mark 14:66–72	2 Corinthians 8:16–24	Psalm 94
☐	95	Numbers 2	Proverbs 29	Mark 15:1–15	2 Corinthians 9:1–5	Psalm 95
☐	96	Numbers 3	Proverbs 30	Mark 15:16–32	2 Corinthians 9:6–15	Psalm 96
WEEK 17						
☐	97	Numbers 4	Proverbs 31	Mark 15:33–47	2 Corinthians 10	Psalm 97
☐	98	Numbers 5	Ecclesiastes 1–2	Mark 16	2 Corinthians 11:1–15	Psalm 98

☐	99	Numbers 6	Ecclesiastes 3–4	Matthew 1:1–17	2 Corinthians 11:16–33	Psalm 99
☐	100	Numbers 7	Ecclesiastes 5–6	Matthew 1:18–25	2 Corinthians 12:1–10	Psalm 100
☐	101	Numbers 8–9	Ecclesiastes 7–8	Matthew 2:1–15	2 Corinthians 12:11–21	Psalm 101
☐	102	Numbers 10	Ecclesiastes 9–10	Matthew 2:16–23	2 Corinthians 13	Psalm 102
WEEK 18						
☐	103	Numbers 11–12	Ecclesiastes 11–12	Matthew 3:1–12	Romans 1:1–7	Psalm 103
☐	104	Numbers 13	Song 1:1–2:7	Matthew 3:13–17	Romans 1:8–17	Psalm 104
☐	105	Numbers 14	Song 2:8–3:11	Matthew 4:1–11	Romans 1:18–32	Psalm 105
☐	106	Numbers 15	Song 4:1–5:9	Matthew 4:12–25	Romans 2:1–11	Psalm 106
☐	107	Numbers 16	Song 5:10–7:10	Matthew 5:1–16	Romans 2:12–29	Psalm 107
☐	108	Numbers 17–18	Song 7:11–8:14	Matthew 5:17–32	Romans 3:1–8	Psalm 108
WEEK 19						
☐	109	Numbers 19	Amos 1:1–2:3	Matthew 5:33–48	Romans 3:9–20	Psalm 109
☐	110	Numbers 20	Amos 2:4–2:16	Matthew 6:1–18	Romans 3:21–31	Psalm 110
☐	111	Numbers 21	Amos 3:1–4:5	Matthew 6:19–34	Romans 4:1–12	Psalm 111

☐	112	Numbers 22	Amos 4:6–5:17	Matthew 7:1–14	Romans 4:13–25	Psalm 112
☐	113	Numbers 23	Amos 5:18–6:14	Matthew 7:15–29	Romans 5:1–11	Psalm 113
☐	114	Numbers 24–25	Amos 7–8	Matthew 8:1–17	Romans 5:12–21	Psalm 114
WEEK 20						
☐	115	Numbers 26	Amos 9	Matthew 8:18–34	Romans 6:1–14	Psalm 115
☐	116	Numbers 27	Hosea 1–3	Matthew 9:1–17	Romans 6:15–23	Psalm 116
☐	117	Numbers 28	Hosea 4–5	Matthew 9:18–38	Romans 7:1–6	Psalm 117
☐	118	Numbers 29	Hosea 6–7	Matthew 10:1–15	Romans 7:7–25	Psalm 118
☐	119	Numbers 30	Hosea 8	Matthew 10:16–33	Romans 8:1–11	Psalm 119:1–24
☐	120	Numbers 31	Hosea 9–10	Matthew 10:34–42	Romans 8:12–17	Psalm 119:25–48
WEEK 21						
☐	121	Numbers 32	Hosea 11:1–12:1	Matthew 11:1–19	Romans 8:18–30	Psalm 119:49–72
☐	122	Numbers 33	Hosea 12:2–13:16	Matthew 11:20–30	Romans 8:31–39	Psalm 119:73–96
☐	123	Numbers 34	Hosea 14	Matthew 12:1–14	Romans 9:1–18	Psalm 119:97–120
☐	124	Numbers 35	Jonah 1–2	Matthew 12:15–32	Romans 9:19–19	Psalm 119:121–144

☐	125	Numbers 36	Jonah 3–4	Matthew 12:33–50	Romans 9:30–10:4	Psalm 119:145–176
☐	126	Deuteronomy 1	Micah 1	Matthew 13:1–17	Romans 10:5–21	Psalm 120

WEEK 22

☐	127	Deuteronomy 2	Micah 2	Matthew 13:18–30	Romans 11:1–10	Psalm 121
☐	128	Deuteronomy 3	Micah 3–4	Matthew 13:31–43	Romans 11:11–24	Psalm 122
☐	129	Deuteronomy 4	Micah 5–6	Matthew 13:44–58	Romans 11:25–36	Psalm 123
☐	130	Deuteronomy 5	Micah 7	Matthew 14:1–21	Romans 12:1–8	Psalm 124
☐	131	Deuteronomy 6	Isaiah 1	Matthew 14:22–36	Romans 12:9–21	Psalm 125
☐	132	Deuteronomy 7	Isaiah 2	Matthew 15:1–20	Romans 13:1–7	Psalm 126

WEEK 23

☐	133	Deuteronomy 8	Isaiah 3–4	Matthew 15:21–39	Romans 13:8–14	Psalm 127
☐	134	Deuteronomy 9	Isaiah 5	Matthew 16:1–12	Romans 14:1–12	Psalm 128
☐	135	Deuteronomy 10	Isaiah 6–7	Matthew 16:13–28	Romans 14:13–23	Psalm 129
☐	136	Deuteronomy 11	Isaiah 8:1–10:4	Matthew 17:1–13	Romans 15:1–7	Psalm 130
☐	137	Deuteronomy 12	Isaiah 10:5–34	Matthew 17:14–23	Romans 15:8–13	Psalm 131

☐ 138	Deuteronomy 13–14	Isaiah 11–12	Matthew 17:24–18:9	Romans 15:14–21	Psalm 132

WEEK 24

☐ 139	Deuteronomy 15:1–16:20	Isaiah 13	Matthew 18:10–20	Romans 15:22–33	Psalm 133
☐ 140	Deuteronomy 16:21–18:22	Isaiah 14	Matthew 18:21–35	Romans 16:1–16	Psalm 134
☐ 141	Deuteronomy 19–20	Isaiah 15–16	Matthew 19:1–15	Romans 16:17–27	Psalm 135
☐ 142	Deuteronomy 21	Isaiah 17–18	Matthew 19:16–30	Ephesians 1:1–14	Psalm 136
☐ 143	Deuteronomy 22	Isaiah 19	Matthew 20:1–16	Ephesians 1:15–23	Psalm 137
☐ 144	Deuteronomy 23:1–24:4	Isaiah 20–21	Matthew 20:17–34	Ephesians 2:1–10	Psalm 138

WEEK 25

☐ 145	Deuteronomy 24:5–25:19	Isaiah 22–23	Matthew 21:1–17	Ephesians 2:11–22	Psalm 139
☐ 146	Deuteronomy 26	Isaiah 24–25	Matthew 21:18–32	Ephesians 3:1–13	Psalm 140
☐ 147	Deuteronomy 27:1–28:14	Isaiah 26–27	Matthew 21:33–46	Ephesians 3:14–21	Psalm 141

☐ 148	Deuteronomy 28:15–68	Isaiah 28	Matthew 22:1–14	Psalm 142
☐ 149	Deuteronomy 29	Isaiah 29	Matthew 22:15–33	Psalm 143
☐ 150	Deuteronomy 30	Isaiah 30	Matthew 22:34–46	Psalm 144
WEEK 26				
☐ 151	Deuteronomy 31:1–29	Isaiah 31–32	Matthew 23:1–36	Psalm 145
☐ 152	Deuteronomy 31:30–32:47	Isaiah 33	Matthew 23:37–24:2	Psalm 146
☐ 153	Deuteronomy 32:48–33:39	Isaiah 34	Matthew 24:3–14	Psalm 147
☐ 154	Deuteronomy 34	Isaiah 35–36	Matthew 24:15–31	Psalm 148
☐ 155	Joshua 1	Isaiah 37	Matthew 24:32–51	Psalm 149
☐ 156	Joshua 2	Isaiah 38–39	Matthew 25:1–13	Psalm 150
WEEK 27				
☐ 157	Joshua 3–4	Isaiah 40	Matthew 25:14–30	Psalm 1
☐ 158	Joshua 5–6	Isaiah 41	Matthew 25:31–46	Psalm 2

☐	159	Joshua 7	Isaiah 42	Matthew 26:1–16	Philippians 2:12–18	Psalm 3
☐	160	Joshua 8	Isaiah 43	Matthew 26:17–35	Philippians 2:19–30	Psalm 4
☐	161	Joshua 9	Isaiah 44	Matthew 26:36–56	Philippians 3:1–11	Psalm 5
☐	162	Joshua 10	Isaiah 45	Matthew 26:57–75	Philippians 3:12–4:1	Psalm 6
WEEK 28						
☐	163	Joshua 11	Isaiah 46–47	Matthew 27:1–23	Philippians 4:2–9	Psalm 7
☐	164	Joshua 12–13	Isaiah 48	Matthew 27:24–44	Philippians 4:10–23	Psalm 8
☐	165	Joshua 14	Isaiah 49	Matthew 27:45–56	Colossians 1:1–14	Psalm 9
☐	166	Joshua 15	Isaiah 50	Matthew 27:57–66	Colossians 1:15–23	Psalm 10
☐	167	Joshua 16–17	Isaiah 51	Matthew 28	Colossians 1:24–2:5	Psalm 11
☐	168	Joshua 18	Isaiah 52–53	Luke 1:1–25	Colossians 2:6–15	Psalm 12
WEEK 29						
☐	169	Joshua 19–20	Isaiah 54	Luke 1:26–38	Colossians 2:16–23	Psalm 13
☐	170	Joshua 21	Isaiah 55	Luke 1:39–56	Colossians 3:1–17	Psalm 14
☐	171	Joshua 22	Isaiah 56	Luke 1:57–66	Colossians 3:18–4:1	Psalm 15

☐	172	Joshua 23	Isaiah 57	Luke 1:67–80	Colossians 4:2–6	Psalm 16
☐	173	Joshua 24	Isaiah 58	Luke 2:1–21	Colossians 4:7–18	Psalm 17
☐	174	Judges 1	Isaiah 59	Luke 2:22–38	Philemon	Psalm 18

WEEK 30

☐	175	Judges 2:1–3:6	Isaiah 60	Luke 2:39–52	1 Timothy 1:1–11	Psalm 19
☐	176	Judges 3:7–31	Isaiah 61	Luke 3:1–22	1 Timothy 1:12–20	Psalm 20
☐	177	Judges 4	Isaiah 62	Luke 3:23–38	1 Timothy 2:1–7	Psalm 21
☐	178	Judges 5	Isaiah 63	Luke 4:1–13	1 Timothy 2:8–15	Psalm 22
☐	179	Judges 6	Isaiah 64	Luke 4:14–30	1 Timothy 3:1–7	Psalm 23
☐	180	Judges 7	Isaiah 65	Luke 4:31–44	1 Timothy 3:8–16	Psalm 24

WEEK 31

☐	181	Judges 8	Isaiah 66	Luke 5:1–16	1 Timothy 4:1–5	Psalm 25
☐	182	Judges 9	Nahum 1	Luke 5:17–32	1 Timothy 4:6–16	Psalm 26
☐	183	Judges 10	Nahum 2	Luke 5:33–6:5	1 Timothy 5:1–16	Psalm 27
☐	184	Judges 11	Nahum 3	Luke 6:6–19	1 Timothy 5:17–6:2	Psalm 28

☐	185	Judges 12	Zephaniah 1	Luke 6:20–36	1 Timothy 6:3–10	Psalm 29
☐	186	Judges 13–14	Zephaniah 2	Luke 6:37–49	1 Timothy 6:11–21	Psalm 30
WEEK 32						
☐	187	Judges 15	Zephaniah 3	Luke 7:1–17	Titus 1:1–4	Psalm 31
☐	188	Judges 16	Habakkuk 1:1–2:1	Luke 7:18–35	Titus 1:5–9	Psalm 32
☐	189	Judges 17–18	Habakkuk 2:2–20	Luke 7:36–50	Titus 1:10–16	Psalm 33
☐	190	Judges 19	Habakkuk 3	Luke 8:1–15	Titus 2:1–15	Psalm 34
☐	191	Judges 20	Jeremiah 1	Luke 8:16–25	Titus 3:1–11	Psalm 35
☐	192	Judges 21	Jeremiah 2:1–3:5	Luke 8:26–39	Titus 3:12–15	Psalm 36
WEEK 33						
☐	193	Ruth 1	Jeremiah 3:6–4:4	Luke 8:40–46	1 Peter 1:1–12	Psalm 37
☐	194	Ruth 2–3	Jeremiah 4:5–31	Luke 9:1–17	1 Peter 1:13–25	Psalm 38
☐	195	Ruth 4	Jeremiah 5	Luke 9:18–36	1 Peter 2:1–12	Psalm 39
☐	196	1 Samuel 1	Jeremiah 6	Luke 9:37–50	1 Peter 2:13–25	Psalm 40
☐	197	1 Samuel 2	Jeremiah 7:1–8:3	Luke 9:51–62	1 Peter 3:1–7	Psalm 41

☐ 198	I Samuel 3	Jeremiah 8:4–17	Luke 10:1–12	I Peter 3.8–17	Psalm 42
WEEK 34					
☐ 199	I Samuel 4–5	Jeremiah 8:18–9:26	Luke 10:13–24	I Peter 3:18–22	Psalm 43
☐ 200	I Samuel 6:1–7:2	Jeremiah 10	Luke 10:25–42	I Peter 4:1–11	Psalm 44
☐ 201	I Samuel 7:3–8:22	Jeremiah 11	Luke 11:1–13	I Peter 4:12–19	Psalm 45
☐ 202	I Samuel 9	Jeremiah 12	Luke 11:14–36	I Peter 5:1–14	Psalm 46
☐ 203	I Samuel 10	Jeremiah 13	Luke 11:37–54	Hebrews 1:1–6	Psalm 47
☐ 204	I Samuel 11–12	Jeremiah 14	Luke 12:1–21	Hebrews 1:7–14	Psalm 48
WEEK 35					
☐ 205	I Samuel 13	Jeremiah 15	Luke 12:22–34	Hebrews 2:1–9	Psalm 49
☐ 206	I Samuel 14	Jeremiah 16	Luke 12:35–48	Hebrews 2:10–18	Psalm 50
☐ 207	I Samuel 15	Jeremiah 17	Luke 12:49–59	Hebrews 3:1–6	Psalm 51
☐ 208	I Samuel 16	Jeremiah 18	Luke 13:1–17	Hebrews 3:7–19	Psalm 52
☐ 209	I Samuel 17	Jeremiah 19–20	Luke 13:18–35	Hebrews 4:1–13	Psalm 53
☐ 210	I Samuel 18–19	Jeremiah 21–22	Luke 14:1–11	Hebrews 4:14–5:10	Psalm 54

WEEK 36

☐ 211	1 Samuel 20	Jeremiah 23	Luke 14:12–24	Hebrews 5:11–6:12	Psalm 55
☐ 212	1 Samuel 21	Jeremiah 24	Luke 14:25–35	Hebrews 6:13–20	Psalm 56
☐ 213	1 Samuel 22–23	Jeremiah 25	Luke 15:1–10	Hebrews 7:1–10	Psalm 57
☐ 214	1 Samuel 24	Jeremiah 26	Luke 15:11–32	Hebrews 7:11–19	Psalm 58
☐ 215	1 Samuel 25	Jeremiah 27	Luke 16:1–17	Hebrews 7:20–28	Psalm 59
☐ 216	1 Samuel 26	Jeremiah 28	Luke 16:18–31	Hebrews 8:1–7	Psalm 60

WEEK 37

☐ 217	1 Samuel 27–28	Jeremiah 29	Luke 17:1–19	Hebrews 8:8–13	Psalm 61
☐ 218	1 Samuel 29–30	Jeremiah 30	Luke 17:20–37	Hebrews 9:1–10	Psalm 62
☐ 219	1 Samuel 31	Jeremiah 31:1–30	Luke 18:1–14	Hebrews 9:11–22	Psalm 63
☐ 220	2 Samuel 1	Jeremiah 31:31–40	Luke 18:15–30	Hebrews 9:23–28	Psalm 64
☐ 221	2 Samuel 2	Jeremiah 32	Luke 18:31–43	Hebrews 10:1–4	Psalm 65
☐ 222	2 Samuel 3	Jeremiah 33	Luke 19:1–10	Hebrews 10:5–18	Psalm 66

WEEK 38

☐	223	2 Samuel 4–5	Jeremiah 34	Luke 19:11–27	Hebrews 10:19–25	Psalm 67
☐	224	2 Samuel 6	Jeremiah 35	Luke 19:28–40	Hebrews 10:26–39	Psalm 68
☐	225	2 Samuel 7	Jeremiah 36	Luke 19:41–20.8	Hebrews 11:1–7	Psalm 69
☐	226	2 Samuel 8–9	Jeremiah 37	Luke 20:9–26	Hebrews 11:8–16	Psalm 70
☐	227	2 Samuel 10	Jeremiah 38	Luke 20:27–40	Hebrews 11:17–31	Psalm 71
☐	228	2 Samuel 11	Jeremiah 39	Luke 20:41–21.4	Hebrews 11:32–12.2	Psalm 72
WEEK 39						
☐	229	2 Samuel 12	Jeremiah 40	Luke 21:5–19	Hebrews 12:3–17	Psalm 73
☐	230	2 Samuel 13	Jeremiah 41	Luke 21:20–38	Hebrews 12:18–29	Psalm 74
☐	231	2 Samuel 14	Jeremiah 42	Luke 22:1–13	Hebrews 13:1–6	Psalm 75
☐	232	2 Samuel 15	Jeremiah 43	Luke 22:14–30	Hebrews 13:7–19	Psalm 76
☐	233	2 Samuel 16	Jeremiah 44	Luke 22:31–46	Hebrews 13:20–25	Psalm 77
☐	234	2 Samuel 17	Jeremiah 45–46	Luke 22:47–62	2 Timothy 1:1–7	Psalm 78
WEEK 40						
☐	235	2 Samuel 18	Jeremiah 47	Luke 22:63–23.5	2 Timothy 1:8–18	Psalm 79

☐ 236	2 Samuel 19	Jeremiah 48	Luke 23:6–25	2 Timothy 2:1–13	Psalm 80
☐ 237	2 Samuel 20	Jeremiah 49	Luke 23:26–49	2 Timothy 2:14–26	Psalm 81
☐ 238	2 Samuel 21	Jeremiah 50	Luke 23:50–24:12	2 Timothy 3:1–9	Psalm 82
☐ 239	2 Samuel 22	Jeremiah 51	Luke 24:13–35	2 Timothy 3:10–17	Psalm 83
☐ 240	2 Samuel 23	Jeremiah 52	Luke 24:36–53	2 Timothy 4:1–8	Psalm 84

WEEK 41

☐ 241	2 Samuel 24	Lamentations 1	Acts 1:1–11	2 Timothy 4:9–18	Psalm 85
☐ 242	1 Kings 1	Lamentations 2	Acts 1:12–26	2 Timothy 4:19–22	Psalm 86
☐ 243	1 Kings 2	Lamentations 3	Acts 2:1–13	2 Peter 1:1–15	Psalm 87
☐ 244	1 Kings 3	Lamentations 4	Acts 2:14–28	2 Peter 1:16–21	Psalm 88
☐ 245	1 Kings 4	Lamentations 5	Acts 2:29–47	2 Peter 2:1–11	Psalm 89
☐ 246	1 Kings 5	Obadiah 1–21	Acts 3:1–10	2 Peter 2:12–22	Psalm 90

WEEK 42

☐ 247	1 Kings 6	Joel 1	Acts 3:11–26	2 Peter 3:1–7	Psalm 91
☐ 248	1 Kings 7	Joel 2	Acts 4:1–12	2 Peter 3:8–13	Psalm 92

☐	249	1 Kings 8:1–53	Joel 3	Acts 4:13–22	2 Peter 3:14–18	Psalm 93
☐	250	1 Kings 8:54–9:28	Daniel 1	Acts 4:23–31	Jude	Psalm 94
☐	251	1 Kings 10	Daniel 2	Acts 4:32–5:11	1 John 1:1–4	Psalm 95
☐	252	1 Kings 11	Daniel 3	Acts 5:12–26	1 John 1:5–10	Psalm 96

WEEK 43

☐	253	1 Kings 12	Daniel 4	Acts 5:27–42	1 John 2:1–6	Psalm 97
☐	254	1 Kings 13	Daniel 5	Acts 6	1 John 2:7–14	Psalm 98
☐	255	1 Kings 14	Daniel 6	Acts 7:1–16	1 John 2:15–17	Psalm 99
☐	256	1 Kings 15:1–32	Daniel 7	Acts 7:17–34	1 John 2:18–27	Psalm 100
☐	257	1 Kings 15:33–16:34	Daniel 8	Acts 7:35–53	1 John 2:28–3:10	Psalm 101
☐	258	1 Kings 17	Daniel 9	Acts 7:54–8.8	1 John 3:11–24	Psalm 102

WEEK 44

☐	259	1 Kings 18	Daniel 10	Acts 8:9–25	1 John 4:1–6	Psalm 103
☐	260	1 Kings 19	Daniel 11	Acts 8:26–40	1 John 4:7–21	Psalm 104
☐	261	1 Kings 20	Daniel 12	Acts 9:1–19	1 John 5:1–5	Psalm 105

	#					
☐	262	1 Kings 21	Ezekiel 1	Acts 9:20–35	1 John 5:6–12	Psalm 106
☐	263	1 Kings 22	Ezekiel 2–3	Acts 9:36–10:8	1 John 5:13–21	Psalm 107
☐	264	2 Kings 1	Ezekiel 4–5	Acts 10:9–33	2 John	Psalm 108
WEEK 45						
☐	265	2 Kings 2	Ezekiel 6–7	Acts 10:34–48	3 John	Psalm 109
☐	266	2 Kings 3	Ezekiel 8	Acts 11:1–18	Revelation 1:1–8	Psalm 110
☐	267	2 Kings 4	Ezekiel 9	Acts 11:19–30	Revelation 1:9–20	Psalm 111
☐	268	2 Kings 5	Ezekiel 10	Acts 12:1–19	Revelation 2:1–7	Psalm 112
☐	269	2 Kings 6	Ezekiel 11	Acts 12:20–25	Revelation 2:8–11	Psalm 113
☐	270	2 Kings 7	Ezekiel 12	Acts 13:1–12	Revelation 2:12–17	Psalm 114
WEEK 46						
☐	271	2 Kings 8	Ezekiel 13	Acts 13:13–25	Revelation 2:18–28	Psalm 115
☐	272	2 Kings 9	Ezekiel 14–15	Acts 13:26–41	Revelation 3:1–6	Psalm 116
☐	273	2 Kings 10	Ezekiel 16	Acts 13:42–52	Revelation 3:7–13	Psalm 117
☐	274	2 Kings 11:1–20	Ezekiel 17	Acts 14:1–18	Revelation 3:14–22	Psalm 118

☐	275	2 Kings 11:21–12:21	Ezekiel 28	Acts 14:19–28	Revelation 4	Psalm 119:1–24
☐	276	2 Kings 13	Ezekiel 19	Acts 15:1–21	Revelation 5:1–10	Psalm 119:25–48

WEEK 47

☐	277	2 Kings 14	Ezekiel 20	Acts 15:22–35	Revelation 5:11–14	Psalm 119:49–72
☐	278	2 Kings 15	Ezekiel 21	Acts 15:36–16:5	Revelation 6:1–8	Psalm 119:73–96
☐	279	2 Kings 16	Ezekiel 22	Acts 16:6–24	Revelation 6:9–17	Psalm 119:97–120
☐	280	2 Kings 17	Ezekiel 23	Acts 16:25–40	Revelation 7:1–8	Psalm 119:121–144
☐	281	2 Kings 18	Ezekiel 24	Acts 17:1–15	Revelation 7:9–17	Psalm 119:145–176
☐	282	2 Kings 19	Ezekiel 25	Acts 17:16–34	Revelation 8:1–5	Psalm 120

WEEK 48

☐	283	2 Kings 20	Ezekiel 26	Acts 18:1–17	Revelation 8:6–13	Psalm 121
☐	284	2 Kings 21	Ezekiel 27	Acts 18:18–28	Revelation 9:1–11	Psalm 122
☐	285	2 Kings 22	Ezekiel 28	Acts 19:1–10	Revelation 9:12–21	Psalm 123
☐	286	2 Kings 23:1–35	Ezekiel 29	Acts 19:11–20	Revelation 10	Psalm 124
☐	287	2 Kings 23:36–24:20	Ezekiel 30	Acts 19:21–27	Revelation 11:1–14	Psalm 125

☐	288	2 Kings 25	Ezekiel 31	Acts 19:28–41	Revelation 11:15–19	Psalm 126
WEEK 49						
☐	289	Ezra 1–2	Ezekiel 32	Acts 20:1–16	Revelation 12:1–6	Psalm 127
☐	290	Ezra 3	Ezekiel 33	Acts 20:17–38	Revelation 12:7–17	Psalm 128
☐	291	Ezra 4	Ezekiel 34–35	Acts 21:1–16	Revelation 13:1–10	Psalm 129
☐	292	Ezra 5:1–6:18	Ezekiel 36	Acts 21:17–26	Revelation 13:11–18	Psalm 130
☐	293	Ezra 6:19–7:28	Ezekiel 37	Acts 21:27–36	Revelation 14:1–5	Psalm 131
☐	294	Ezra 8	Ezekiel 38:1–39:24	Acts 21:37–22:11	Revelation 14:6–13	Psalm 132
WEEK 50						
☐	295	Ezra 9	Ezekiel 39:25–40:49	Acts 22:12–21	Revelation 14:14–20	Psalm 133
☐	296	Ezra 10	Ezekiel 41–42	Acts 22:22–29	Revelation 15	Psalm 134
☐	297	Nehemiah 1–2	Ezekiel 43	Acts 22:30–23:11	Revelation 16:1–16	Psalm 135
☐	298	Nehemiah 3	Ezekiel 44	Acts 23:12–22	Revelation 16:17–21	Psalm 136
☐	299	Nehemiah 4	Ezekiel 45	Acts 23:23–35	Revelation 17:1–10	Psalm 137

☐ 300	Nehemiah 5:1–7:4	Ezekiel 46–47:12	Acts 24:1–9	Psalm 138

WEEK 51

☐ 301	Nehemiah 7:5–73	Ezekiel 47:13–48:35	Acts 24:10–27	Psalm 139
☐ 302	Nehemiah 8	Haggai 1	Acts 25:1–12	Psalm 140
☐ 303	Nehemiah 9	Haggai 2	Acts 25:13–27	Psalm 141
☐ 304	Nehemiah 10–11	Zechariah 1–2	Acts 26:1–11	Psalm 142
☐ 305	Nehemiah 12	Zechariah 3–4	Acts 26:12–23	Psalm 143
☐ 306	Nehemiah 13	Zechariah 5–6	Acts 26:24–32	Psalm 144

WEEK 52

☐ 307	Esther 1	Zechariah 7–8	Acts 27:1–12	Psalm 145
☐ 308	Esther 2	Zechariah 9–10	Acts 27:13–26	Psalm 146
☐ 309	Esther 3–4	Zechariah 11–12	Acts 27:27–38	Psalm 147
☐ 310	Esther 5:1–6:13	Zechariah 13–14	Acts 27:39–28:10	Psalm 148
☐ 311	Esther 6:14–8:17	Malachi 1:1–2:16	Acts 28:11–16	Psalm 149
☐ 312	Esther 9–10	Malachi 2:17–4:6	Acts 28:17–31	Psalm 150

NOTES

1. E. D. Hirsch, Joseph F. Kett, and James Trefil, *The New Dictionary of Cultural Literacy: What Every American Needs to Know,* Revised Updated Edition (Boston: Houghton Mifflin Harcourt, 2002), 1.

2. Benson Bobrick, *Wide as the Waters: The Story of the English Bible and the Revolution It Inspired* (Simon & Schuster, 2001), 12.

3. Thomas Cahill, *The Gift of the Jews: How a Tribe of Desert Nomads Changed the Way Everyone Things and Feels* (Anchor Books/Nan A. Talese, 1999), 248.

4. As quoted in Isabella D. Bunn, *444 Surprising Quotes About the Bible: A Treasury of Inspiring Thoughts and Classic Quotations* (Bethany House Publishers, 2005), 15.

5. Eugene H. Peterson, *Eat This Book: A Conversation in the Art of Spiritual Reading* (Wm. B. Eerdmans Publishing Co., 2006), 6.

6. As quoted in Isabella D. Bunn, *444 Surprising Quotes About the Bible: A Treasury of Inspiring Thoughts and Classic Quotations* (Bethany House Publishers, 2005), 13.

7. Charles Colson, "Reversing Biblical Memory Loss," *Christianity Today,* 6 August 2001.

8. George A. Lindbeck, "The Church's Mission to a Postmodern Culture" in *Postmodern Theology: Christian Faith in a Pluralist World,* ed., Frederic B. Burnham (Harper & Row, 1989), 44.

9. Stephen Prothero, *Religious Literacy: What Every American Needs to Know—and Doesn't* (New York: HarperCollins, 2007), 38.

10. George Steiner, "The Good Books," *The New Yorker* (January 11, 1988), 94.

11. See the report from the 2003 National Assessment of Adult Literacy (NAAL) concerning Basic Prose Literary Skills.

12. Nicholas Carr, "Is Google Making Us Stupid?: What the Internet Is Doing to Our Brains," *Atlantic Monthly* (July/August 2008), 57.

13. Robert Maynard Hutchins, *The Higher Learning in America: With a New Introduction* by Harry S. Ashmore (New Brunswick, NJ: Transaction Publishers, 1995; orginally published by Yale University Press, 1936, 67–68, 83.

14. In the process of developing each chapter, I conducted a recorded interview with each of our conversation partners. That interview was then transcripted, and I edited the conversation (normally taking the

transcription from over thirty pages down to sixteen to eighteen pages) and at times rearranged the material to make it more readable. Finally, I sent the edited chapter back to the interviewee for his or her edits and final approval. This means that the conversations reflected in *Read the Bible for Life* were ongoing, involving a process of discussion over time. So the final product you have in your hand is the result of ongoing dialogues rather than just a brief conversation of a moment.

15. J. C. Ryle and J. I. Packer, *Practical Religion: Being Plain Papers on the Daily Duties, Experiences, Dangers, and Privileges of Professing Christians* (New York: Crowell, 1960), 94.

16. This is the most famous statement of Johann Albrecht Bengel, a committed follower of Christ and a prominent New Testament scholar of the Eighteenth Century.

17. J. R. R. Tolkein, *The Two Towers: Being the Second Part of The Lord of the Rings* (Boston/New York: Houghton Mifflin Company, 1954, renewed 1994), 697.

18. T. D. Alexander and B. S. Rosner, *New Dictionary of Biblical Theology* (England/Downers Grove, IL: InterVarsity Press, 2000), 164–65.

19. Hebrews 4:1–11 speaks of Sabbath more generally and is not dealing with keeping the Sabbath as in the Ten Commandments.

20. E. Randolph Richards, *Paul and First-Century Letter Writing: Secretaries, Composition, and Collection* (Downers Grove, IL: InterVarsity Press Academic, 2004), 165–69.

21. In chapter 14 Michael Card and the author discuss lament in more detail.

Your Guide to Understanding and Living God's Word.

LifeWay, in partnership with the Ryan Center for Biblical Studies at Union University, has launched one of our most important initiatives of this decade, a biblical literacy initiative called *Read the Bible for Life*. It's more than a series of resources—it's a movement, and in homes, in churches, and in community gatherings across the country, our prayer is that it will help you rediscover, reengage and rebuild your life on the Word of God.

The Read the Bible for Life video curriculum, hosted by Dr. George Guthrie, was created specifically for small groups and includes creative teaching segments, interactive exercises, as well as guest interviews with leading Christian scholars.

Reading God's Story: A Chronological Daily Bible is organized to make clear the step-by-step development of the biblical story and includes helpful introductory articles on each "Act" and "Scene" in that story. Coming October 2011.

A Reader's Guide to the Bible presents a one-year chronological Bible reading plan along with a brief commentary for each day's reading. The *Reader's Guide* coaches the reader day-by-day on how to read the Scripture well and how to apply the Scripture to life. Coming October 2011.

ReadTheBibleForLife.com